This book should be returned to any branch of the
Lancashire County Library on or before the date

- 3 OCT 2016

experienced by foreigners, no matter how knowledgeable or fluent
in the language they are . . . The first pages of this book recount in moving and often exquisite detail – the English translation by Danica Mills
reads very well – how Chen, when still a little boy, was guided by his
slightly older brothers to touch, stroke and almost see trees, flowers,
animals   *rary Review*

'Chen Guangcheng has a life story unlike any other you will ever read. His memoir – eloquent, accessible and necessary – is not only about his improbable path to prominence as a human-rights activist in China. It is, above all, about the universal power of will'

Evan Osnos, author of *Age of Ambition: Chasing Fortune, Truth, and Faith in the New China*

'Chen Guangcheng. The barefoot lawyer from rural China. Think Huckleberry Finn growing up to be Atticus Finch. In this brave and undaunted book, Guangcheng proves himself the very best kind of trouble-maker. He fights monsters. Monsters who hide behind official-dom and party uniforms. Monsters of lazy sadism who flaunt the rule of law and violently oppose any chance for human dignity. A gritty and insanely inspiring story of a man who has been through hell and come out smiling, *The Barefoot Lawyer* represents the ultimate victory over cynicism and cruelty. Tyrants Beware!'   Christian Bale, actor

The
Barefoot
Lawyer

Chen Guangcheng is a Chinese civil rights activist now living in the US. In 2007 he was named one of *Time* magazine's 'Time 100', a list of '100 men and women whose power, talent or moral example is transforming the world'. He is also a laureate of the prestigious Ramon Magsaysay Award, bestowed for 'his irrepressible passion for justice in leading ordinary Chinese citizens to assert their legitimate rights under the law.'

The
Barefoot
Lawyer

The Remarkable Memoir of
China's Bravest Political Activist

Chen Guangcheng

PAN BOOKS

First published 2015 by Henry Holt and Company, LLC, New York

First published in the UK 2015 by Macmillan

This paperback edition published 2016 by Pan Books
an imprint of Pan Macmillan
20 New Wharf Road, London N1 9RR
Associated companies throughout the world
www.panmacmillan.com

ISBN 978-1-4472-6882-6

9 8 7 6 5 4 3 2 1

A CIP catalogue record for this book is available from the British Library.

Maps by Gene Thorp

Printed and bound by CPI Group (UK) Ltd, Croydon, CR0 4YY

For my mother, Wang Jinxiang;
and my wife, Yuan Weijing

In the world as we know it, are there things that are difficult, as well as things that are easy? Through action, those things that seem difficult become easy; with inaction, things that are easy become difficult.

Peng Duanshu (1699–1799), from *On Studying*

Bring forth all that is good in the world, and expunge all that is bad.

Mencius (372–289 BCE), from *Universal Love III*

One who is shut indoors may come to know the world; one who cannot look out the window may understand the Way of Heaven.

Laozi (fifth century BCE), from the *Dao De Jing*

Contents

The World of Chen Guangcheng

Beijing ★

Tianjin ○

Bo Hai

Yellow Sea

Jinan ○   Zibo ○

Tai'an ○

SHANDONG PROVINCE

Qingdao ○

Dongshigu village ○

Linyi ○

Luoyang ○

East China Sea

C H I N A

JIANGSU PROVINCE

Huai River

ANHUI PROVINCE

Yangtze River

Nanjing ○

Shanghai ○

Hangzhou ○

ZHEJIANG PROVINCE

0   100   200
MILES

RUSSIA

MONGOLIA

NEPAL

CHINA

Detail

INDIA

JAPAN

TAIWAN

Philippine Sea

0   1,000
MILES

Map by Gene Thorp

Chen Guangcheng's Escape

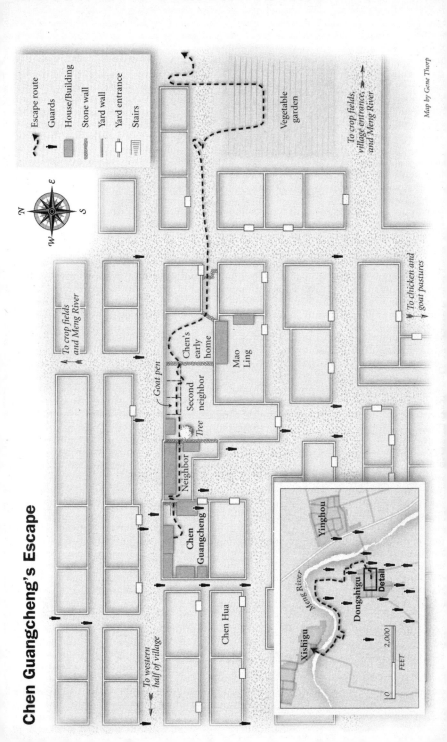

Legend:
- Escape route
- Guards
- House/Building
- Stone wall
- Yard wall
- Yard entrance
- Stairs

Vegetable garden

To crop fields, village entrance, and Meng River

To crop fields and Meng River

To chicken and goat pastures

Goat pen

Chen's early home

Mao Ling

Second neighbor

Tree

Neighbor

Chen Guangcheng

Chen Hua

To western half of village

Yinghou

Meng River

Xishigu

Dongshigu

Detail

FEET

0   2,000

Map by Gene Thorp

Foreword

BY THE DALAI LAMA

I welcome this publication of Chen Guangcheng's memoirs of his life so far. It's a story that should be told because it shows clearly that with determination, confidence in yourself, and a concern for others you can overcome adversity. Chen Guangcheng overcame the significant setback of blindness and social prejudice and gained an education. He put that education to use by helping and advising the poor people in rural areas who have no one else to turn to.

In the clarity of his motivation Chen Guangcheng reminds me of the first generation of communist leaders I met in China sixty years ago, who at the time impressed me with their genuine concern for the welfare of the mass of ordinary people. When his barefoot activism attracted the attention of vested interests he was tried and imprisoned on the contrived charge of disturbing the peace. When, on his release, he discovered that his own and his family's normal life activities were restricted by the authorities, he decided to escape. He succeeded, in as much as he and his family have been able to start a new life in the freedom of the United States; however, he continues to champion for the rights of his fellow brothers and sisters, especially the rights of the rural poor.

During my meetings with Chen Guangcheng I was impressed by his drive and warmheartedness. Helping people help themselves as he did is no threat to the peace and order of society, but can instead contribute to its harmony. I look forward to a time when China is able to embrace and accommodate inspiring and well-motivated people like Chen Guangcheng and Liu Xiaobo; people like them have a positive role to play.

October 18, 2014

The
Barefoot
Lawyer

Escape

We watched them as they watched us. We studied their every move and every habit. We had been planning my escape for over a year, going over the details again and again in muted whispers. We assumed that the house was bugged, that our captors could hear every word we spoke.

If I could just get beyond the village—beyond what had once been a home and was now a private hell, beyond the seventy or more guards laying siege and blocking every possible exit. "Home will be no better than prison," a warden had told me shortly before I was released from jail after being confined for over four years. And he was right: once back in Dongshigu, I had been kept under brutal house arrest, an epicenter within the vast prison that all of China had become.

By now I had already attempted to escape my home numerous times. My wife, Weijing, and I debated and discussed the hazards and benefits of each plan endlessly, and I went through each possible route in my mind, over and over. I was desperate to escape: my life, not just my spirit, depended on it. Gravely ill since prison, I was not allowed to see or even speak to a doctor. My isolation in my own house was almost total: no going out, no visitors, no news, no contact with the outside world. I had severe diarrhea, often with bleeding, and I constantly felt exhausted. Recently I'd been spending about two weeks out of every month in bed, too sick to move. If I finally lost my battle to live, the authorities would say that I had died of such and such illness, at home in my own bed, and who would know the difference? Resolve was all I had.

On April 20, 2012, Weijing and I spent the morning resting in the main room of our house, which was one of four small buildings around a dirt courtyard that made up our family compound. A few days earlier we'd realized that the neighbor's dog was gone. I'd often said that one dog was more dangerous than a hundred guards, and now, with this one away, we focused our attention on the escape route that would take me past that neighbor's house, to the east.

That morning, as usual, I went through the route in my mind, dwelling on every detail—exactly where to turn, the distances between things, the walls, all the minutiae that Weijing had gathered during her daily routines over a period of months. Only she and I knew of our plan, though we agreed that when attempting to get past the guards, I should try to find help in the village, from either a close childhood friend or another good friend who was a carpenter. Both lived along my path of escape, but we had no way of communicating with anyone outside our house. It was too dangerous to tell even my mother about the plan; she strongly objected to the notion that I should try to escape.

Weijing and I had often talked about how I would get word to her once I was safe. We couldn't use written or spoken communication, so the only possibility was to send a sign, a signal. Eventually we decided that if I got out alive, I would have someone deliver six apples to Weijing; in Chinese, "six" can signify success, and the word for "apple" is the same sound as that for "safe." I imagined having someone bring her six big red apples once I got away from our village, and if there were none to be had, I figured I would find a way to get her six of something else so she would know that I was free.

All that morning, Weijing observed the guards from inside the house, watching for an opportunity. Earlier, up on the roof of our flat kitchen building, where we dried corn and aired out our clothes, she'd noticed that the car belonging to the head of the group of guards on duty was gone. There were usually six guards stationed in our yard, perched on tiny stools just outside the door to our house. The crew on duty today sat near our main gate, and only two of them had a direct line of sight to our door. A little before eleven a.m., the moment suddenly came: the guard closest to us slowly stood up, a tea mug in his hand. He was off to fill it with boiled water from one of the thermoses the guards kept outside our yard, and he didn't seem to be in a hurry. On his way, for just a few seconds, he would block his partner's view of me. I would have to hurry out the door and dart across the courtyard to the eastern wall, a distance of about fifteen feet. After a moment, the guard would have his sight line back.

"Let's go!" Weijing whispered, squeezing my arm. I followed her out the door, walking quickly, carefully, across the yard, skipping ahead of her and passing the old millstones where we used to grind grain and other staple foods. I scurried to a stone staircase I knew was hidden from view, then stood at the bottom of those six rough-hewn steps, breathing hard and listening with all my might, straining for any sign of disturbance or recognition from the guards.

My heart raced. The snap of a twig could betray me, resulting in a fresh round of beatings, or worse. For some time, Weijing had been picking up any potential obstacles from the path of my escape, though she was careful not to clear away too much at once and risk arousing suspicion. Every rock, branch, leaf, water bucket, or pan in my way could make a sudden noise that would attract the attention of the guards.

As I stood by the stairs, I heard Weijing gathering dried leaves and grass from our woodpile, only a few steps away; a moment later, she headed back into the kitchen building to light a fire. By then the guard was already back at his post, putting his tea mug on the ground and chatting with his fellow guards as he settled onto his stool again. Then Weijing came back out of the kitchen building to fill our kettle from the outdoor faucet—all pretext, of course—and soon enough I heard the kettle clanking on the stove. Again she came out, this time walking back to the woodpile for larger sticks and branches. Each time she passed me, she whispered a few words, telling me what she was seeing, saying that so far I was safe.

I didn't move. Weijing was extremely anxious, but now that I had made it past the innermost ring of guards, how could I give up? "We have to go forward," I whispered. "We can't fail."

The next time Weijing came out of the main house, she carried an armload of clothes. "I'm going up to take a look," she whispered as she passed. I knew that meant she would climb up to the roof of the kitchen building, where she would have a panoramic view of all the activity around our yard. Over the past few months, she had spent countless hours up there on various pretexts, scouting my initial escape route. A few years back, these "square buildings" had become popular in our village. Now the flat roof gave Weijing an invaluable way to observe my escape route.

A few moments later, she came down and said it was safe for me to go up. By now my breathing had slowed and my nerves were calmer. I walked quietly up the steps, which I knew by heart, and soon I was crouching atop the east wall of our yard, just below the roof of the kitchen building. East was the direction of my freedom, beyond the adjoining courtyard compounds of my neighbors. Fortunately, I knew every inch of the neighbor's yard below, each detail clear in my mind from experience and memory. Aware that the guards patrolling the perimeter just twenty feet away might spot me if I stood up on the wall, I kept low. Moving slowly, I found the bottle Weijing had mentioned, an obstacle placed on top of the wall by the guards. I picked it up, scuttled forward, and put the bottle to one side before straddling the wall. Careful to avoid the least suspicion, I then placed the bottle back in its original spot. Bracing myself between the wall and the side of my neighbor's house, I slowly climbed down into a corner of her yard.

Moving as fast as I could, I scrambled past my neighbor's main house, toward the concrete steps that led to the roof of her kitchen building, whose position in the yard was much like ours. I was conscious now of another set of guards—the ones just outside my neighbor's yard, who might catch a glimpse of me through a crack in my neighbor's main gate. After climbing up the steps to the roof of my neighbor's kitchen and onto the eastern wall, I planned to descend into the next neighbor's yard. Up and down the walls, one yard after another: this was the only way to make it beyond the cordon of guards to open space. I carried nothing, but every detail of the route was clear in my head.

I took my chances and started up my neighbor's steps, feeling for the objects Weijing had warned me about. Here, on the second step, were the two metal buckets, which I passed without a sound. A little farther up, I found the snarl of electrical cables, attached to the equipment that the guards had been using to jam our cell phone signal. Then, a couple steps beyond the cables, I came upon the pan full of bricks Weijing had described. Feeling my way with both hands, I discovered an unstable section of the wall; it was immediately obvious to me that if I tried to climb down the other side of it, the wall would not be able to support my weight and would crumble.

Just then, I heard my neighbor's main gate squeak open. I slipped up onto the roof of the kitchen building and lay flat on my back. If she saw me, she would almost certainly report me. I knew that the guards had been bribing her to keep an eye on me, sharing their extra food with her and maybe giving her money.

For a few minutes I lay there silently, forcing calm on my pounding heart. So far, so good: my deep familiarity with my home's immediate surroundings had served me well. Although blind since infancy, I knew every bit of the terrain around my village in a million ways besides sight: the patterns of sounds, the mix of smells, the organization of space. Memory would play an essential role in my attempt to escape—when you're blind, there's no taking things in at a glance—and I knew that this dependence on memory would only increase as I made my way toward Xishigu, the next village over, where I hoped to get help. The distance was short, but the obstacles were many. In the years before my arrest and imprisonment, I had come to know the walls, roads, and fields of my village in all their elaborate detail and almost infinite complexity. But that was long ago, and now, after seven years in bondage, memory would be my guide.

We had been talking about the escape from the very day Guangcheng came home from prison, and for over a year we had been working on a plan. I often consulted the lunar calendar, scouring its pages for an auspicious day, if only to ease my fears and make the endless days pass just a bit faster. The guards had previously seized almost everything we owned, fearing that we would turn even the smallest scrap of paper to our benefit; we now had only this small calendar for 2012, which Guangcheng's mother had been allowed to purchase while under the watchful gaze of our captors.

I knew the guards might grow suspicious if I spent too much time looking at the calendar, so I would write the number of eggs we gathered from our chickens on the page for each day. Having planned for a protracted period in captivity, we encouraged our hens to sit on some of their eggs. Once the brood finally hatched, we had more than forty chickens to supplement our meager diet. If all else failed, we could kill and eat the chickens; we had to be completely self-reliant. When the guards finally asked me why I consulted the calendar so often, I described my habit of recording the day's harvest of eggs. They accepted the explanation and said nothing more.

Over time, I realized that spring would be the ideal season to attempt an escape. The new leaves on the trees would cover Guangcheng's movements; light winds moving through the trees would muffle the noises he would inevitably make. As I flipped through the calendar, I saw that April 20 would be a *chengri*, a day of success. The God of Wealth, who brings luck and opportunity, would be facing east, one of the possible directions of Guangcheng's escape. On that day, the pig would overcome the snake. This detail had a special significance: Guangcheng was born in the Year of the Pig, and the head of the crew on guard that day was born in the Year of the Snake. On a more mundane level, we had analyzed the different shifts of the guards, and we knew in advance that this group usually sat a little farther off than the others, giving Guangcheng a better angle for escape.

The calendar broke the day into two-hour blocks, auspicious or inauspicious. The block between eleven a.m. and one p.m. would be ideal, but I had no way of knowing exactly when an opportunity would present itself, if at all. Guangcheng himself did not know that I was consulting the calendar; nor was he aware that this day was of particular significance. But as it happened, the guard stood up and went for tea just before eleven o'clock.

I was lying flat on my neighbor's roof, wondering what to do and listening to the guards just outside her yard. I could hear their conversation, as well as the noises from the games they were playing on their phones. I considered the wall in front of me: the drop into the next yard was a sheer twelve feet, and I would have to find a way to climb down. This would have been easy enough when I was younger, but years of captivity had weakened my body—it would be too dangerous and noisy to jump from the top of the wall to the ground. I knew that a tree grew close to the eastern side of the wall; it was only about six or seven inches in diameter, Weijing had told me, but if I could somehow determine its exact location, I could climb down its trunk instead of jumping.

As I lay there, trying to remember precisely where the tree was, I heard a hissing noise from the direction of our house. It was Weijing, up on our kitchen roof with a scoop, under the pretext of gathering some dried corn, which we stored in a sack there.

"Hurry," she whispered frantically. "Get going before they spot you!"

I held my arm out straight, waving my fingers toward the next yard, mimicking an effort to locate the tree. She immediately knew what I was asking.

"It's right near your feet," she said, speaking as softly as she could. Though guards surrounded us on all sides and were never more than a few yards away, they didn't hear her.

After crawling to the edge of the roof, I turned around and started easing my legs over the far side of the wall, feeling for the tree with my toes. Clutching the spaces between the stones in the wall, I had descended just a short way before my arms began to shake with fatigue. I reached back with my foot in hopes of finding the tree. For an instant I felt my toes graze the trunk, but I was too feeble to hold on. I lost my grip, missed the tree, and hit the ground hard. Fortunately, I wasn't seriously hurt, though my dark glasses were broken.

I sat up, bruised but all right. But now I confronted a new problem: the moment I'd fallen, my second neighbor's dog, which was chained in the yard, had started barking. I needed to find a place to hide before the guards came to see what the noise was about. I kept low, crawling across the neighbor's yard, trying to stay out of sight of Chen Guang-feng, my neighbor's mentally ill son. This man, no longer young, lived in a prisonlike room in the yard with bars on an open window. He had been locked up that way for as long as I could remember, and he bayed from morning until night for his mother, who had no choice but to go about her daily routine, as though deaf to his cries. Sympathetic to his plight, I had tried to help him in the past, but now I feared that if he saw me, he might shout my name and give me away.

Moving on all fours, I did my best to stay below the man's window. Just beyond his room, Weijing had told me, stood three animal pens in a row, each one six or seven feet wide. She had mentioned that a gate to the closest pen was on one side of the low wall surrounding the pens, only when I ran my hand along the wall I found nothing. But with the dog barking wildly, I needed to get out of view immediately. By now, I was shaking uncontrollably with fear. I quickly scaled the four-foot concrete wall and fell flat on my back in the pen, exhausted—my frail body was no longer accustomed to such exertion. The front of the pen was closed, as Weijing had described to me, so at least the guards wouldn't see me if they happened to glance into the yard.

Inside the pen were several goats, and I heard them retreat in unison, bleating and shoving one another at the far end of the stall, alarmed at my sudden appearance in their midst. As I lay in the pen trying to make no noise whatsoever, the goats slowly mustered their courage and moved toward me, and after a time two or three of them were chewing on my clothes. Since I'd grown up around goats, this didn't bother me at all. One of them put its front two feet on my chest and bent down to smell my face. When I shifted a little, the startled goats once again retreated to the rear of the pen.

For the moment, I was too anxious and tired to do anything but lie there trembling. I decided to rest for a while—once my nerves had calmed and my shaking subsided, I would look for the chance to make a move.

After trying to help Guangcheng locate the tree, I didn't dare stay up on our roof, and I couldn't risk going up to look for him anymore. A little later, when I heard the barking of the second neighbor's dog, my heart skipped a beat; I was terrified that the animal would give Guangcheng away. With a morsel of food I teased our own dog, chained in the yard, hoping to make it bark to cover the noise and draw attention to us instead. Then, trying to be as casual as possible, I went to have a chat with the guards. Like us, they were farmers and the sons of farmers, and we'd come to know them a little. We exchanged a few words, and I went back inside, my heart racing. Luckily, our chickens chose just this moment to steal the dog's food, which caused such a commotion that the guards paid no attention to the racket two houses away.

For the rest of the day, I listened for the slightest sounds, hoping to hear something, anything that might tell me where Guangcheng was. I was crazed with fear, but I tried to behave as if it were just another day. Each time a guard entered our yard, I would anxiously study his face, looking for some sign that Guangcheng had been captured.

Early that afternoon, my mother-in-law returned from working in the fields. It was her habit to come in for a rest, have something to drink, and check in on Guangcheng. At first she didn't notice that he was gone. She drank some water and then walked to the bedroom and looked in, expecting to see Guangcheng.

"Is Guangcheng sleeping?" she asked me.

I couldn't lie to her. "Ma, Guangcheng has gone," I whispered.

She looked at me in surprise and anger. "How did he leave?"

I didn't answer.

"Isn't this just asking for the worst?" she said. "There's layer upon layer of guards out there. Do you really think he can get away?"

"What could I do, Ma? He's so sick—how long do you think he could go on like this?"

"They'll beat him to death for sure," she said, her voice full of reproach.

"He'll die if he stays here," I replied.

"Once he leaves this house," she said, "we have no way of knowing what will happen to him. They could beat him to death and dump him somewhere and we wouldn't even know it. If we're going to die, we should at least die together."

I covered her mouth and asked her not to speak of such unlucky things. "He'll be fine," I said, trying to reassure her. "There won't be a problem. But we should say some auspicious words and ask the gods to protect him."

My mother-in-law would not be appeased. She felt certain that the escape was doomed, and she held me responsible. "I go out for just a little while and you allow him to leave," she said bitterly. Then she picked up her stool and sat out in the courtyard, watching the chickens and refusing to eat or drink.

I usually don't believe in luck or God or any higher power, but on that day I believed in anything that might help us. As the afternoon went on, I returned to the kitchen several times to pray to the image of the Kitchen God on the wall, beseeching him to protect Guangcheng. I would glance through the door to see if any of the guards were watching, then quickly prostrate myself in front of the image. "Kitchen God, I beg you," I said. "Please ask all the other gods to watch over Guangcheng."

Leaning back against the wall of the goat pen, I listened hard for any indication that the guards had noticed my absence and were pursuing me. The dog was still barking; now, suddenly, Chen Guangfeng began to yell for his mother. The rhythm of his periodic cries had long since become a natural part of the village landscape, like the calls of birds and insects. I relaxed a little, hoping that his yelling might mix with the dog's bark and return a sense of normalcy to the late morning sounds.

After a while it went quiet again. As my nerves eased I began to collect my wits; wondering about the time, I realized that my talking watch, made especially for the blind, had broken in my fall. I sat up straighter and allowed my head to rise just to the top edge of the wall, but the dog began barking frantically again. Guangfeng immediately noticed me as well, and his cry changed from *"Niang! Niang!"* ("Mother! Mother!") to *"Li Hong! Li Hong!"* (he seemed to think I was his little brother). I quickly ducked back down.

An hour or so later, I heard the guards taking lunch. They shifted in their chairs, chopsticks clinked on metal bowls, and then came sounds of them getting up—they were going to wash their dishes. A post-meal quiet settled over them, and I could tell that the guards' attention was now elsewhere. More than a dozen of them were stationed on the other side of my neighbor's wall, in an unused space between this home and another.

Sensing an opportunity, I scrambled as quickly and quietly as possible over the wall between the first and second animal pens; except for a little stove, the second pen was empty. I explored the space, found a door on one side, and then listened for a while, trying to determine when to move and also what was in the third stall. I threw a handful of sand over the wall, and the sound the sand made revealed to me the basic contents of the pen: scattered corn stalks and a collection of farm tools. I took my chances and scurried into the third pen.

Once there, I came up against another wall, this one much more challenging. On the eastern side of this wall was a whole other family compound, one I happened to know very well. For a couple of hours I bided my time, calculating, listening. I heard the guards going about their business only a few feet away, chatting aimlessly, flicking open lighters, smoking cigarettes. As far as I could tell, they'd seen nothing amiss.

My watch was broken, but I had grown up using nature to tell time and I could still guess it accurately down to the hour, sometimes the half hour, by being alive to temperature, sounds of the natural world, and, above all, the human routines around me. About three p.m., four hours after I'd left my house, I heard Guangfeng's mother come home and begin to work in the yard. He continued crying, *"Niang! Niang!"* and eventually she brought him food, which I knew she would pass to him through a space in the bars. Soon after he finished eating, he began to shout for water and cigarettes.

I crouched in the pen and felt up and down the contours of the old and crumbling wall with my hands, trying to determine the best place to cross over. There was a shed along the northern side of the pen; just beyond it sat a guard, and I knew he would see me if I climbed to the top of the wall. The stones on the eastern side of the pen were very loose; I was sure they would not support my weight, so I decided to move close to the southeast corner, where I would have better handholds. Testing the wall, I put my palms flat on the rough surface and slowly pulled myself up, using my toes to find the best crevices. I explored every inch of that part of the wall, memorizing the exact location of each hold—where the first step would be, then the second, then the third. Once I reached the top, I would be completely exposed, so I could make no mistakes while climbing. Any noise at all and the guards would spot me. It would be over.

As the afternoon wore on, I heard a neighbor who lived across the road from Chen Guangfeng and his family open the door to her yard and roll her motorcycle into the road; a moment later she drove off. I knew she was going to pick her daughter up at school, which meant that it was now about four-thirty. Twenty minutes later, the motorbike came back down the road.

Soon the guards would be eating dinner, and my original plan had been to try climbing over the wall while they ate. Then I remembered that earlier in the morning I had heard a tractor coming from the north, the noise of its engine getting louder as it rumbled along the narrow road. The tractor had turned east, and the guards posted just outside the wall of the shed had scooped up their stools and made way as it passed. The tractor would almost certainly come back the same way, probably this very evening.

No distraction could be better for my attempt to climb this dangerous wall; the guards would inevitably turn their attention to the tractor. My chance would come, I reckoned, just as darkness was falling.

Our daughter Kesi, almost seven years old at the time, came home from school that afternoon a little before five. (At the time, our nine-year-old son, Kerui, was living with my mother in another village and going to a different school.) I worried that Kesi would be shocked and upset by her father's sudden disappearance—every day after returning home, her habit was to call out, "Baba! I'm back!" and go looking for him.

As she entered the house and dropped her school bag, I pulled her close to me and whispered in her ear: "Kesi, don't call for Baba or ask why he's not here. Your baba *has left."*

"Where did he go?" she asked, her voice loud with alarm.

"Quiet," I whispered urgently. "Your father has escaped."

I asked her to behave as if nothing had happened. Understanding, she nodded her head. Kesi knew about our previous attempts to escape, and sometimes she would even give us ideas. She talked to us about the tunnel we had dug the previous year, imagining which route it should follow and how we should run quickly once we all emerged from the other end. And she had watched the guards beat both of us, so she knew how serious the situation was.

Around five-thirty, I made noodles for dinner. Kesi nibbled at the food in her bowl, but neither Ma nor I could eat a thing. I continued to go through all the usual motions, at times talking out loud as if Guangcheng were there. "Let's wash your feet," I said, having filled a basin with water from outside. I took out the chamber pots and emptied them in the out-house. Later, we turned in for the night, but none of us could fall asleep. By now Kesi was terrified of what might happen to her father; she sobbed in her grandma's bed and covered her head with a quilt to muffle the sound. "I miss Baba," she whimpered quietly. I tried to comfort her, say-ing, "We'll see Baba very soon." Eventually she cried herself to sleep.

The hours seemed endless, but finally, just before dark, I discerned the sound of the tractor off in the distance. As it approached the inter-section, the guards began to move their stools, just as I'd hoped. This was my chance. I had only a few seconds to climb the wall while the tractor, my unknowing accomplice, distracted the guards and masked any noises I might make.

As quickly and quietly as possible, I climbed the wall's cobbled sur-face, picking my way up the rough footholds. At the top, I turned my body and hung my feet over the other side. I knew that the drop to the ground was around six feet, a manageable distance. And once I got beyond this wall—as soon as I landed—I would find myself in a famil-iar courtyard.

Long ago, my own family's home had stood in this spot. I had been born here, and for years I had lived in this compound with my parents and four older brothers. The house and courtyard now lay in ruins, but every detail, every memory I had of the spaces around me would be vital once I landed on the other side of the wall.

I let go and dropped. Instantly a stabbing pain exploded in my right foot. The tractor's noise had drowned out the sound of my fall, and somehow I managed to stifle the wail that rose up inside me. Sprawled out on the ground, I discovered that a pile of large rocks lay at the base of the wall, precisely where I had just landed. The pain was overwhelm-ing, but I knew I had to move beyond the opening between the walls, so I rolled along the ground until I came to yet another wall, this one on the north side of the courtyard. Again I tried to rise to test my foot, but the pain was too intense. In agony, I fell back to the ground.

If my escape had seemed risky before, now it could only be utter madness. Lying there, I sized up my situation: I was blind, alone, and beyond the help of my family or friends. In the hours since I had left home, I had traveled only a hundred feet or so, and my foot was almost certainly broken. Though it was nearly dark, there were still more guards at the edge of the village, and they would be patrolling all night. The world was too rough, too full of hazards. How could I make my way to the next village, still almost a mile away? And why had fate made my escape yet more difficult? But I was determined not to yield to the pain or my fears; no matter what, I would not give up. Instead, I concentrated on the way forward, thinking only of how to overcome the obstacles that lay ahead. Somehow, I would find a way to send those six luscious apples to Weijing.

CHAPTER ONE

A Child Apart

I cup my hands together, cradling a hard-boiled egg my mother has given me. It's still warm. I am three or four years old and rarely given my own egg, so I hold off as long as I can before eating it. Wandering outside, I find the millstones where we grind our food, feeling for the top stone, carefully placing shell and rock together. I listen to the sounds of the village children laughing and playing in the yard, relatives and neighbors coming and going. I head back inside, climb onto a stool, and gently set the egg on the table. It begins to roll, but I can't see it well enough to stop it. I hear the dull crack of shell against the dirt floor, then silence. If something bounces, rolls, makes a sound, I can use my ears to locate it, often with ease, but now I am at a loss. I strain my eyes, hoping to spot the egg, but all I can see are undifferentiated shapes. The neighbors and the children in the room don't come to help me; instead they gawk at my trouble. Only my mother hurries over. She peels the egg, then folds it inside a *jianbing* crepe with some salted pickles and places it in my outstretched hands.

I was born in a remote Chinese village called Dongshigu on November 12, 1971, in the midst of the Cultural Revolution, a time of hardship and great bitterness. I was healthy at birth, but after five months a terrible fever set in, and we had no money for the hospital. Despite being acutely worried about my condition, my mother also had to feed and care for my four older brothers, aged five, eight, eleven, and fourteen. My father was working far away at the time, and we had no access to telephones; her in-laws, meanwhile, were consumed with their own affairs.

Making do on her own, my mother attended to every aspect of our lives. Each day she had to fetch water from a well near the Meng River, carrying buckets that swung on a pole over her shoulder. Before dawn she spent hours grinding food at our mill wheel to make the batter for the day's *jianbing*. During the day, when she was not out working in the fields, she gathered wood and kindling for the cooking fire up in the hills. And always, she adhered to the strict work orders from the commune that organized how we worked, lived, and ate.

Her heart torn by my wild crying after I came down with the fever, my mother wrapped me in some old cloths and nestled me in a basket in the yard near where she worked. She would need two yuan to take me to a doctor at the local hospital, the only place with real medical care. But that was a substantial sum, for we had almost no money—my father earned only eighteen yuan a month at his job. In desperation, my mother set out to borrow the money from the head of her production team, who sent her to the bookkeeper, who sent her to the man responsible for financial matters. "How can you borrow money from us?" the man asked her incredulously. "You owe us money, and you haven't earned enough grain points." The communes were divided up into production brigades and even smaller production teams, and within the production team you earned points based on how much work you got done. You had to contribute at least as much as you ate, but with my mother the only adult working full-time, our family often fell behind. No points, no money, no doctor. The man told my mother to get a letter from the head of the production team, but she knew he was just trying to get rid of her.

Discouraged and distraught, she went to friends and relatives and tried to borrow money, but there was none to be had. The village "barefoot doctor," a farmer who had received very basic medical training to provide care in remote rural areas, had no idea how to bring down my fever.

I cried for two whole days and two whole nights, my tiny body burning and squirming in my mother's arms. On the third day, my mother was up at her usual early hour, preparing food for the family, when she heard my terrible wailing begin again. She picked me up to breast-feed me but recoiled in terror when she saw the blue masses clouding my dark eyes. She rushed me to an old woman in a nearby village who had some experience with home remedies. Her cure, after examining me, was to blow on my eyes; of course, there was no change in my condition.

My parents never knew the nature of my illness or why my fever caused me to go blind. After returning home a month later and learning what had happened, my father arranged to take me to the local clinic. By then it was too late for my eyes, but my father was determined to find a cure, and over the next several years my parents took me to doctor after doctor, each time in vain. One said it was keratitis, another said glaucoma, but they all concluded that there was nothing they could do.

Whatever the cause of my fever, the results were unforgiving. In my earliest memories I see only splashes of color, and only if an object is right in front of my eyes. Sometimes I like to say that I was blinded by communism—or, more specifically, a wave of unrealistic, empty propaganda that swept the country continually for decades. The Communist Party, the bringer of "scientific development," liked to boast about its hospitals and its free health care, about how well people were treated and how much better things were now than in the past. But the truth is that we lacked the most basic medical care and were always at the mercy of illness. Death came for us often. Two years before I was born, in fact, my mother had given birth to a baby girl, the daughter she'd been longing for after bearing four sons. When the baby sickened, she had no money for the hospital, and finally there was little my mother could do but wait and hope. My sister had what the villagers called "the seven-day sickness," and, indeed, she was dead after eight or nine days. If the girl had survived, my mother later told me, I would probably never have been born.

Now four years old, I am hanging suspended between heaven and earth. As my brother pulls from above, I rise in the air. Three, five, ten feet up—no fear, only joy. Higher up in the persimmon tree, I can hear everything, every sound etched in the air. I hear the reverberating calls of birds, their overlapping, melodic lines spinning through the trees, and the sounds at a spring nearby, where the villagers are using ladles to scoop up water, the liquid splashing into the buckets and jugs; I can distinguish the minute changes in pitch, from the first plashing into an empty bucket to that quickening sound when it's almost full. All around I hear a chorus of life: songbirds trilling, animals lowing, bleating, barking, each one with its particular intensity, its own pattern of rising and falling, each moving in and out of rhythm with the others.

We have done this before, Third Brother and I. He loves to climb trees and catch birds, and this is how he takes me with him. He secures one end of a rope around my waist; holding the other end, he climbs up the tree and ties the rope tight at the fork of two sturdy branches. I stand beneath the tree, waiting. He strains to pull me up, little by little, until I reach that fork in the tree, where I can sit in perfect contentment. At first I simply hold the branch, but soon I grow bold, touching everything around me.

Above me are persimmons, branches lined with them. I ask my brother to pick one for me. "You know you can't eat them," he says. "They're not ripe yet, and you can die from eating an unripe persimmon." "I know," I reply. He climbs up to a higher branch to pick out the biggest and roundest one he can find. My hands are so small that I can barely hold the persimmon in one hand while still hugging the tree with the other. My enchantment is complete—I stare at the brightness of the fruit's reds and yellows, feeling in my palm its smooth and finely textured skin. I hold the persimmon close to my face, almost touching my lips. The feel and smell are so enticing that I can no longer help myself: I take a small, secret bite off the pointed tip. At first the taste is sweet, but when I take a second, larger bite, my lips pucker, and I remember my brother's warning. I spit out the second bite quickly.

Seeing that something is wrong, Third Brother climbs down to me and asks, "Did you eat it?" I am afraid he will be angry with me, so I hold the part I'd bitten inside my palm, out of sight. In a small voice I lie, saying I hadn't. "Let me see your persimmon," he says, prying open my hand and finding it. "Why did you eat it?" he asks. I had promised not to, so I don't know what to say.

"How do persimmons grow on branches?" I ask my brother a few minutes later, when he is once again scampering up above me. He bends a branch laden with fruit toward me, close enough to touch. With one hand I hold the fruit I've already bitten; with the other I feel my way across the slippery bark, finding two glossy persimmons that are growing together. I grab one of them and twist it, but my brother warns me not to pick it and tells me to let go. As soon as I do, the branch snaps back into place, the persimmons trembling.

Someone approaches from along the road, footsteps shuffling rhythmically on the packed dirt. "How on earth did that child get so high up in that tree?" a woman calls out. "Don't you know that's dangerous?" Third Brother replies, "It's okay. We've done this many times before at home."

When I've finally had enough, I shout, "Let's go down!" My brother slowly uncoils the rope, length by length. I reach out to touch the tree bark one more time. When I am close to the ground, I start swinging and spinning back and forth. I am not afraid—I am thrilled. I feel nothing but freedom, all the way down.

Dongshigu Village, Shuanghou Township, Linyi Prefecture, Shandong Province, China. A bow in the Meng River embraces the village along its east and north sides; to the south is a landscape of rolling hills, and to the west is a stream that winds down from the hills into the Meng. The Menglianggu Mountains rise in the distance to the north. We liked to say that water flowed on three sides of us, with hills on the fourth. A patchwork of walled yards enclose thatch-roofed or clay-shingle cottages and kitchen buildings, woodpiles, dogs, goats, chickens, mill wheels, and outhouses. A short walk through the crooked dirt lanes and footpaths between yards brings you quickly to the edge of the village; continue past the family garden plots and through a forest of young poplars and you will come to the quiet waters of the Meng, the gateway to our village. The river is our lifeblood, our source for everything from drinking and irrigating to laundry and bathing water, at least for part of the year. Flip off your shoes and roll up your pants to cross the river—which is what we all did until a bridge was finally built in 1996—and you come to the road that connected us to the outside world. Walking north, south, or west from the village, you will come to our crop fields, which stretch out across the floodplain in a checker-board of corn, sweet potatoes, tobacco, and sorghum.

Summer and fall were the preferred seasons for farmers, in part because after a long day in the fields we could take a trip down to the river to bathe. As the days shortened and the temperature began to drop, the river water turned icy, leaving people with no way to get clean. Until 1980, the only public bath available to villagers was in the county capital, thirty miles and a prohibitive bus fare away. Heating water in a pot for a bath wasn't a good alternative, either, as it was just as frigid inside as outside. As the cold weather descended, the dirt settled in bit by bit, layer by layer; given the time and the price, people simply stayed home, not taking a single shower or bath the entire winter, until well after the New Year—celebrated in January or February—or even past late April, when the trees began to bud and new grass first greened the hillsides. By late May, the river would still be chilly, but by then people were finally willing to brave the cold water to get clean.

I have exquisitely vivid memories of that first bath of the season. The feeling of lying on the riverbank with the spring sunshine warming my body is almost indescribable: tingling, relaxed, wonderfully alive.

I don't know when my ancestors first settled in Dongshigu, but I know that we've been there for generations. Around half the roughly five hundred villagers share the surname Chen. Besides our family name, my brothers and everyone else of our generation in the village share the "generation name" Guang, or "Light," chosen and recorded by our village ancestors centuries ago. My parents didn't bother to give me my own name at birth or as a child, so I chose one for myself when I was a teenager: Cheng, or "Sincere." Before that, I was simply Little Five, since I was my parents' fifth son.

From the time I was a boy, Dongshigu felt like an extended family, a village of people I would call "Uncle" and "Grandma" and "Cousin" whether they were actually kin or not. This was partly out of closeness and partly out of respect for elders and an understanding of where each stood in relation to others. When I was small, every home was open, and only two families had wooden gates to their yards. In greeting each other we most commonly said, "Did you eat yet?" reflecting years of hardship and common concern for our family, friends, and neighbors. Almost no one said "please" or "thank you"—it wasn't the custom—but we expressed gratitude and warmth in other ways, such as the simple exclamation "Oh, you're here!"

In spite of the close-knit relationships, the people in my village lived on a knife edge of survival until the last few decades. For generations, wars and social upheavals ignited famines, and famines led to power struggles and political battles, wrenching the common folk along a path of scorching instability. Dongshigu was no exception.

Like many rural Chinese, our family owned just a tiny sliver of land, not enough to let us scratch out even a basic living, and we endured the most desperate sort of poverty. When he was young, my father possessed a single pair of pants, and they were badly torn—until his teens, a neighbor once told me, he went around "with his ass hanging out." When my father heard this description, he laughed and said, "Where could you get clothes in those days?" In the cold winter months, my grandmother stuffed the legs of his pants with cotton wads to keep him warm, as many people still do in the Chinese countryside. The villagers made what they wore, and they wore what they'd made until their clothes were completely threadbare, often going without shoes even in the dead of winter.

When he was about ten, my father was considered old enough to help with the family mill wheel, getting up every morning as soon as the cocks started crowing, well before dawn. For two or three hours each morning he walked in a circle, straining to turn the family's millstones. Pouring water through a hole in the top stone, he ground sweet potato or a bit of corn—or, in lean times, grass or even tree bark—into batter for the day's *jianbing*. My grandmother would then spread the batter onto a convex *ao* griddle about three feet in diameter, frying up a huge, paper-thin crepe, our local comfort food. Her *jianbing* were often the family's one consistent meal, so they ate as much as they could at the start of the day.

When there was no food, my father and his siblings sometimes grew so weak that they couldn't get out of bed. Scouring the land for anything edible, the people in our village stripped the trees bare, devouring the leaves of elms and poplars and locusts, gnawing the bark to ease their raging bellies. This only made them sicker. When he was eighteen, my father nearly died of starvation, suffering gravely with edema;

at one point, he became terribly ill after eating cotton seeds, a desperate measure. Nobody spoke of education or the opportunity for a better life; sheer survival was all anyone could hope for.

Occasionally, when her children were especially hungry, my grandmother would swallow her pride and beg a few *jianbing* from the neighbors, a somewhat better-off peasant family. It was a time of incredible bitterness. When my father told me stories from those days—tales of poverty, affliction, and upheaval in which any relief was short-lived—he always wept.

My mother grew up in Sangyuan, a village about five miles from Dong-shigu, a significant distance at the time. She never learned to read or write. After losing her mother at age sixteen, she was raised by her father. In the late 1940s, when the civil war between the Communists and the Nationalists reached Sangyuan, he took her and her surviving brothers up into the mountains. They hid under a rock cliff by day and returned to their village at night to get food. The sight of a soldier who'd been blasted by a missile, tumbling across the mouth of their cave, was seared in her memory forever.

Liberation—that's the name the Communist Party uses for its victory in 1949, when the Communists grabbed power and the Nationalists retreated to Taiwan—brought yet more trouble to Dongshigu. With its policy of land reform, the party began its rule by inciting the people to antagonize the landlords in a massive class struggle. They distributed all land to the farmers, in tiny but truly independent parcels. That independence didn't last long—in effect, all the little landlords were replaced by one big monopolistic landlord, the Communist Party, which soon took back the land, along with villagers' possessions, in the name of collectivization. The result was even worse than the feudalism that had come before; under the old system, if a landlord treated you unfairly, you could always try to go work for someone else. Under communism, there were no alternatives.

My mother met my father through her aunt, who, a few years earlier, had married into our village and come to live with her husband's family, as the bride always did. My parents married in 1955 and had my eldest brother in 1957, on the eve of the Great Leap Forward, a political campaign launched by Mao Zedong that became a man-made catastrophe on a massive scale.

Today, both Chinese and Western experts estimate that roughly forty million people died premature deaths between 1958 and 1961, primarily due to starvation as a result of the party's policies. Mao called for China to "walk on two legs," which meant developing agriculture and industry simultaneously, but he quickly brought the country to its knees. His announced goal was for China to surpass the United Kingdom and America in industrial output within a matter of decades. A slogan at the time went, "If you think big, your crops will be big." The effort to keep up with his program for development pushed people to absurd levels of competition, with production brigades, villages, and towns all reporting wildly inflated agricultural output. In some regions the production brigades claimed that they were reaping up to 800,000 pounds per acre, even though the most fertile lands could produce no more than 4,500 pounds per acre. When illusion finally met reality, the economy responded by contracting. The collectivization of society and the establishment of people's communes were an unmitigated disaster.

In 1958, three years after my parents married, the harvest promised to be outstanding, with bumper crops of grain, corn, soybeans, and sweet potatoes growing in the fields. But everyone's energy and labor were focused on producing steel: Mao had ordered every village to set up its own "backyard furnaces" to smelt steel, gathering anything with the least bit of iron—woks and door locks included—for the communal collection, and no one could avoid the countless hours of work this involved. The people of Dongshigu were pained to see the unharvested crops rotting on the land, even as they went hungry. Some people tried to gather up the harvest, but if you took anything from the fields, you were punished. The next year people dug up and ate the buried, rotten sweet potatoes, which poisoned some of them. For three years there was almost no food, and sometimes people were forced to eat tree bark, which itself became scarce. Full-fledged famine began.

The party served what food there was in the communal canteen, everyone eating from the same big pot, everything shared. If smoke was seen coming from your house, you fell under immediate suspicion and your house might be searched. Were you cooking in secret? Were you hoarding food? Harsh punishment followed for those who took the "capitalist road" by trying to feed themselves.

Access to food was power. One time, my mother told me, she stayed up until the early morning hours making *jianbing* for the commune; then, around dawn, she went to the canteen to cook. There were few clocks in the village, and people had to rely on signs of nature to keep time. Because my mother hadn't heard the rooster crowing, she arrived late. She was interrogated by the party secretary, who put food in her bowl but withheld it from her with a taunt: "What were you doing this morning?"

"I was up cooking until very late last night," she replied.

He poured her bowl of food back into the pot. It didn't matter how hard she had worked or how exhausted she was. Arriving after the appointed hour meant getting nothing to eat, and staying up late while cooking for the commune was no excuse. My mother had no choice but to go hungry and hope that she would finally be given some food later in the day.

I am five, and Fourth Brother is ten. We have been out playing in the fields while our mother works. When it's time to go home, my brother and I race ahead. "Let's get some *guobing*!" he cries as we run. I know the village so well that I have no fear of running into anything.

We have no money, so we search for something to trade. My brother takes the top off the ceramic vessel where we keep our family ration of grain: we can use wheat. He makes me scoop out the grain to give to the person at the shop who makes the delicious wheat cakes called *guobing*; since I am so much younger, I am less likely to get in trouble. The supply meant to last our family a full year is nearly gone, but we pay no heed, now salivating at the thought of the *guobing*.

At the shop, the baker swears and laughs at us for bringing such a meager offering. She weighs the wheat, calculating the size of the slice it will buy us.

By then our mother is almost home, and she meets us on the road. "How dare you give away our wheat for *guobing*!" She is furious, and bends down to pick up a stone to throw at Fourth Brother. I know she won't hit me—I am the baby in my family. My brother runs back to the house, crying. My mother feels bad, knowing how thin and hungry we are. She calls to Fourth Brother, but he stands his ground, angrily staring out the window. She breaks the *guobing* into two pieces, one for each of us, but I balk, wanting to first feel which piece is bigger. She gives him the smaller, and I am pleased. My mother has worked all day in the fields, but she takes nothing for herself.

Sighted people take so many things for granted. What does a bird look like? What's the difference between a sparrow and a swallow? How does a kite fly? What makes two trees different? Other children were able to understand these things in the blink of an eye, but I had to find alternative ways to take in the world. Since my mother worked in the fields and my father was often away, my brothers played an important role in my education, helping me develop a full breadth of knowledge about how things work, about animals, and about life itself. They never failed to bring me along on their adventures, whether those trips involved climbing trees, catching insects and birds, or exploring the woods beyond our village. Whatever they wanted me to know about, they would put directly in my hands. Thanks to my brothers, I learned as a child what other blind people may not learn over an entire lifetime.

We made our own toys—there were no others to be had—by packing mud and clay from the fields into balls or cars, or crafting bows and arrows and slingshots from bamboo and wood we found in our yard. Sometimes, to entertain or comfort me, Third Brother would take me up a tree. After breaking off a branch, he would hand it to me, and I would hold it, feeling the softness of the leaves and the roughness of the bark, understanding from the texture and shape how this tree was different from others. Often I would taste the leaves, and after long experience I could tell many trees apart and give their names confidently. When I was older, my brothers taught me to trap fish using a plate and a piece of cloth; later, as I learned the life cycles of fish, I became quite skilled at catching them. My knowledge of these things was intimate and physical; I came to know the world in a way that most sighted people could never comprehend.

Once, when I was about three or four, Third Brother and I were swimming in the Meng River near the village when my brother spotted a woodpecker landing in its hole in a great willow tree on the opposite side of the riverbank. Third Brother climbed the tree, grabbed the woodpecker, and brought it back to me. I held its wings in my hands, amazed at its huge beak and its smooth tongue, which came slithering out into my hand. It escaped when we got home, but my brother went after it, running through the village, through the fields, until he finally caught it and brought it back, triumphant. The story of his perseverance became legend in the village, but in fact we would often chase a single bird over the course of an afternoon, desperate to cradle it in our hands, in all its softness and vulnerability.

I grew to love the songs of birds and to admire their habits, and for years every spring I would climb into the trees to be with them. Some fledglings I took home to raise myself, feeding them insects or wheat and teaching them tricks—I did everything I could think of to make them sing and stay with me. At night we kept the birds in little pots we left partly covered to keep the mice away. As the birds got older, we let them fly around the courtyard and the house; we laughed when they perched on chairs and tables and shoulders, a natural part of our home.

Swallows built exquisite nests under the eaves of the houses in the village, daubing mud collected from the riverbank one beakful at a time. I had a special love of swallows because of their tireless method of building, the way they worked day after day to create something both durable and beautiful. Farmers also treasured swallows, as they ate harmful insects and bugs. Sparrows, on the other hand, made flimsy nests of straw taken from the thatch in our roofs, often leaving holes that leaked in a hard rain. They also ate grain from the fields and plundered the elegant swallows' nests, grabbing and pecking the swallows, forcing them to abandon their homes. The sparrows would then push the swallow eggs or their young out onto the ground and lay their own eggs in the nest. In my heart I loved all birds, but as children we grew incensed at this injustice and often tried to catch the sparrows, climbing up to the roof to reach into their nests.

Some birds ate corn or millet, not insects. That made it much easier to raise and care for them, and they would fatten up nicely. Even after I got married, I loved raising birds such as the *banjiu*, or turtledove. I liked to keep them for a while; when they seemed healthy and strong, I would let them go. I felt a joy in setting them free but also sadness at losing them, feeling their wings brush my hands for the last time as they took off in flight.

This time I'm five or six years old. It's summer, and boys my age don't wear any clothing: we stay naked all day long. In the morning I spring out of bed, quickly tear at a *jianbing*, then head out to find my friends. I run, the wind rushing over my skin, my bare feet hitting the ground rhythmically. On the open roads and paths around the village, I have nothing to fear, and my speed gives me freedom. I don't mind the small rocks or twigs.

If there is a wall, I climb it. Any wall is a challenge and a joy, my fingers seeking pockets in the rocks, the moisture cooling my toes. Short walls, high walls, old and new: I come to know them all. Sometimes I climb a neighbor's roof and shimmy down the tree on the other side. People seem surprised at my ability, and this makes me happy.

As my friends and I head to the river, the older men scything grass on the side of the road joke with us, pointing between our legs. "Hey! You've got something growing there! What is it? I'll cut it off for you!" They pretend to come after us with their scythes. I learn to swim with my friends, first with their help; later, when they go off to school, I move through the cool waters on my own, reaching down to the bottom of the river to feel the smooth layers of sand between my fingers.

As a boy, I encountered evidence of nature's laws all around me and found that many of these laws applied to people, too. If you buy a pig and put it in a pen and then it escapes, even just once for a day or two, you'll have a very hard time getting it back in again. Rural people know this instinctively, and it's true of cows, horses, dogs, chickens, and many other animals—including humans, as I came to understand as an adult. There are rhythms of the natural world that should not be ignored, and the habits and customs of everything from birds to insects and plants should be respected.

Of course, when we were children, upsetting the natural order meant excitement. Our parents used a familiar phrase to warn us to behave: "Whatever you do, don't go after wasps' nests," meaning that we shouldn't look for trouble that could be avoided. But we loved doing precisely that, opening up wasps' nests just for the thrill. Wasp and bee larvae are delicious (especially when fried up in an omelet), and they made excellent nutrition for the birds we kept at home, particularly since we didn't always have anything else on hand to feed them with. We knocked the nest down with sticks and rocks, shrieking with excitement as dozens of wasps swarmed straight at us. They could easily overtake a child, but we learned to run in zigzag patterns and make sudden turns to throw them off. We discovered that they see bright, contrasting colors more easily than dark ones, and that we could escape from them in the mottled shade of a corn or sorghum field; older children who sometimes wore shirts knew not to wear white.

With a nest in hand, we set about divvying up the larvae, counting how many compartments in the comb were open and how many had been blocked off. If a compartment was still open, that told us that the wasps had still been delivering food to the larva within, which meant that the larva's digestive tract contained feces and so was unclean. When the larvae develop to a certain point, the wasps close off the compartments and stop bringing food; the larvae then starve into "cleanliness," eventually metamorphosing into adulthood. We split our spoils according to who had shown the most bravery and fortitude in the struggle to bring down the nest.

Our parents berated us when we returned home covered in stings; because I was blind, my mother was often particularly worried about me. She would say, "Every day you come home with new cuts on top of the old ones!" But no matter how many times I hurt myself opening nests and running from angry wasps, I could never get enough of the excitement that came with it.

As a boy I loved all kinds of animals; at times I turned our home into a small menagerie. When I was around six years old, I got a little black dog from an uncle who was moving away. Especially with my mother off in the fields and my brothers all in school, my dog was my constant partner and playmate. We would often lie together in the yard, and I would gently touch her belly, her ears, her mouth, her teeth; sometimes I'd pick up her hind legs and we'd race together across the dirt. I put a bell around her neck, so I could hear her wherever she went.

"You're closer to that dog than you are to your mother," an aunt said to me once, only half-joking.

After Mao's death, in 1976, the party followed the Two Whatevers policy, the leaders announcing they would "resolutely uphold whatever policy decisions Chairman Mao made, and unswervingly follow whatever instructions Chairman Mao gave." This included murdering dogs, on the pretext that they spread rabies. In 1978, when I was seven, the party stepped up its barbaric anti-dog campaign. "Every family with a dog should kill it or sell it," blared the village propaganda. Almost every family had a dog; they were a part of our lives. Some villagers stalled, hoping the campaign would end, while others went ahead and sold their dogs. But few were willing to kill their own dogs themselves.

I continued to insist that we had to keep my dog, but one day my mother finally said, "We have to sell it!" I lay on the ground, weeping in despair. My dog was later taken away with a rope tied around her neck; then, just before the exterminators could hang her from a nearby tree, she ran back to our house. My mother wouldn't let her in, but I pushed my mother aside so my poor dog could hide under a table, where she waited, panting, with the rope still around her neck. Finally Elder Brother took her away, back to the dog killer. I mourned her for a long, long time.

At one point I was given a little goat by a relative. The kid quickly came to see me as her mother, and when she couldn't lay eyes on me, she would cry desperately. At night I couldn't bear to tie her up in the yard, so I would undo her rope, but then I could hear her dragging the rope around our yard as she searched for me. By day, I took her everywhere with me, and together we would wander the village paths and walk down to the river, where she would graze the thick grass. She knew to run when I touched her tail and would slow to my pace, showing me the way.

With her first pregnancy, when I was eight or nine, I experienced a kind of rapture I'd never known, and I become completely swept up in the changes in her form. Her belly grew full and round, and her udders swelled. Every day I would gently pat her body, her stomach, and her udders to see if there was milk yet—this was the sign of impending labor—and I couldn't wait for her to give birth. I stayed nearby during the labor, wanting to help, but my goat delivered twins on her own.

After she had licked the two white kids clean, grunting and nudging their tiny bodies, one of the kids instinctively tried to move under his mother's belly, expending a great deal of effort and falling down in the process. I knew he wanted to drink his mother's milk, but he couldn't stand up all the way on his shaking legs, and he seemed too weak to raise his head high enough to suckle. He made an anxious, plaintive bleating noise. I tried to push the teat into the kid's mouth, just as I'd stuffed worms into the mouths of birds I was raising, but I could tell I wasn't doing it correctly. I also worried that the mother would crush her own kids with her powerful hind legs, something that occasionally happened.

Later that day a friend's father, whom I called Fourth Uncle, came to see us. He was experienced at raising goats, so I told him about the birth and my worry that the kids weren't suckling yet. Fourth Uncle was not at all soft and tender with the animals, as I had been. He squatted down in the dirt to get a good angle, dragged the kid under the mother's belly, and used four of his fingertips underneath the kid's lower jaw to pry open its mouth. With his other hand he stuffed the teat into the kid's mouth.

Of course I couldn't see any of this, but I put my hands on his to feel what he did. I had my left hand on his left, my right hand on his right. I began to understand. "If it falls out," said Fourth Uncle, "you push it back in. When he tastes the milk and it tastes good, he'll drink."

I then went to the other side of the mother with the other kid, gently holding it in my arms. I tried to imitate what Fourth Uncle had done, positioning the kid's head with one hand and pushing the nipple in with the other. The kid immediately began suckling, and with my fingers under the kid's jaw, I could feel him drinking and swallowing milk. I reveled at the feeling of this new life taking in nourishment from his mother, who now and again turned her head to watch, grunting in a way I had never heard before but that I knew represented the intense bond a mother can feel for her child.

I have no memory of what it is like to truly see the world. When I was a young boy, colors had a special importance to me, since I could see swaths of pure colored light, but only if something was right in front of my eyes or if it was something very large, like the canopy of a tree on a bright day. In every other way, I was completely blind. As I grew older,

I finally lost the ability to perceive light and color altogether, so if not for those early years I wouldn't understand the concept of color at all.

My parents spent many years looking for a cure for my blindness. They tried everything they could think of, and I'm sure their efforts depleted their meager savings. The first operation took place when I was four years old. I was taken to a hospital in a neighboring county, where a man wrenched me away from my mother as I screamed and cried. To prepare for the surgery, I couldn't eat all day, so I was not only afraid but very hungry. I was laid out on the operating table with a face mask covering my nose; then someone pulled a cloth over my entire face. Sobbing, I inhaled the medicinal smell of ether as I drifted into unconsciousness.

My father later told me that the operation lasted for four hours. When the nurses wheeled me to my room, I was breathing quietly and my eyes were bandaged. I didn't regain consciousness until late in the afternoon the next day; as I came awake, I immediately cried out that a hat was attached to my face. Tearing at the air, I pleaded with my mother. "Help me get it off!" I shouted.

The doctor put medicine on my eyes for several days after the operation, and it hurt terribly. But what caused the worst pain was the bright light he would shine in my eyes—light had become a torment. My mother and father would hold my hands when the doctor shined his light at me; they tried their best to comfort me and take my mind off the pain.

When I first started going outside after the operation, I had to cover my eyes and look down at the ground because the daylight hurt so much. I spent two weeks in the hospital, and the bandages stayed on for almost a month. When it finally came time to remove them, my parents stood beside me anxiously, then immediately asked if I could see anything. I told them it was the same: there was no change in what I could see. My parents refused to believe me and began holding various objects in front of me. I could just make out a vague black blur where my mother stood. She cried bitterly.

The next year we tried again. My maternal grandfather had written to my mother about a new treatment in a hospital where he now lived, far to the south in Hangzhou, in Zhejiang Province. So many details of our journey and our stay there are still etched in my mind—never before had I experienced so much or traveled so far. My cousin came with us on our journey, as my mother couldn't read and wouldn't know how to get to her father's new home.

Leaving our village one summer morning, we hitched a ride on a 50-horsepower tractor that happened to be drawing water from the river for its radiator just as we were passing by. I remember seeing that the front of it was bright red—my favorite color at the time, the same as the buses that sometimes came near the village, the same as a little plastic Mao badge we had. The driver was heading to Dongzhou, about forty miles away, where we could catch the train for Zhejiang. Vehicles like this were few and far between, and I was thrilled. Climbing into the wagon hitched at the back, I ran my hands over every inch of it, trying to understand how everything worked and fit together. How many pieces of iron had been used to make the wagon? Were they held together with screws? Soon my hands were completely covered in oil and grime—we had no water, so my mother cleaned my hands with an apple core.

We rode in the wagon all the way to Dongzhou, where we spent the night before boarding the train the next day. I had never experienced anything like a train before. When the locomotive eased into the station, I heard the *hudong, hudong, hudong* sound of its wheels, and I was sure that only something with angles could make that noise when rolling on the ground. I knew that when I spun a screw with a square or six-sided head it would make that kind of sound, as would a square-sided stone if I flipped it on the ground. I couldn't see the train's wheels, but I sensed that they were there, and I desperately wanted to feel if they were round or square. Before we boarded the train, I tried to step forward to touch the wheels, but my mother yanked me back, yelling that the train would run me over if I wasn't careful.

Once on the train, I started touching everything around me—the window and the seats and the tray table. A loudspeaker played "The East Is Red" and other such songs. I was intensely alert while waiting for the train to move, and I kept asking my mother if we had left yet. "Not yet, not yet," she replied.

When we finally got under way, I was entranced. At one point another train whooshed past from the opposite direction, and I could feel the shadow and the flickering as the two trains swept past each other, bands of sunlight flashing as the windows momentarily aligned. I wanted to touch the other train and thought I could stretch out my hand through the open glass. I was furious when my mother made me bring my hand inside and my cousin quickly shut the window.

A day later, we arrived at my grandpa's home. Grandpa lived on the first floor of an apartment building. It was a simple space, with just a small stove and a table for furniture. He was thrilled to see me, and I ran into his arms. Also living with Grandpa were my step-grandmother and my uncle, who agreed to go to the hospital with my mother and me to see an experienced ophthalmologist.

Early in the morning, we set out for the hospital. My uncle, my mother, and I drove there in a truck, whose sides, headlights, and hood I first touched extensively and whose every quality I was alive to. I declared my intention to learn how to drive, but everyone immediately made it clear that this option was forever closed to me. That response made me long for it even more; I told my mother that I was determined to drive a car someday, and I still am.

We stayed with Grandpa for about a month. One day, while visiting the little store near Grandpa's house, my mother spotted a pair of scissors in a glass case. The shopkeeper took them out for her to examine, and she fingered the blades, opening and closing them. All of our clothing was made by my mother, as there were still no clothes to be bought in stores, and no money to buy them with if there had been. At home, the scissors my mother used were old and dull and could no longer cut well. She longed for that new pair of scissors, but we simply could not spare the few yuan to buy it.

At Grandpa's, I had unending opportunities to take in the exotic particularities of my surroundings. For the first time I tasted sugarcane, which immediately reminded me of how at home I would eat corn stalks for their sweetness, peeling off the skin with my teeth and fingers. I was also fascinated by the water buffalo my mother described to me. He would walk back and forth along a steep side of a gulch near Grandpa's house, and I worried that he would fall into the water at the bottom. But when the herder shouted, *"Hui lai!"*—"Come back!"—the buffalo would immediately shift its position and head back up the gully, never ceasing its grazing for a moment.

One day we took a bus to a different hospital, and once again a doctor opened my eyes wide with his fingers and began to shine his flashlight at my pupils; it felt as if someone were electrocuting me by plugging wires into my eye sockets. I screamed and pushed his flashlight away. "Okay, okay, so you're afraid of light," he said calmly. "I won't shine the light in your eyes again." He then positioned his flashlight on the side of my face, which felt much better. He was the first doctor who understood and tried to reduce the pain I was feeling, a compassionate response I never forgot. But he, too, said nothing could be done for me, suggesting that my mother take me to Beijing.

Soon after, we set out on the long journey home. When I got dressed that morning, I put on the new pair of sneakers Grandpa had bought for me, the first factory-made pair of shoes I had ever owned. At first I couldn't figure out which sneaker went on which foot; until then I'd owned only the cloth shoes my mother made for me at home, which could be worn on either foot.

Grandpa, my step-grandmother, and my uncle accompanied us on the long walk to the bus station, ignoring my mother's pleas that we were fine, that they should go back home. Their courtesy and consideration were in the best Chinese tradition: you always see a loved one to the very last place you can reach, until finally you have to part. After we arrived at the bus station and I took my seat on the bus, there was a little tap on my window. Then I heard Grandpa call to me. "Little Five," he said in a wavering voice, "please come again." I didn't yet understand how precious this visit was, and I never got the chance to go back. My mother cried as the bus drove away.

In the years following this trip, my parents made yet more attempts to restore my sight. We visited another barefoot doctor; he instructed me to drink a strong potion three times a day, but it had no effect on my eyes. There was a famous doctor in a nearby county who was recommended by one of my father's colleagues. He was very kind, but he didn't even suggest that I take any medicine, which to my mother meant that there was no hope at all.

Even so, my father made one last effort when I was nine. After hearing about a new method for curing blindness, he took me to a doctor in Jinan, the provincial capital. Again we endured the routine of hopes being raised and then dashed: after examining me, the doctor said there was nothing he could do. He wrote a letter referring us to another expert in the city. We went to see him, too, but the result was the same.

As we walked out of that last hospital, onto the streets of Jinan, I could hear the shouts of hawkers selling ice pops. My father felt wretched; as I held his hand, he cried, and I didn't quite understand why. I desperately wanted an ice pop, but I didn't dare ask my father, given his mood.

A man on the street asked my father why he was crying.

He held my hand up and exclaimed, "There's no way to cure my son's blindness!"

As we looked for a hotel in which to spend the night, my father finally noticed that I kept turning my head in the direction of the hawker's cries. *"Binggun! Xuegao!"* he was shouting, "Ice pops! Ice cream!" My father bought me an ice pop, and soon we checked into a small room, which we would share with several other guests. Later he went to buy train tickets—we would be leaving the next day—and returned with a bunch of bananas, a new experience for me. I was rapt, eager to feel all the bananas together in a single bunch, just as they must have been when they came off the tree. I felt the five fruits from top to bottom, and then I ate one, relishing the new flavor and texture. The next morning, before boarding the train, I couldn't stop myself from eating just one more, which left one for my father and two to bring home to my mother, who had never seen a banana.

After that trip, there were no more visits to doctors, and there was no more talk of cures. My parents were heartbroken, and I was deeply disappointed. Being blind had often made me feel like a child apart, and now that I was older my disability meant being alone more than ever.

CHAPTER TWO

By Nature's Hand

When I was six or seven, I started noticing that my friends were becoming unavailable during the day: they were starting school, heading off each morning carrying a stool under one arm and a handmade book bag over the other. No one made mention of education for me. It was assumed I would not go—after all, I couldn't see—and, in fact, I wasn't even allowed in the village's two-room schoolhouse, where my friends attended class. Sometimes I followed the other children to the school, sitting alone on the stone step just outside the classroom, taking in the day's lesson and the quiet of the room as the teacher scratched characters in chalk on the blackboard.

As I waited for my friends to come out and play, I often found that I already knew what the teacher was talking about. One day the topic was waterfalls. After making the students close their books, the teacher asked, "What does a waterfall look like?" Silence. "What are you doing?" he shouted to them. "Haven't you learned anything? I'll bet even Little Five can answer this," he said, pointing at me.

"It looks like a screen of pearly beads," I replied, recalling an earlier lesson I'd overheard. Though delighted by my answer, the teacher bellowed at the class, enraged that a small blind boy who didn't go to school and didn't have a single textbook could answer a question that his own students could not.

Perhaps in part because school was off-limits for me, I developed an intense curiosity, thirsting for information about the physical world: how things worked, the cycles of nature, the land around us. When I came across something I didn't understand, I would ask anyone who would listen, pestering people until I felt like I had probed the depths of their knowledge, then moving on to someone else who might be able to fill in additional details for me. Sometimes, with a burning question on my mind, I might sit for hours at the side of the road, waiting for a particular person who could provide missing pieces of information. Of course, I couldn't be sure who was approaching until I heard a voice, and I would have to wait until their footsteps had almost reached me to call out a greeting. "Hi, Uncle!" I would say. "You're back from the fields!" After I heard the person's reply and was sure it was who I'd been waiting for, I would fall in behind him, matching my pace to his and making small talk before launching into my line of questioning, committing his words to memory.

In the village there was a man named Chen Guangsheng; I called him "Older Brother," although he was actually older than my father. When Dongshigu was still organized as a commune, his job was to manage our forest; this was known as "tree work." The forest stretched along the river for a few miles, and Guangsheng would walk the length of the woods, making sure no one was cutting down trees and stealing our wood or making off with the fallen leaves, which we used for fuel. Guangsheng was tall, with a bellowing voice, so people often called him "Big Horse."

Every day he would set out early, following the bend in the river to a place at the very southern point of our forest where a huge tree had been removed, leaving a gaping pit about four yards in diameter. Guangsheng liked to sun himself there, lying down against the protected walls of the hole and closing his eyes for a nap, then waking up in time to get back for lunch.

One morning Guangsheng stopped by our house before heading out to his tree work, and on a whim he asked me if I wanted to go with him, probably not expecting that I would leap at the chance. My heart thrilled to hear my mother say, "Why don't you go along?" I knew my way around Dongshigu quite well, but I rarely had the chance to go beyond the perimeter of the village, as there was no one to take me.

Older Brother Guangsheng took my hand in his, leading me along the river through the forest. We chatted as we made our way, and he quizzed me on my knowledge of birds and trees, praising me for all I knew.

Guangsheng had once been in the army, and he still had his soldier's gait. I was small and had to trot along quickly to keep up with his pace. With his slow, thumping steps and my tripping feet we made a steady musical rhythm, crunching through the underbrush in a clear 4/4 time. We wended our way to the pit, where he immediately lay down and made himself comfortable. I asked him to tell me stories, and he obliged, drawing on his knowledge of old Chinese tales and classic fables. The sun was warm, despite the winter weather, and soon Older Brother Guangsheng was asleep, snoring loudly. I was too excited to rest, tossing and turning, playing in the dirt. Suddenly, I heard a sound, and stood up to listen.

Even though it was winter, there were still a lot of dried leaves on the ground that could be used for fuel, but these were allotted according to the strict rules of the production team. This fuel was an absolute necessity and a scarce resource to be tightly controlled. Each family was allowed to come out only at a certain time with a rake, baskets, and a carrying pole to collect the leaves.

Older Brother Guangsheng was still asleep. The *shuashuashua* sound was unmistakable: someone was stealing leaves! I poked his arm. "Wake up, quick! Someone's stealing our leaves!" I said.

He awoke with a start. "Where?" he asked.

"Listen," I said. "Over there!"

He couldn't hear what I heard, but as soon as he stood up he saw them: four or five people with rakes and baskets scooping up leaves. He was not pleased. "What makes you think you can take our leaves?" he called out, confronting them. They were from a neighboring village.

"Just a few," one replied. "We don't have any fuel at all at home."

"If I let you, then what's to stop someone else from coming and taking more, and then what will we use for ourselves?"

"Okay, okay, we won't take any more. We'll just leave with what we've collected already."

They walked over to talk to Older Brother Guangsheng, stopping near the pit where I stood. They said they'd come all this way barefoot, fording the icy waters of the Meng River in the dead of winter to gather fuel. Noticing me, one of them remarked, "I'll bet you can't get out of there on your own, from the northern side. I'll pull you up the last bit if you make it that far."

I knew they didn't think I could do it, that they doubted my abilities because I was blind. I'd already researched the entire space and knew the north side was the steepest. Of course I can climb out, I thought to myself, but I'm not going to give them the satisfaction of making me try on command. Older Brother Guangsheng said, "I wouldn't look down on him if I were you—I'm pretty sure he can do it just fine."

As they talked I heard the villagers continue to rake up leaves and stuff them in their baskets. I couldn't understand why Guangsheng didn't stop them. He'd already said they could keep what they had, but did they need to take more? I felt around in the sand and found a small stone about the size of a chestnut, fingering its contours as I considered the situation. Suddenly I raised my arm and threw with all my might— beyond my expectations the rock hit one of them squarely on the hand.

"What? You can't see, and you hit me, hard!" cried the villager.

Guangsheng burst out laughing.

"My hand is all red! What's so funny about that?"

Guangsheng just laughed, waving them off until they eventually made their way back over the river. We headed home for lunch, talking and joking the whole way. From then on Older Brother Guangsheng and I had so many stories about our times together, so many adventures.

Not being able to see, and not having access to school, I found that I was drawn to exploring and understanding things by making them, and I became adept at crafting my own inventions or developing those of others. If I wanted to know about something or wanted to play with something, I couldn't go to a store and buy it; I had to make it entirely from scratch. I made all kinds of things out of mud, using my hands to try to mold things I had come across or heard about. Once I felt I had thoroughly understood an object or a machine from the inside out, I quickly moved on to the next obsession.

At one point I became particularly fascinated with guns. When I was young, a plastic pistol had been a favorite toy of mine, the envy of the village kids; later someone gave me a toy gun made of metal that shot plastic pellets. I began wondering if I could make a gun myself, asking anyone I could pester to explain the different parts of a pistol.

A few farmers in our village had *tupao,* the old-style local guns they used for hunting.

"What's this part for?" I would ask one person.

"That's the barrel, where the bullet comes out," came the reply.

"And what about this?" I asked someone else.

"That's the trigger—it makes the gun go off," he explained.

Examining one of these guns, I found the chamber for bullets in the back and figured out how the hammer hit the back of the bullet, making it travel down the barrel and come out the other end. When I blew down the barrel I immediately understood how it worked. But what propelled the bullet? I wondered. Finally someone explained that the back of the bullet carried a bit of gunpowder, which could be made from sulfur, saltpeter, and charcoal. I couldn't find a piece of pipe long enough for a rifle, so I made a pistol with a bicycle chain, wire, and some rubber from a bicycle inner tube. I found a few bullet shells and packed them with small stones from the riverbed, along with paper and some match heads. I also bought some gunpowder from a neighbor, with money I borrowed from a friend who had just sold some eggs at the market. Gunpowder was common in the village, since farmers used it to blast stone in the quarries.

One day I went down to the river to try out my contraption. I aimed upward and pulled the trigger. Shocked by the blast—it was like a clap of thunder under my ear—I felt the barrel; it was hot. Success! Soon friends began helping me perfect my homemade invention; we called ourselves the Pistol Gang. The guns were a big hit in the village, and I made dozens of them, instructing people on what materials to procure and then putting a firearm together for them.

Inevitably my fascination with guns led to trouble. By the time I was fourteen, I had been playing with guns for several years. That spring, when the grass around the village was growing thick and plentiful, my nephew Chen Kegui and I took a basket and went to gather grass for my goats. I stuck my homemade gun in my pocket, along with a little gunpowder, so we could keep ourselves entertained. After we'd gathered all the grass we needed, I put some gunpowder inside my gun and foolishly packed the weapon with pellets while resting it on my leg. Somehow the gun went off, and all the pellets ended up inside my leg, opening up a serious wound.

I was taken to the nearest hospital, where I had to undergo surgery to remove the shot. The cost of the procedure was 200 yuan, an amount I remember because that year Elder Brother had spent 190 yuan on an electric fan, a luxury for our village back in those days. I stayed in the hospital, recovering, for more than a week, and even then the wound didn't fully heal. After leaving the hospital, I had to have my bandages changed every day for two months—a serious burden for my family, because someone had to take me to the hospital and back each time.

While I was still in the recovery room, some of the other patients laughed when they learned that a blind kid had gotten hurt while playing with guns, but I could tell that they were surprised and impressed that I had become the local gunsmith. My parents, however, insisted that I give up on my gun making, and I reluctantly obliged.

Sometime later I developed a new interest that didn't pose a danger to anyone. I had first observed other people flying kites when I was just four or five years old, and after my injury I wanted to make my own. Again, I had to locate all the materials myself: bamboo strips from discarded packaging for the frame, old twine from the crop fields for the string, and paper from a used dry cement sack for the covering. I curved my bamboo strips into large ovals for rounded butterfly wings, laying the paper carefully across the frame and securing it with glue I made from flour and water. I affixed a rubber band between the two antennae for sound—after all, without any noise, what fun was in it for me?—and constructed a tail out of strips I'd pulled from a flax plant. But when I tried to launch the kite, I found that it kept crashing to the ground and landing on one side. I assumed that the side hitting the ground first was too heavy, so I balanced the kite on two needles to see which side weighed more. To my surprise, the lighter side had fallen first. I adjusted the weight, and after that my kite soared. Though I couldn't see it as it climbed, I heard the wind buzzing through the rubber band, and when

I plucked the string, I heard the vibrations travel all the way to the kite. I felt the many physical forces at work, and in the process I learned about wind currents and the basic physics of flight.

As more and more of my friends my age drifted away, I began spending time with a deaf boy named Du Dezhen, who lived near us in the village. People wondered how we could possibly communicate with each other, but between his sounds and my gestures we somehow found a way. One winter, standing by enviously as other children played on the frozen river, we decided to make our own sled to go sliding on the ice. We asked the advice of some woodworkers in the village, and they suggested that we use willow for the runners, for both its strength and its flexibility. As we walked down to the woods near the river, I took Dezhen's hand to lead him to the kind of tree I wanted to use, and then with my hands I showed him how long and how thick a piece I was looking for. That was how we communicated.

We climbed up into the trees, searching exhaustively until we found just the right branches. I was quite a perfectionist at the time, taking the branches home and carefully sawing off the ends until they were absolutely flat and squared. I wanted the sled to look right, not just be fast. I used an ax to split some of the branches in half for the seat; despite being blind, I was comfortable with an ax and had figured out how to use it safely. When the result wasn't fast enough for our taste, we lined the sled's runners with No. 8 wire until we were zooming along, speedier than a bicycle. It was so fast! Soon everyone else wanted a sled like ours.

Despite my will to understand the world, I faced unending prejudices, which revealed themselves in large and small ways. Being blind was simply not understood or accepted. People with disabilities of any sort were considered intrinsically lacking; they were thought of as not whole, not even fully human. I constantly had to prove my worth as a member of the community, and to myself. People recognized that I was smart, but what good was I to anyone if I couldn't see?

When I played with other children, my playmates and the adults nearby sometimes found it easy to forget that I was different, but more often than not, people viewed me as some sort of curiosity. On occasion

I would reach out to pick up something sitting on a table and another child would quickly snatch it away, thinking I wouldn't notice. The child found this amusing, and the adults present usually laughed along, not considering the lessons they were teaching their children.

Once I was playing on the banks of a little pond, looking for the frogs that lived there, which would jump into the water when people approached. Some children tried to trick me by throwing stones into the pond, then exclaiming, "Oh, look! There's one!," not realizing that I could hear each of them bending down, picking up a stone, and jerking their bodies to launch the stone. I might not have been able to see, but people had no idea that my ears provided information that sighted people were blind to.

Sometimes when I left our yard, I found other children putting stones or branches from thornbushes in my path, hoping to watch me stumble. They didn't realize that I could hear them, even from a distance, and could usually make out the general location of their obstacles, though occasionally I did trip and fall.

Other times I would be out playing on my own in the village and a kid would come up to me without a word and hit me, hard, then run away, knowing I couldn't make chase. Children did this for fun, or to make themselves feel big in front of other people; often, adults made no effort to admonish them. I seethed, but I made it a habit to show no reaction. Instead, I waited for the kid to strike again; when I heard him coming, I would grab him and throttle him back. Only then would the adults react vigorously. All this infuriated me, of course, especially since these people seemed unconcerned with how I might feel and saw no problem with the way I was treated.

Fortunately, I had the opportunity to imagine myself in different circumstances, and this proved vital to my development. In the early 1960s, my father had attended evening classes for adults, and he had finally learned to read and write, just before the schools were closed during the Cultural Revolution. If not for those classes, he would have remained illiterate, like my mother and so many others in the world I grew up in. When I was little, my father often read aloud to me when he was home, and after he retired from his job at the Communist Party school, I got more time with him. Every night, my father and I would sit under the kerosene lamp as he read aloud, making out the words in a halting rhythm, his voice rough and low.

My father was a lifelong party member, and for the most part he believed in the superiority of socialism, but as we discussed his readings I learned to take a critical view of both the texts and the accepted learning. The enchanting, homespun folktales he told and the Chinese classics he read aloud were inherently critical of those in power, describing the rise and fall of dynasties, the great deeds and grievous crimes of ancient heroes and villains. Every child in China knows the names of these stories from an early age: *Outlaws of the Marsh, Journey to the West, Romance of the Three Kingdoms, The Dream of the Red Chamber, Romance of the Sui and Tang Dynasties, The Seven Heroes and Five Gallants.* A special favorite of mine was *Investiture of the Gods*, with its glorious pageant of gods and goddesses, its immortals and its strange spirits, its riveting tale of how King Wu of Zhou deposed the cruel ruler King Zhou of Shang and established a new dynasty, ushering in a mythic golden age for the ancient Chinese world.

As we moved from myth into history, my father's stories reflected the long-held Chinese belief that all unjust rulers will eventually face the people's wrath. He told of Zhu Yuanzhang, the founder and first emperor of the Ming dynasty, who led the Chinese people in a war of national liberation, heroically driving out the Mongol invaders. He described the last days of the Sui dynasty, when the court had forgotten the people's well-being and the officials turned terribly corrupt, fueling the people's rage.

Again and again I learned that however absolute the power of emperors may seem, no dynasty can survive without the support of the people, and eventually even the most powerful autocrats come tumbling down. Why, I wondered, were the beginnings and the ends of dynasties so different? Things always seemed so promising at the start of a new dynasty, when the new rulers used their mandate to try to lift up the common people from their suffering. But the dynasties always seemed to crumble after a time, descending into despotism and corruption like the previous ones. I came to see that most of Chinese history is a long succession of one group of dictators replacing another.

The stories my father read to me served as a counterpoint to the official party line and the usual propaganda. Just as important was that my father's stories and our discussions about them gave me an organic education in ethics, providing a framework with which to understand my experience as a disabled child. The stories I heard when I was young allowed me to imagine myself in the position of the characters, to consider how I would react if faced with similar challenges, to devise my own responses and then to compare them with what actually took place. From the many examples in history, myth, and folktale, I saw the power of perseverance and the importance of struggling for what is right and just. Chinese history is full of examples of the disempowered overcoming the odds through wit and daring. Though I lacked the conventional education of my peers, I also avoided the propaganda that was part and parcel of the party's educational system. Instead, my father's tales became my foundational texts in everything from morality to history and literature and provided me with a road map for everyday life.

When I was a child my family had a small radio, a real novelty in our village at the time. Beginning in the late 1970s, I listened to countless stories on this radio; I also absorbed news and information that most people had no access to, and this greatly broadened my horizons. By the early 1980s, people in Dongshigu were crazed for radios, and most families were eventually able to get one. From then on, radio began to play a significant role in the development of Chinese society, spreading knowledge about the law, science, agriculture, nature, and many other things. The radios in our village were battery-powered—Dongshigu still had no electricity—but every evening around six-thirty, you could hear people tuning in.

I was ten the year the village leaders announced that we would install electricity. Despite the buzz of excitement, it would prove a difficult, tortuous process, one that was held up by politics, lack of funds (the village had to pay for the project, with no help from the government), and the challenge of having to organize the villagers to perform the manual labor, including digging holes for the poles by hand. Not until early 1984, three years after the initiative began, did we finally find our homes filled with light. Everyone was thrilled.

Of course, once electricity made it into their houses, the villagers began to want more than just lightbulbs. But most people were severely cash-poor, making only a few cents per pound from crops such as sweet potatoes, corn, and wheat. There was no extra money for anything remotely luxurious.

It so happened that I was at a neighbor's house playing when the first television in Dongshigu arrived. It was the winter of 1986; everyone was excited, gathering expectantly at six o'clock, when the first program would come on. No one knew what it would be, but no one cared, either. The neighbor carefully lifted the set out of its box, placed it on a table, and plugged it in. He turned the knob with great caution; I heard it go *che-che-che* as he tried to find a channel. By that time I couldn't see at all, but I knew that if there was a channel I would hear voices talking normally, and if there was no channel there would be a *shhhhhh* sound. No matter how many times the knob was turned, there was no channel, only *shhhhhh*.

After two hours of fruitless efforts to get the TV working, an electrician was summoned. He walked into the house, marched right up to the TV, and with a flick of his wrist—*ka-ka-ka*—turned the knob roughly, as though it were any old thing, not a delicate, fragile instrument to cherish. When there was still no reception, the electrician turned the set over, fiddled with something on the back, and pulled up the antenna. The result was immediate: a channel came in with perfect clarity. Everyone cheered.

For days people watched the TV with a nearly religious devotion, piling into the neighbor's house every night, some sitting, some crouching, some in the doorway or just outside, on tiptoes peeking through cracks or a space between people's heads. When someone in front had to go to the bathroom, it was quite a bother for them to squeeze all the way through the crowd to get to the outhouse.

I was terribly curious about the TV. I couldn't see the programs, but I could hear, and I enjoyed being there with everyone else. The fact that I couldn't see the screen made some people angry. "You can't see, so what are you doing here? You're taking up a spot someone could actually use."

This hurt me deeply, but I didn't react or refute the statement. It was true: I couldn't see, and I was taking up space other people could use. Maybe they thought my silence was tacit agreement. But this was blatant prejudice, and at the time I had no way of entering into a dialogue with people about it. The only thing I knew to do was to remain silent. But I swore to myself that should there come a day when I had the slightest advantage, I would not use it to get the better of other people; I would try to be generous and treat others with respect. In the end, my only recourse was to stay away, and I spent more time in the glorious out-of-doors, enjoying and learning about nature and living things.

Blind people in China's countryside have few options for employment and few means to support themselves. When I was growing up, a blind person could become a fortune-teller or a storyteller or both. If you were a little successful, you might be able to stay home and have others come to you for their fortunes, especially after the Chinese New Year, when people want to hear what to expect in the coming year. In this way you might even make a decent living, at least comfortable enough, given the circumstances. Otherwise, you had to wander from village to village, along unmarked paths and uncertain ways, banging a small copper cymbal to announce your arrival. Most blind people, however, rarely if ever left the confines of their family's home.

As a young boy, I liked to listen to the stories told by a blind, itinerant storyteller who would spin his tales by the side of the road. Each market day, a crowd of people would gather around to listen. Every time the storyteller reached the end of a section in his story—usually after half an hour or so—he would take a rest. This was the cue for people in the audience to give him a few coins. Locals would offer the storyteller a place to stay the night, and other families would bring food for the storyteller, to lighten the burden on the hosts.

I still remember the day a blind man in his forties came to Dongshigu and gave a long performance for a sizable crowd. Afterward, everyone went uncomfortably quiet, knowing it was time for someone to offer food and a place to stay. No one wanted to help, and I could feel the poor storyteller growing ever more anxious as night fell and the crowd began to melt away. I was deeply embarrassed, but there was really no way for him to stay with us, since two families were already squeezed into our home at the time; even so, my father told me to bring him home if no one else did. Finally, another villager stepped forward and invited the storyteller to his family's home.

The next morning we made *jianbing*, and my father told me to bring some to the blind man. Later, an old villager and I collected grain and dried sweet potatoes from other villagers, who were usually more willing to give food to a storyteller than pay him money from their meager supplies of cash. We collected a large sack of staples, which I carried over my shoulder.

Soon after we gave him the food, the storyteller sold it off to people in the village who needed it. This was the typical process: how else could he make use of a large bag of goods, especially since he was unsure of what lay ahead? Then, with some change in his pocket, the storyteller picked up his cane and headed off to the next village to ply his trade. In China there are few public safety measures in place, and railings on bridges or fences near gullies are rare, so he would have to depend on the kindness of strangers to remind him to "look out for the ditch over there" or "be careful, there's a river just ahead." Such is the life of a blind person in rural China.

By the time my father returned home, in 1982, life in our village was beginning to change. We still lived in dire poverty, sometimes barely subsisting, but following years of fear and stagnation the countryside was slowly coming back to life. Economic reform brought new opportunities. The household responsibility system, which gradually phased out the communes, gave farmers more latitude in how they used their land and invested their own labor. Our village bought one tractor in 1978 and a second tractor in 1981—events of major significance, anticipated for months in advance. We waited for hours by the riverside for each of the tractors to arrive; once it did, we swarmed over it, then chased it into the village.

Despite these modernizations, the life of a farmer was still precarious and unforgiving. How to improve our lot was a question my father and other villagers pondered at length. Some, like my father, decided to try to raise pigs to sell at the market. We were enthusiastic about the prospects. It was my job to mill slices of our dried sweet potatoes with water and then boil them into slop. But when we finally brought the pigs to market, we were paid less than one yuan per pound, which didn't even cover the cost of the feed, let alone our labor and other expenses. We all felt a sense of defeat.

By that time, my brothers were married or gone from the house, and I was the only one around to help my father and mother in the fields. I did farmwork like everyone else; after all, as people often said, you have to work if you want to eat. My father was as hard on me as he had been on my brothers; it didn't matter to him that I was blind. I did everything: I harvested and hoed peanuts, got the feed corn ready, weeded the fields in the spring and summer. At home, I made fried bread and wrapped dumplings. When something broke, I fixed it. My father would sometimes compare me to able-bodied children my age—"Look at what they can do and you can't," he would say—which seemed deeply unfair at the time. I see now that he was training me to confront and overcome the seemingly impossible. He held me to a simple ethic: if other people can do it, you can do it; if others can't do it, you should still be able to do it. "Figure out the principle at work and find a way!" he would say. He was especially pleased whenever I could do something that my brothers, all of whom had normal vision, couldn't do.

One year my father decided that we would grow tobacco as a cash crop. When the leaves were ripe and ready for roasting, I put on a pair of plastic sandals, the common footwear of rural China, and waded unsteadily across the wet field. Soon my sandals were caked with mud, so I kicked them off and went barefoot. But now I encountered a problem: how was I supposed to tell which tobacco leaves were ripe? Color is the usual way, but by then I'd lost my ability to discern colors and could see nothing at all.

I struggled with this challenge for a long time, trying to figure out a system. You can't distinguish the ripe leaves with your nose; anyone who has ever walked in a tobacco field knows the overpoweringly pungent smell of the crop. My father suggested that I simply pick the bottom three leaves from every plant, because they ripened first and most plants would have roughly three ripe leaves. But that seemed too wasteful, so I started investigating with my hands, touching every leaf and learning with my fingertips just how each one should feel. I discovered that the texture of the leaves changed in subtle ways as the plant moved through its life cycle, though most sighted people might not be able to discern the difference.

My father watched me learn. "Why don't you pick that one?" he asked of a particular leaf that I had touched and then ignored.

"It's not ripe," I replied with confidence.

"Oh, you can tell the difference by feeling!"

The first year we grew tobacco, the sale of our harvest went well: the grades of the leaves were clear, and the price differential between them was substantial. A year later at harvesttime, we farmers found that government officials had begun using their connections to take advantage of us to make a profit. When we went inside the market hall to sell the tobacco, we were told that our leaves were of low quality and would reap a low price according to the government-established standards. This ruse was transparent: everyone knew that we had produced high-quality leaves. Frustrated, we all went outside, only to be met by relatives of the officials who had just disparaged the value of our crop; brazenly, they offered to buy the leaves at a marginally higher price than was being offered inside. The government had a complete monopoly on tobacco, and there was nowhere else to sell it legally. Having no choice, we sold our crop at a loss.

Government corruption infected the entire chain of distribution, and party officials engineered a glut by encouraging us to grow more and more tobacco, only to later refuse to buy our tobacco leaves at a reasonable price. It took a long time for most people to understand that they were being cheated, and they continued to believe the government propaganda advertising potential profits in tobacco. "Maybe this year will be different," they would say, my father included, and then the vicious cycle would start all over again.

One year we sold a whole season's crop for just 200 yuan—$25 at the time—barely enough to pay for roasting the leaves, let alone to cover the costs of the fertilizer, the pesticides, and our own labor. And we were not alone. Unfortunately, this is the situation that farmers—who make up over 70 percent of the total population of China—still face. They perform endless work for paltry rewards, and they have few options for a better life.

Finally, by the late 1980s, no one believed in the annual propaganda campaign anymore, and the tobacco-roasting ovens began to collapse from neglect. The patience of the Chinese people can be exhausted, and gradually many of the villagers—and my family—came to understand that you simply couldn't trust the government with your basic survival or your well-being. If you didn't sell your tobacco, you couldn't fill your stomach with it. In a quiet rebellion, people began planting watermelons. Living standards started improving, though this trend didn't last long in places like Dongshigu, because by then the party had already begun shifting its focus to the cities. Meanwhile, some villagers continued to believe in the central government, saying the corruption had been the fault of local officials. Others would retort, "Don't speak of who's good and who's evil; all crows under heaven are black." Evildoers everywhere are the same.

As I reached my late teenage years, my parents began to worry. What kind of future did I have? Would I ever be able to support myself or live on my own? No matter how much I worked in the fields or helped at home, they saw me as a dependent. The bias against handicapped people was strong in the countryside; even members of my own family could never entirely break free of it. Though being blind sometimes meant that I received special treatment from close friends and family, the internal prejudice was hard to expunge. People had looked down on me from the time I was small: I was defective, incapable of providing for myself, not worth investing time and effort in. Being blind was a physical problem, of course, but it was also a social problem. Because many people thought of me as useless, I was nearly invisible. I practically didn't exist.

The expected paths loomed ahead. Whenever someone suggested to my father that I tell stories for a living, I protested loudly that this form of entertainment would soon all but disappear, replaced by radio and then television. Once people started hearing higher-quality programming, I argued, they would no longer be satisfied by street performers. What's more, listening for long periods by the side of the road can be uncomfortable and tiresome, and it's difficult to hold on to a sense of continuity when a story unfolds over many days. Just as important, the villagers have to work their fields and don't necessarily have the time to sit and listen all day every time there's a market.

But people knew what kind of status was accorded to the disabled in the countryside: no matter what you contributed in terms of chores and farmwork, you were dependent on your family's support, especially as we were all required to pay taxes and fees, as well as contribute labor to the government. If I could make a little of my own money from storytelling or fortune-telling, the logic went, at least I could contribute something to the household that was supporting me. In my heart, though, I knew that most people looked down on storytelling and fortune-telling as just another form of begging.

Some things were clear to me in a way that many others would not understand. Most sighted children grow up under the watchful eye of their parents, gradually gaining new capabilities as they mature. They see the ways in which they can help other people, how their "use" in society can translate into respect and esteem. As they grow older, they are increasingly valued by society. But when they become elderly and start to weaken, their perceived "usefulness" to society declines to the point where they need other people to help them; especially in rural areas, they are seen as "useless," which often leads to extreme poverty at the end of life. People like to talk about respecting elders, but this doesn't reflect reality—for many older people in China the most they'll get are a few kind words.

In my life, I knew the feeling of "useless" from the very beginning. By the time I was seventeen, the people who'd kept telling my father that I should study fortune-telling had finally convinced him. A blind master fortune-teller lived just a few miles away, and my father made plans for me to study with him. I was completely against it, trying to persuade my father that he had to come up with better ideas, pointing out that even my mother agreed that I should not study fortune-telling. I argued that instead we should find a way to cure my blindness. I dug in my heels and absolutely refused to go.

One day in the fall of 1988, Fourth Brother came home with unexpected news. Gao Bo, a blind boy I had known as a child, was going to school. My brother had seen Gao Bo on television, learning to read Braille.

"Where is he in school?" my father asked. "And exactly how is he able to go to class?"

"He's at a school for the blind in Linyi," replied my brother.

"Well," said my father, "we should be there, too."

Until the early 1980s, there were only five schools for the blind in China, all located in the largest and most developed cities: Beijing, Shanghai, Nanjing, Tianjin, and Qingdao. The latter two had been founded by missionaries but had been taken over by the government after 1949. The school in Qingdao was the closest, but we had little regular communication with the outside world and no information about such things. It was only when we heard about Gao Bo and the Linyi School for the Blind—which at that point was only three years old—that we realized formal education could even be in the realm of possibility for me.

I was conflicted; in fact, I found the news about Gao Bo deeply depressing. I had never given up hope that someday my blindness would be cured; every day I lived with the hope that somehow, somewhere, a doctor would invent a miraculous way to fix my eyes. Attending a school for the blind would mean admitting that for the time being my eyes could not be fixed, which is why, for all my passionate curiosity about the world, I really didn't want to go to Linyi.

But in the end I changed my mind, realizing that I could at least get a basic education, which would give me a solid foundation for my studies if my blindness was later cured. My parents, realizing that this was my only hope for a better future, decided that they would somehow find a way to pay the school's low tuition. My father's feelings about my prospects brightened: he was confident that after graduating I could at the very least support myself as a teacher at a school for the blind—that this would be my "iron rice bowl," a lifetime source of income, security, and respect. This was certainly a better option than itinerant fortune-telling.

In 1989, some in our village still scoffed at the idea of wasting an education on a blind child. Besides, I was now nearly eighteen, and officially I would be starting elementary school. "Going to school isn't that useful even for normal children," our neighbors would say to my father. "What's the use in him going?" Middle school was as far as most rural children ever got, and the idea of advancing to college was unthinkable for a child, much less a blind one coming from a place like Dongshigu.

All that summer I tried to imagine the dramatic changes that lay in store for me. Once the fall arrived, I would be spending most of my days at school. Each term would last for at least four months, and I would hardly have any time for myself. After roaming freely among rivers and trees all my life, I would be living in a dormitory with other blind students. Some of the older villagers had never gone far beyond Dongshigu, and many others had done so only to perform collective work. Now, for months at a time, I would be living away from my family and my village.

The evening before I left for school, I decided to go for a swim in the river, wanting to give myself a last little memory of home. No one else was there—it was already mid-September—so I had the river all to myself. The air was no longer warm, but I took off my clothes and left them on the shore, choosing a spot where I could easily find them again. Everything around me was deeply familiar, and I felt the rush of cool water flow over my body and heard the gurgling of the river as I floated comfortably in its depths. I knew from what people had told me that the sand at the bottom was white and very clean; submerging myself, I lay for a moment on my back on top of that sand, making a little pile of it to serve as an underwater pillow. A few moments later, the current washed the pillow from under my head.

I had played this game with the river from an early age—nothing could be more natural to me. As I swam that evening, I was filled with nostalgia and longing. In my mind's eye I was small again: bathing in the river, fishing in it, frolicking with my friends. Stillness and peace were everywhere; I listened with every part of my being to the ripple of flowing water, the sound of waves splashing on the shore, the buzz of insects flying in midair and chirping in the grass by the river.

The temperature grew still cooler, and as soon as I'd finished my swim I hurriedly put on my clothes. Walking home along the little path that followed the shore, I mused about all the changes ahead of me. I thought about the path itself, where I used to run naked and barefoot, joking and laughing with my friends, all of us chasing each other and making a racket. But this moment seemed particularly quiet, and I thought of how a person's life proceeds in stages, one after another, and how no stage can be repeated. Once a stage is over, there is no going back.

The next morning I was up at dawn. My mother made me some noodles, then handed me a quilt and a small bag with some hand-me-downs from my brothers. She also gave me a container full of boiled peanuts drizzled with soy sauce and sprinkled with fennel seeds and salt. As a going-away gift, Third Brother brought me some baked sesame seed cakes. The only other thing I brought with me was a chipped enamel tea mug that commemorated my father's work on a railroad back in the 1950s.

My father and I took the bus to Linyi, some forty miles to the south of Dongshigu. Since there were no seats left, we stood the whole way, bumping along for the entire two-hour trip. My mind kept raising endless questions about the future. What would the school be like? Would I get along with the other students? I tried to imagine my new life, right down to the little tactile details. What kind of floors would the school have, brick or pounded earth?

Once we arrived in Linyi, a busy, bustling city, no one could tell us where the school for the blind was. We hired a pedicab driver, but he left us at a school for the deaf. When we finally found the Linyi School for the Blind, my heart sank; I immediately sensed a certain coldness. I stood in front of the building, aware that the forecourt was paved with bricks. I heard the sudden ringing of the school bell and then the slapping steps of several students coming down the stairs, one of whom asked if I'd just arrived.

Turning right in the building's lobby, we came first to the office of Xue Keming, the educational director, who greeted us and took my hand. He explained the school procedures, and my father handed him the acceptance notice the school had sent us, as well as my tuition money. Director Xue told us about the curriculum, stressing that it was almost the same as the curriculum in the regular schools.

Director Xue called over the teacher in charge of our class, who took my father and me up the stairs to the building's third floor, which served as the boys' dorm. On the way, we passed the second floor, where the classrooms and the girls' dorm were; all my classmates fit easily into a single building. I entered the room where I would sleep and discovered that it measured twenty feet by twenty and held ten beds. I was the first new student to arrive. We chose a bed in the southeast corner of the room, where there was a nightstand that had a drawer and a small cupboard. The area beneath the bed served as a storage space, and this is where I stowed the clothing I'd brought from home. All the beds in the dorm were new, and there were screens inside the glass windows. This place was nothing like the primitive stone schools in the countryside.

By the time I'd settled in, it was already nine forty-five in the morning, and the second class of the day was over. As the class let out, I pulled open the screen—it was full of dust and hadn't been swept in ages. Beyond the window I could hear the students doing exercises in the courtyard, following directions broadcast over the loudspeaker. My father was impressed. "You'll even be doing calisthenics!" he said. I listened carefully to the man's voice on the loudspeaker, trying to make out what he was saying, knowing that soon I'd be doing such exercises myself.

My father went out to buy me some supplies: an enamel washbasin, a thermos for hot water, a towel, and some soap. He even bought me a toothbrush and toothpaste, though I'd never brushed my teeth before. I tried the toothbrush later that day; with my mouth tingling and my gums all sore, I thought, This is really a whole different way of living!

Soon my father said it was time for him to leave; he promised to return for me when the school holiday came. With no phones in the village, there would be no way for us to communicate during the intervening months. As we walked to the gate, I held my father's arm and realized then that age and the long days of manual labor had taken a toll. My father's arm was no longer the strong, firm arm I had always held as a child—it was already much thinner, and the skin was beginning to loosen.

As we reached the school gate, my father said, "Go back to the dorm—you don't need to walk with me any farther. Study hard, and if you have any problems, talk to your teachers. Do what they tell you."

He gave me almost all the money in his pockets, leaving himself just enough for the bus ride back home. He tore off a few ration tickets for food and handed these to me as well.

As my father walked away, I heard his shoes dragging on the pavement. His footsteps echoed against the school's walls, making his movements seem even slower. After a moment he turned around and told me once more to go back to the dorm. I said okay, but I didn't move. I stood there until the sound of his footsteps was gone.

CHAPTER THREE

An Uncommon Education

I walked slowly and carefully back to the building, making my way up the steps to my dorm room, beginning the process of memorizing my surroundings. I found myself wondering at the myriad changes in my life, large and small, that kept jolting my awareness. For instance, at home there was no echo when we talked indoors. But here, every noise brought a responding *wengwengweng* sound that grated on my ears. Even my footsteps in the concrete stairwell reverberated loudly. I realized that noise was just one of the many things I would have to get used to.

Back on the third floor, I decided to get to know the room, feeling with my hands where my bed was in relation to the other beds, the walls, and the window, and where the door was. Going through the door, I stepped into the hallway, feeling the railings on both sides of the walls, counting the doors along the hallway. I found the bathrooms but discovered that the doors were locked. How strange, I thought. Why would they not allow people to use the toilets?

That afternoon, Gao Bo came to my dorm room to greet me. I was anxious to know about our classes and what we would learn. Gao Bo brought me to his classroom and showed me one of his textbooks—this was the first time I had felt Braille letters. Even though classes hadn't begun yet for new students, I decided to ask some upperclassmen to help me get started learning Braille, which in Chinese has fifty-two basic Braille letters, plus several more to mark tones and punctuation. Over time, I learned to write using the Braille board—a small metal grille with rows of tiny holes in groups of six—by impressing dots into thick paper with a stylus to form words from right to left. To review what you have written, you turn the paper over, reading by feeling the bumps from left to right. The process is slower than writing with a pen, but we had no other way to put words to paper.

Soon we began our regular classes. Because Linyi had been open for only a short time—my class would be the fourth to matriculate—the school at first offered a limited range of courses, mainly for the primary grade level. We studied such subjects as language, math, geography, history, physical education, thought and ethics, music, and handicrafts. I took a particular interest in history, but before long I realized that my view of China's past was sometimes quite different from the teacher's, and that what we were spoon-fed in class was far simpler than what I had learned in discussions with my father under our old kerosene lamp.

As I grew more comfortable with Braille, I found it profoundly liberating to run my fingers over a page of text and so begin to shake my dependence on sighted readers. Soon I was devouring every Braille book the school had. I was particularly taken by a popular series known as *The 100,000 Whys*. Nothing could have suited me better, and as I tore through the books on astronomy, geography, biology, and physics, I discovered that my years of exploration in the village had given me a natural understanding of these subjects. While reading about the moon, for instance, and how gravity kept it revolving around the earth, I recalled its cold white glow, which I had still been able to see as a small child. When *The 100,000 Whys* explained centrifugal and centripetal forces, I thought of one of my childhood projects, a toy made from a length of string and some clay I had collected from the fields. When the clay was still wet, I patted it around the string into the shape of a ball; after the sphere had dried, I swung it round and round, feeling the physical forces pull the clay ball outward.

The rhythm of life at the Linyi School for the Blind was highly structured, and we had little time of our own. Outside of classes and meals, the only free time available to us was the half hour or forty minutes just before bed. During these precious moments, many students would take their flutes out, playing pop or folk melodies as they wandered through the halls and out in the yard. The cement walls inside made a great surface for echoes, and all the flutes together created a wonderful cacophonous symphony.

One evening, standing in the hallway, I listened to the students playing songs I recognized from the secondhand record player my father had purchased some years back. I had never learned to play an instrument, and after a while I approached a student who played the flute well. I asked his name, then asked if he would teach me how to play.

"Sure," he said.

I then admitted that I didn't have a flute.

"Well, why don't you just buy one?" he said.

I was silent. How could I spend money on a flute? The one yuan was just too much for me.

Before the lights went out, at bedtime, we all had to rush to brush our teeth on the first floor and use the bathroom outside in the courtyard. Not only were the toilets on our floor permanently locked, but at night each floor as well as the entire building were locked, so we were unable to go out to use the bathroom until morning. No one had an answer as to why the school locked the doors, and there were times during that first semester when people got sick and had no choice but to relieve themselves in the hallway.

Before long I came to realize that the Linyi School for the Blind was not at all what I had imagined. My family and I had heard that government-run schools provided disabled people with an excellent education, and we were sure that the government would do much more than simply meet the basic needs of disabled students, as evidence of the superiority of socialism we all believed in. The reality was very different. Severely underresourced, the school provided no extra support for the students, which came as a complete surprise to my parents and me.

Within days of my arrival at the school, I realized that it would be very difficult to survive on the twenty-six yuan my father had given me when he left. The school's cafeteria, for instance, still functioned according to the planned economy model and used a system of ration tickets purchased by students at the start of the semester. But I quickly calculated that I would run out of money in just two months if I ate what would be considered normal, adequate meals at the cafeteria. What's more, I needed money for things besides food, such as writing paper and other school supplies. Once I did the math, I decided I would have to eat primarily steamed buns and corn bread, supplemented by a container of the cheapest salted pickles available, which I asked a teacher to buy for me from outside.

I also encountered other problems with food and water at the school. Because of insufficient water pressure, the taps throughout the entire school were often dry, meaning that we had no water for such things as washing or brushing teeth, and the cafeteria had no water for cooking. To compensate, teachers would organize those students who were partially sighted to fetch water from outside. Meanwhile, the kitchen staff was supposed to boil the water brought in from outside before giving it to us to drink, but we discovered that before pouring the water into our thermoses, they used it to steam bread. Every day, we also faced daunting challenges involving hygiene: with no water in the plumbing, we couldn't use the toilets inside the dorm, and we had no way to fill our basins to bathe.

During my first year at Linyi, I was selected as a student representative to participate in meetings with the administration about student life. I raised the issue of our limited access to water, feeling it was my duty to let the school administrators know where there were problems so they could fix them. I could tell that they were unhappy to hear my comments, but they put on a nice face and told me I had "some good suggestions." When the school failed to respond to these concerns, I sought out Linyi's municipal education department, hoping someone there would step up to improve our lot. Again, nothing changed, but my complaint so angered the school's principal that he, in turn, reported my behavior to the education department. He even confronted me one day when we were outside in gym class, insisting that if there was a problem I should talk directly to him. "Do you really need us to explain these things to you?" I asked. "From the start of the school year to now," I continued, "no one has been able to bathe. I'd like to ask you, Mr. Principal: how many times have you bathed this winter?" He seemed shocked by my directness, but I did not back down.

Students started complaining that the school sometimes seemed like a jail. Unless accompanied by a family member, we were forbidden from leaving the school grounds to buy food, or for any other reason. But most of the students were from the countryside, and their families rarely, if ever, visited. My family, for example, took me to school at the start of each semester the first few times, but after that I traveled from home on my own, seeing my family at school only when they came to pick me up for winter and summer break. The school's excuse was that it was too dangerous for us to go out: the traffic was terrible, and there were bad people in the world who would try to take advantage of us.

I argued that we couldn't live like prisoners and said that sooner or later we had to go out into the community. After all, besides providing us with an education, the school had a responsibility to help us learn how to participate in society. If we were never allowed to leave the school, how could we ever adapt to unfamiliar surroundings? I wondered if the school might be violating the law by restricting our freedom of movement, and one day I mentioned this to one of the teachers. "Oh," she said with surprise, "so you even know about the law!"

We continued to press for more independence, and after nearly two years we finally managed to convince the administration to allow me and a friend to leave the school unaccompanied. The administration and staff didn't take kindly to my efforts, however, and they made their opinion of me known in different ways: for almost two years the kitchen staff gave me small or leftover steamed buns at meals; and when my classmates voted me a "Three Goods" student for "good academic performance, good morals, and good health," the school refused to give me the award and instead told my parents that I was a troublemaker with unruly ideas.

Despite the school's poor facilities and my conflicts with the administration, I was grateful for any opportunity to study, given how few schools for the disabled existed at that time. There were fewer than forty students in the entire school, about a fifth of whom were female.

We worked extremely hard, and our teachers were very conscientious about their classes. Though our living conditions were unacceptable, this wasn't the fault of our teachers, who were caring and warm and always willing to help us however they could. Against the odds, and with very few resources, the teaching staff at Linyi struggled mightily to give us the best education possible.

In 1992, I started spending Saturdays studying vocal music at a nearby arts school, and soon I was pressing for a more serious arts curriculum and real performance opportunities at our own school. I argued that for one thing we needed more instruments—and, to his credit, the principal borrowed money to buy them. As our musical abilities improved, we began earning top honors at competitions with other schools for the disabled in Shandong Province. Hoping to raise the school's profile, I started phoning journalists and inviting them to visit and report on our concerts. This made the principal uncomfortable; he called me into his office and reprimanded me for contacting journalists on my own initiative.

With the arrival of a new principal in my fourth year at Linyi, basic conditions finally improved; soon we had adequate plumbing and better food. The new principal successfully applied for funds and had a three-hundred-foot-deep well drilled to resolve our water problem. He even managed to get money from the Civil Affairs Bureau to buy the school's students a year's supply of flour, meaning that we no longer had to spend our own money on ration tickets. This thrilled my father, who thought that these changes decisively proved the superiority of socialism. Unfortunately, it also led my father to conclude that I no longer needed any money from him, so that semester I ate less than ever, living almost solely off steamed buns and corn bread. I became seriously ill, and for several days I couldn't attend classes; I lay in bed shivering and shaking, and the medicine I took didn't help. Eventually I was hospitalized, and the doctors told me that malnutrition had seriously exacerbated the effects of a bad cold.

While I was sick, my teachers were remarkably kind and considerate. One teacher gave me an apple and a pear, and another gave me some white sugar. Normally I would have been eager to eat just about anything, but at the time everything tasted bitter. A third teacher brought me two raw eggs; he made me put them in my tea mug and stir in some tepid water. It wasn't appealing, but I forced myself to drink the concoction for the nutrition.

During my illness, the school's authorities told me they needed to notify my family. My mother and Elder Brother came to the school, and my mother cried when she saw how terrible I looked.

"Why don't you buy anything besides bread?" she said. "If you ate a few more vegetables and some protein, wouldn't you be all better by now?"

"What else can I buy?" I replied angrily. I reminded them that no one had given me any money for the semester; I had begun the school year with only twenty yuan from Third Brother, plus a little bit that I had been able to cobble together myself. After this painful conversation, my mother and Elder Brother managed to come up with another twenty-three yuan for me.

Back at home over break, I learned that my father was enraged at the government's lack of attention and support for the school. "If socialism can't take care of you disabled people," he said to me, "how is it superior to other systems?" Clearly the government wasn't interested in making a serious effort to educate and care for the disabled, and the fact that students like myself lived under economic duress was not taken into consideration. The hard truth was that without money, I would have nothing to eat—and without food, how could I possibly get an education?

While I was away in Linyi in the autumn of 1990, party cadres came to our house in Dongshigu to collect taxes and fees. As they have for over two millennia in China, the tax collectors went door to door with a list in hand, noting how many people lived in a given household and what kinds of taxes they should pay. Despite my disability and the fact that at the time I couldn't get a job, from birth I was still required to pay a tax as a resident of the village, as all rural residents were. What's more, every year the government demanded that each member of a household contribute a number of days of "voluntary" labor to do such things as help build bridges and fix roads. If you were very young or very old or disabled, your family either had to do the work for you or had to pay money on your behalf. In addition, farmers had to "pay" the state a certain amount of grain every year, again according to how many people lived in a household.

It so happened that earlier that year, my father had read an article in the newspaper about a new law that the government was promulgating: the Law on the Protection of Persons with Disabilities.* In truth, the law was little more than a document that encouraged people to treat the disabled with respect, although it did include language suggesting that the disabled who were unable to work (which included the blind) "shouldn't have to bear additional material burdens." Few clauses in the law had any practical use; one that did help stated that the blind should be allowed to ride metropolitan public transportation for free.

Although my father had paid the annual tax on my behalf ever since I'd been born, the law made him rethink the situation. Now he argued that forcing me to pay was inhumane; if anything, the government should be doing something to help me and other disabled citizens, not adding to their troubles. I had long felt frustrated by the fact that we disabled had to rely on others for our basic needs, but the "voluntary labor" requirement made our circumstances all the more painful. We had already internalized society's message that we were useless, or at least considerably less valuable than "normal" people; now, whenever the labor requirement came up, we were reminded that society saw us as fundamentally inadequate.

When my father tried to talk to the cadres about the new law and the Chinese constitution, which guarantees protection to the disabled and stipulates a citizen's right to material support from the government in times of need, the tax collectors simply shrugged and repeated the orders they'd been given. Having no choice but to submit, my father paid the tax.

That winter, when I was back home from school over break, my father and I began to piece the new law together statute by statute, trying to understand its most important points. Once I returned to

---

* The Law on the Protection of Persons with Disabilities has been revised since its earliest inception. Unless otherwise noted, I refer in this narrative to the original 1991 version.

Linyi, some school friends and I decided to investigate whether the section on transportation was actually being enforced. By now the school had relaxed its rule prohibiting us from going into town unless accompanied by a family member, so we decided to take a short bus trip just to see what would happen.

No sooner had we stepped onto the bus than the ticket collector demanded to see our tickets. We mentioned the new law, but the woman was unmoved. "I've never heard of such a thing," she shouted. "And if everyone rode for free, how would we operate?" Then the bus driver chimed in: "What, you don't want to pay for a ticket? Next you'll be trying to get a free meal from a restaurant—eat all you want and just walk right out."

At the next stop the driver refused to open the doors, and the other passengers started to get angry. Eventually he let us out, and later we asked the school to help us get a copy of the text of the law—in print, not in Braille. From then on I carried it in my pocket wherever I went.

We didn't go out again to test whether Linyi's transportation system was supporting the Protection Law. For one thing, it was extremely uncomfortable to be yelled at in front of other passengers, even with the law on our side. For another, we already knew what the outcome of any further tests would be: a vicious, stubborn, and uninformed response. Instead, we reported what had happened to us to the two heads of our school, believing that they, in turn, would pass on our concerns to the relevant government bureaus. After all, we had been hearing a steady stream of government propaganda: "Enthusiastically implement the national policies and law! Protect the rights of the disabled!" and so on. But nothing changed, and I continued to hear about blind people having to pay for their bus tickets.

After the Law on the Protection of Persons with Disabilities officially took effect, in May of 1991, I hoped to see some small improvements, though I knew that substantial, system-wide change would take time. But in the spring and fall of 1992 cadres again came to collect my portion of the annual tax from my father, as though oblivious to the law. During the winter holiday that year I went with my nephew Kegui to the village offices, then worked my way up the chain of authority, pushing to get the Protection Law implemented. I argued that the government should desist from demanding money and services from the disabled, in accordance with the new law. Without exception, the officials ignored me, and they continued to demand money from the indigent and the disabled. Disabled people who refused to pay taxes were visited by "little work teams" of cadres, who would beat up entire families and brazenly steal from their homes.

While attending school in 1993, I called the Linyi branch of Canlian (also known as the China Disabled Persons' Federation), the quasi-governmental organization responsible for protecting the rights of the disabled. With ample funds from the government—including fees paid by businesses that don't employ the requisite number of disabled people—the Canlian has offices in every city and every county across China. Just as the All-China Federation of Trade Unions "represents" China's workers and the All-China Women's Federation "represents" Chinese women, the Canlian purports to represent all of China's disabled. In truth, the organization is an arm of the party and takes money that should be used to help the disabled. It employs few disabled people itself and contributes almost nothing to the struggles waged by ordinary disabled people for justice, dignity, and livelihood.

When I told Canlian workers on the phone about what was happening to me and others I knew, they practically yawned. I then began going in person to the local, county, and city Canlian offices, as well as other government offices; one official I met hardly raised an eyebrow at my descriptions of how the law was being flouted. "There are so many disabled people," he responded when we put our complaint on his desk. "If they were all exempt, where would we get our money?"

For a long time I couldn't figure out why I was making so little progress: what on earth were the officials at the Canlian, who were charged with managing the affairs of the disabled, doing all day? Even the slightest bit of effort from those who held such jobs should bring about gradual improvement. As we say, "At the very least, a monk should strike the gong a few times a day"—if it's your job, you do it.

By 1994 my family was still paying taxes they could barely afford, so I turned again to the Canlian. I persisted in my quest to find someone who would listen and take my complaint seriously; with Kegui and several classmates, I first visited the provincial levels of Canlian offices, and eventually decided that we should take our complaint directly to the offices of the Central Canlian, in Beijing. But a classmate was skeptical: "Don't you know how difficult it is for disabled people to actually get inside the Central Canlian gate? When you get there and say you want to meet so-and-so, they'll just say, 'He's not here now, he's busy.'"

Nonetheless, I talked my way into a meeting with a senior official at the Central Canlian who was himself blind. But this conversation, too, proved pointless: the official just sat there listening to the complaints I and my classmates put forward, hardly saying a thing, completely noncommittal. One comment made by a high-level official at the Central Canlian office is representative of my entire experience with them, the endless runarounds: "You should go back and petition your local office. Ask for their help."

I was flummoxed. Finally a cynical, unusually well-read neighbor explained the situation to me: "China has no law," he said. "The legal system is under the control of the administrative branch of government, which answers to the party." In contrast to what goes on in Western countries, he explained, the law cannot be considered a fully established field in China. "What about criminal law or constitutional law?" I asked. My neighbor just scoffed. "Compare it to other countries," he said. "In America, for instance, even the president is subject to the law, but in China such a thing would be unimaginable." At the time, I thought a president was the same as an emperor, able to act with impunity. "Read more books and you'll learn," my neighbor advised.

In time, I did learn. For one thing, I came to understand that the Protection Law was never truly implemented. Even down to the present day, it remains an empty promise, another lie the nation tells itself. Although it was passed the same year as the Americans with Disabilities Act, the Protection Law is vague and toothless, falling far short of its American equivalent. An attempt to make China appear civilized and progressive in the eyes of the world, the law is brimming with enlightened language, like so much of the country's legislation. But China on paper is not China in the streets, and simply because a certain piece of legislation exists does not necessarily mean it will be translated into reality. Did the Canlian ever have any real intention of implementing the Protection Law and doing something concrete to improve the lives of more than one hundred million disabled Chinese, three-quarters of whom live in the countryside? We will never really know, but the evidence suggests that right from the start the law was just for show.

During my five years at Linyi School for the Blind, I moved rapidly through the primary school curriculum. Both the spirit and the commitment of the teachers were wonderful, but we continued to suffer from a lack of resources, and we had few course offerings. Hoping for more, I decided to transfer to the Qingdao School for the Blind, where conditions were supposed to be good and there was a greater openness to the outside world. A well-established academic institution originally founded by missionaries, the school offered a full range of courses, including subjects like physics and chemistry, which many people believed the blind could never learn.

Qingdao required that I take entrance exams—both of which I passed—but they took an unusually long time to let me know whether I had been accepted. When Second Brother called the school on my behalf, the principal said he'd forgotten to get in touch. He then told my brother that I was welcome to attend but the tuition was high. My family would have to make major sacrifices to come up with the money, but they fully supported my decision to go.

On September 3, 1994, Second Brother and I made the nearly eight-hour journey by bus to Qingdao only to learn that the school was demanding a 1,000 yuan "training replacement" fee on top of the normal tuition, because I was from out of town. "You should think a little more about whether you want to study here," the school administrators told us.

At first Second Brother agreed to pay the necessary amount, but after thinking it over he hesitated. I could feel the pressure he was under from the sound of his voice. His own wages at the time were less than 200 yuan a month, and my father's pension was then around 200 yuan per month. Even so, my brother eventually agreed to cover both the tuition and the extra fee. During my years in Qingdao, Second Brother selflessly helped me a great deal, not just with tuition but with living

expenses and medical expenses. Recognizing the hardship I was causing him and my parents, I did everything I could to keep my costs as
low as possible.

My first weeks at the Qingdao School for the Blind were difficult, in
part because the administration initially insisted that I repeat a year of
primary school, under the assumption that a student coming from
another school couldn't possibly be at the same level as their own. I
managed to convince them that I could keep up, and I was able to stay
on track. But between the completely new environment, the competi-
tiveness of the classes, and the much higher tuition, the pressure was
enormous. Gradually, however, I adapted to my new surroundings.

At Qingdao, I felt my horizons expand: I had more freedom, I met
other talented and driven fellow students, and our classes were more
formal and demanding. The courses were much like those at any other
Chinese middle school—we studied such subjects as history, geography, math, and chemistry, as well as music, "hand work," and "life
skills." We also took specialized classes in acupuncture, moxibustion,
and massage, as preparation to work or continue our studies in the field
of traditional Chinese medicine, the only career major, outside of
music, available for blind students. I undertook a rigorous study of the
bodily meridians (also called "energy channels," through which the life
force *qi* flows) and the hundreds of acupuncture points found throughout the human body.

Sighted people might wonder how blind students study, what tech-
niques we use in class to remember and engage with the material. I
can't speak for others, but as far as I was concerned, taking notes in
class with the Braille pad actually made it harder to really listen to
what the teacher was saying. When studying physiology, for example, I
would listen carefully and in my mind re-create a map of the body
according to what the teacher was describing. That way, having already
understood the structures of the body and the principles by which it
operated, I wouldn't need to take too many notes, and the information
stood out clearly in my head. When I had a free moment, back in my
room, I would jot down some of the important points from class using
the Braille pad. I could feel my memory improving as I did this, my
mind working more swiftly and retaining more firmly whatever it was I

wanted to grasp. It may be that sighted students who rely strictly on note taking do so at the expense of developing memory.

I took a great interest in all of my courses, but I soon developed a special love of physics. Our teacher reminded us from the outset to think hard about the problems he presented to us, yet he also encouraged us to ask questions. During one class, we discussed the principle of the lever and the famous comment about it made by Archimedes: "Give me a long enough lever and a fulcrum, and I will move the world." With leverage, our teacher stressed, a small force could lift a heavy one.

One day a lesson on gravity got me thinking about a problem. I asked my physics teacher what would happen if a tunnel were constructed straight through the center of the earth, between Qingdao, in Shandong Province, and New York City, and I fell in. Assuming gravity would pull me inward, would I come to a stop at the center of the earth or swing back and forth between New York and Qingdao?

My teacher was stumped, and for a long time I was unable to get an answer. Many years later, I asked a friend who was well versed in this type of question. "I think you probably already know the answer," he said. "Assuming your tunnel is a perfect vacuum, you would swing back and forth like a pendulum, pulled from Shandong to New York and back again forever, never stopping."

Besides studying harder, I was determined to get out into the world. For a blind person, though, nothing is more daunting than navigating an invisible locale and grappling with the countless uncertainties of physical space. A sighted person, walking through a teeming city wearing a blindfold, will soon discover that the surroundings seem either very wide or very narrow. As a boy, I had come to know Dongshigu by heart, but after I left my village every step had to be studied, and in a big city my sense of independence vanished. For sighted people, learning to walk is a matter of learning how to move your legs, but for the blind it's much more complicated. Walking without assistance can be a torturous process, requiring deep experience and sometimes exacting a heavy price. From childhood I had become practiced at making smooth turns without any guideposts; I had also grown skilled at interpreting how sound waves were reflected by objects in my environment and understanding what they told me about things in my vicinity. But this skill was severely compromised in the city, and I found myself trying in vain to use my ears to pick my way amid the throngs of people, honking cars, rumbling trucks and buses, and construction sites.

One day a favorite physics teacher, Cui Beihong, asked me if I'd ever been off campus alone. "Not alone," I admitted, "just with fellow classmates." He told me I would have to be more independent if I ever wanted to become a part of society and make an impact. Up until then I had never used a cane, but I decided to visit the school's principal, who took me to a storeroom where he kept a number of canes. After buying what seemed to be a good one, I approached a classmate of mine who often went out into the city to purchase a few things or make a phone call; he agreed to take me with him the next time he left the campus. A few days later, we walked together through the city, and I found that if anything he moved too slowly, which gave me a surge of self-confidence.

I soon became convinced that the school should equip us with canes and show us how to use them off campus, and other students agreed with me. I practiced with Teacher Cui; as he followed behind, I walked through the streets of Qingdao and figured out how to cross them, navigated the crowded market and visited the city's beach, and even climbed a mountain path with no one guiding me. Few teachers were willing to take on such a responsibility, but Cui showed genuine courage, not only by helping me but also by convincing the school administrators that this kind of learning should be part of our curriculum. Once the school began to teach us how to make our way in the world, our ability to go beyond the school gate and participate more normally in society improved rapidly. I felt my world expanding exponentially.

I also began reaching out to the wider world in other ways, especially through my habit of listening to a radio I had purchased while at school in Linyi. Radio programs had always provided me with a vital source of news and information; at Linyi they also convinced me that if I wanted to go further in life I would need to study English, and for this I would need a tape recorder, as there were no books in Braille.

Acquiring a recorder, however, was not easy. In my early days at school, I'd assumed my father would help me buy one; I was sure he would understand how important a tape recorder would be for me and my education. I was stung when he refused; wasn't he interested in helping me realize my full potential? Still, I was determined to buy a recorder, even if it meant spending my own savings. For more than a decade I had been slowly and carefully squirreling away money—a few cents at a time—by doing such things as selling fur from my Angora rabbits and medicinal flowers I had harvested from a village tree and helping in a relative's apple orchard. Two or three years after I first seized upon the idea of getting a tape recorder, I finally had enough money to buy one on my own. Unfortunately, soon after buying the machine, I discovered that the English-language tapes were too expensive for me to purchase, and I couldn't find anyone who would lend me tapes. Still, I was able to use the recorder for studying and reviewing class material.

While listening to the radio in Qingdao, I found myself especially intrigued by local shows focusing on the law, one of which was *Lawyer Hotline,* a program that encouraged people to call in and ask for legal advice. Because of my efforts to enforce the Protection Law, and as a result of witnessing the many injustices taking place around me, I was becoming increasingly interested in the law. Listening to the radio also helped me begin to understand the power of the media, and a trip into Qingdao during my first year at the school brought this lesson home in an especially powerful way.

The national Protection Law mandated that blind people could ride metropolitan public transportation for free. Most times, we went out without any form of ID or government-issued tickets, and in Qingdao (unlike Linyi), we had no problems with the bus system—people there have a reputation for being particularly kind and courteous. Thus we were shocked when one day a ticket collector insisted that my friends and I pay to ride the bus.

After being forced to buy tickets, we used a public phone to call a local radio station and described what had just happened. A journalist got in touch with the bus company, and the next day one of our teachers interrupted class to tell us that three representatives of the bus company were in his office, ready to apologize and return our bus fares. (They also gave us two used wall calendars, which came in handy because we later took them apart and used the thick sheets as Braille notepaper, which was quite expensive.) This was the first time I had witnessed this kind of problem being resolved through the media, and it taught me an invaluable lesson about the media's crucial role in promoting social justice.

If tape recorders could help educate the blind, I was sure that computers would have an even deeper impact. In the fall of 1996, a classmate told me that a professor at Tsinghua University, in Beijing, had developed a talking computer, and the news drove me to distraction. I hounded our school principal to find out more about this machine, but in the end I had to track the professor down myself, finally reaching him by telephone. When I called, a gentle voice answered on the other end: "This is Mao Yuhang." I told him I was a student at the Qingdao School for the Blind who wanted to come to Beijing and learn how to use the computer he'd developed. To my surprise, he immediately agreed, proposing that I visit him for two weeks at the start of the long Chinese New Year holiday in early 1997.

Going out alone in Qingdao was one thing, but voyaging several hundred miles by train to Beijing proved to be quite another. I traveled with a blind classmate, and we quickly learned that you can't take anything for granted under such circumstances. Buying a train ticket, finding a bathroom, getting a meal—everything is painstaking work. In Jinan, the provincial capital, we had to change trains, which meant going across town to another station. We set out into the city, tapping our canes in front of us. We weren't sure where to go. At one point, we headed down into a pedestrian underpass, and I felt as if I'd entered a cave. Water was dripping somewhere, and people were racing back and forth, their voices echoing chaotically. We asked the first pedicab driver we encountered to take us to the city's other railway station, where we planned to either catch the train to Beijing or find a place to spend the night. But the driver tried to pick our pockets, abandoned us by the side of the road, and left us deeply shaken and scared.

Soon we found another pedicab. Getting in and out of the cab, I felt the sleeve of the driver's cotton-padded jacket, which reminded me of home. I instinctively believed that he was a man we could trust, and fortunately I was right: he took us to the local school for the disabled, where he knew we could spend the night, and he refused to accept our money. Even today I remember his name—Wang Xiaoqing—and his warmth of spirit. Just before he pedaled off, I touched his pedicab with my hands, wanting to remember it. I noticed a glove on the handlebar and thought about how difficult it must be to drive the cab on frigid winter days. As we parted, I said, "Please give my regards to your family." He responded, "You have a long way to go, and I hope people will help you."

The next day we finally arrived in Beijing, where the main square in front of the train station was packed with people. We realized we had no way to locate Professor Mao. I had the idea of raising our canes up in the air, as our "bright sticks" should be easy to spot. Some locals jeered at us, calling us names and telling us that we looked lost. At last we were approached by Liu Ning, Professor Mao's assistant, who had come to find us. After two exhausting days on our own, it was an immense relief to have her guide us.

Liu Ning took us to the famous Tsinghua University campus, where I heard magpies flying and voices singing; I sensed a great expanse, and I reveled in the knowledge that I stood inside the walls of this hallowed institution, revered by scholars and students throughout China. Then she escorted us to the small hotel that Professor Mao had booked for us. The man behind the reception desk was taken aback. "How can they stay here?" he asked Liu Ning. "Don't worry," I said, "it won't be a problem. Just bring us to our room and show us where the bathroom is." The underground passageway that led to the bathroom was like a rabbit warren. But though the bathroom was hard to reach, the reward was a shower that stood right next to the toilet—and it had hot water.

When Professor Mao came to our hotel that evening, he asked us if we'd ever used, or even seen, a computer. I told him that I'd seen one once—I had been in its presence and even touched it—but that was it. "Can it read books?" I asked excitedly. Professor Mao laughed, saying that although this wasn't possible now, it would be in the future. We were hugely excited to know that we would spend the next two weeks learning basic computer skills under his direction.

The next morning we went to his office, and I was thrilled to run my hands over the entire computer. I knew that this computer was like any other, with one crucial exception: Professor Mao's software enabled it to read aloud the words we typed. The sound quality was awful, the computer was painfully slow, and I found the keyboard layout to be completely illogical. But over the next two weeks we learned the almost impossible art of typing things you can't see, as well as basic word-processing skills like copying, deleting, and editing text. Hard as it was to learn these skills, the experience was revolutionary: we didn't have to redo everything when we made a mistake, and we could show other people our work. When you write Braille, your audience is severely limited, and "translation" into regular writing is laborious.

Although we had no immediate prospect of using a computer once we returned to Qingdao, we felt deeply grateful for Professor Mao's generous instruction. On our last day in Beijing, Professor Mao invited us to have dinner with him and his family in his apartment. That night and throughout our visit, I never sensed that he felt embarrassed to be with us, as so many people often were. He was unfailingly warm and considerate, and he seemed to understand some of what we'd had to overcome to be there to study with him.

"Use your minds and think deeply about things," he counseled us that final evening. "I know you have great aspirations and lofty ideals, but it's difficult in China under the current circumstances."

"It is," I replied, "but if you don't have the courage to face difficulties, your life will never amount to anything."

After dinner, Professor Mao walked us back to our hotel and asked us to send his regards to our families. The next morning we gathered our belongings and, as planned, headed off with Liu Ning to an old part of Beijing called Yongdingmen; there we said our good-byes.

On our own again, my classmate and I made our way down an alley to the State Bureau for Letters and Visits, also known as the "petition office." In a Chinese tradition that has carried over from imperial times, petitioners come to these special offices to report their deepest wounds and grievances, hoping against hope that someone in power will listen and bring them justice. If China had a good legal system, you wouldn't need a petition office; as it is, all you can really do is go there to beg for help. The only thing the Chinese people receive for their efforts in this place is the understanding that petitioning is pointless—but I didn't know that back then and was still hopeful.

In some ways, that winter morning was the culmination of six years of protest. I was now twenty-six years old, a blind student without an independent livelihood. Already all but crushed by the cost of supporting me at school, my family still had to pay taxes on my behalf and make up for my "volunteer labor service" every year. The Protection Law had been officially in place for six years, yet it had brought about no real change in my life or my family's life, and no real easing of hardship. Now, taking advantage of my trip to Beijing to visit with Professor Mao, I was bringing my complaint directly to the central government, to the petition office down this ancient alley. On the one hand, I was acting in the tradition of the "loyal subject" who works through established channels; on the other, I was pursuing a bold and risky protest that could easily land me in hot water with officials back home, who might lose face because of my petition. In recent years, many petitioners have been beaten, detained, and kidnapped by their local officials after they've returned from Beijing.

My classmate and I stood in the petition office among the desperate and disaffected, trying to claim our rights as disabled people. After waiting in line for a long time, we filled out a form, explaining our purpose in petitioning. Eventually an official directed me to one room and sent my classmate to another. The man I met with wrote something on a slip of paper and handed it to me, saying that I should deliver it to a government office at the provincial level. He didn't tell me what he'd written, and of course I couldn't read it. "Don't show this document to anyone else," the man warned.

He then stood up to exit the room, but I blocked him. "You can't just get up and leave without doing anything," I said.

"Get out of my way," he retorted. "I told you what to do."

For the past five years, I had visited all of the lower-level petitioning offices, including the village, township, city, county, and provincial offices. Now I was at the national level, at the state bureau, and I had nowhere else to go, short of breaking into Zhongnanhai, the closed compound that belongs to the party leaders. With the shock of full recognition, I finally understood that the petition system was worth-less and that the Communist Party would never do anything for me. From that day on, I decided that a better way to address social inequi-ties would be to take legal measures, to seek justice through the law itself.

My classmate and I left the office, heading for the train station. As we walked back down the alley, a man approached us and asked if we had just been inside the petition office. He seemed friendly enough, so I took out the slip of paper and asked if he would read it to us. "'Chen Guangcheng has come to see us to report on a problem in Shandong,'" the man read. "'We hope you can take care of this issue.'" The man told me that except for my name the rest of the form was all preprinted, and there was no signature or seal to indicate who had written it. It hardly mattered; I knew no one would bother to read the document anyway.

As it turned out, my frequent protests and my petition in Beijing did not escape the notice of local officials. Later that year, while I was back at school in Qingdao, the local government sent a representative to our house in Dongshigu, a man who blithely announced to my father that the government would no longer demand taxes from me. He then informed my father that now, instead of collecting taxes, the govern-ment would give me 200 yuan every year I was at school; all my father had to do was sign a document on my behalf. My father did so, relieved to be free of the tax at last and happy that my trip to Beijing had been fruitful.

At the time, many rural people used a personal seal, or chop with red ink, as a signature. When signing an official document, the correct practice was to place one's chop as close to the last word of the docu-ment as possible, preventing others from inserting any additional text. My father didn't understand this, and he put his chop off to one side. Taking advantage of this error, the official would later add four crucial words before my father's seal, making it appear as though my father agreed that I was "unreliable, providing false evidence," though it would be some time before we knew what had occurred.

That spring, during the time when farmers begin preparing their

Just a few months old, I sit on my mother's lap; Fourth Brother stands beside us. This is the only photograph of me as a child, and the only one taken at a time when I could still see.

In early 1988, my family gathered as we always did to celebrate my grandmother's birthday. My grandmother sits front and center, with my father and mother to her left; my uncle is to her right, with my nephew Chen Kegui sitting on his lap. My brothers and I are in the second row; right to left, Elder Brother, Second Brother, Third Brother, and me, just sixteen. In the back row are my brothers' wives and two cousins.

A view of our yard from the main gate. Our house is at the center of the photo; the kitchen building is on the right. Our family mill wheel sits under the overturned bucket at the intersection of the two buildings.

My father sits on a stool outside our kitchen building, cooking a meal. He retired from his job at the Communist Party school when I was ten. I was fortunate to be able to spend a good deal of time with him after that.

I finally learned to read at age eighteen, after I began my formal education at the Linyi School for the Blind in 1989. Here, I'm reading a book in Braille out in our yard.

My mother with a handmade basket full of fresh peanuts; Elder Brother wields a hoe behind her. Farm labor is still done primarily by hand in rural China.

After a paper mill was built upstream from Dongshigu, our beautiful Meng River became terribly polluted. With the help of Caroline Wilson at the British embassy in Beijing, we were able to dig a proper well so we could all "eat clean water." Here, I am listening to the well's pump.

Yang Ziyun

My informal education in the law made me an ad hoc legal expert in our area, where lawyers were scarce. I began organizing events like this one to spread information about the law in rural areas; here, I am giving a presentation with attorney Jiang Tianyong to a group of farmers and disabled people.

As my work continued, I met many disabled people who lived in unimaginably difficult circumstances. The mother of the two disabled children by my side in this photo singlehandedly cared for them as well as the children's blind grandparents; she also performed all the family's farm labor.

Li Wei

In 2002, on the day we filed a class-action lawsuit in protest of illegal taxes against the disabled, fellow barefoot lawyer Li Zhizeng and I led a group of disabled people and their families to court.

Soon my legal work in the countryside began to attract the attention of the wider world, including the international media. In 2002 *Newsweek* featured me in an article about China's barefoot lawyers.

After a tumultuous courtship Weijing and I were married on February 8, 2003. As is typical in China, we had photographs taken at a studio where we posed wearing outfits we borrowed from the studio.

Weijing and me with our son, Kerui, then just a few months old, after we returned from a trip to America in 2003 at the invitation of the U.S. Department of State.

Teng Biao

In 2005 I launched an investigation into the government's abusive enforcement of the One-Child Policy with the help of a few friends and activists; pictured here with me is Guo Yushan (right). I was horrified by the stories we heard.

A government propaganda banner promoting the One-Child Policy reads: "Beat it out! Abort it out! Drag it out! Whatever you do, do not give birth!" Slogans like this one were a common sight throughout rural areas.

In September 2005 I was kidnapped in Beijing and brought home. These guards stationed outside our house were among dozens posted throughout the village to prevent me from continuing my investigation.

Yuan Weijing

In 2006 two of my attorneys, Li Jinsong and Li Subin, were stopped when they tried to enter Dongshigu to investigate the circumstances of my detention. Activist Hu Jia took this photo just before the guards flipped over the car—with my attorneys inside.

Hu Jia

A day before my first trial in 2006, dozens of supporters gathered outside the courthouse wearing T-shirts emblazoned with an image of my face. Later, the shirts were torn from their bodies. Left to right: attorney Gao Zhisheng, university professor Sun Wenguang, and democracy activist Deng Yongliang.

I was still in detention after my sentencing when two of my attorneys traveled from Beijing to try to meet with me; they were beaten mercilessly. Li Fangping, pictured here after being taken to a hospital, sustained serious head injuries.

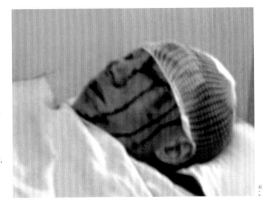

The Linyi Prison, where I spent forty-three months following two sham trials. To the left of the blue sliding door is the entryway to the visiting room.

Hu Jia

Within two hours of returning home after more than four years in prison, I found I was prohibited from leaving my yard. Once again, my home had become my prison.

Desperate to communicate with the outside world, Weijing and I recorded a video in which we described our circumstances. In this still from the video, I am holding the bouquet of leaves that my daughter, Kesi, and Teng Biao gave me before I went to prison.

Chen Guangxin

Guards constantly patrolled the corner of National Route 205 and the road into Dongshigu; they built the white house pictured here as a surveillance post and used the cars as roadblocks. Anyone who tried to enter the village after I returned from prison was stopped and beaten.

In another still from our secretly recorded video, Kesi and I look out our front door. My family suffered under house arrest just as I did. Kesi was rarely allowed out of the yard.

Danica Mills

After our video got out the guards beat us and ransacked our home. I secretly jerry-rigged an old AA battery charger to charge a cell phone I'd kept hidden, which allowed us to send out one final message. Pictured here is a re-creation of the device.

In the summer of 2011 the authorities began converting Second Brother's old home into a prison built especially for us. That fall, they told us to prepare to move into the prison, but fortunately they held off, likely due to pressure from the outside world.

land for planting, we discovered that the government had taken ownership of two-thirds of my land—the roughly quarter of an acre allotted to each villager during the reform era. With no warning or legal basis whatsoever, the government had rented it out to other villagers for a profit.

I protested repeatedly, confronting the village party secretary and writing complaints to government officials, but this land grab appeared to be a done deal. For years, the government had been stealing my money through unlawful taxation; with this move it had confiscated my land in a flagrant display of deep-rooted corruption. The official's cheap sleight of hand showed that, despite the law, nothing had changed except the means of extortion, and now the government would consider my case effectively closed. Years of effort, culminating in the petition I'd filed in Beijing, had been made moot by this deceptive bureaucrat's pen behind the cover of closed doors. In time, the government would take control of the remainder of my land, too, on the absurd excuse that I had moved away for school.

By 1998, I was seriously considering going to college. That spring, still at Qingdao, I heard that Nanjing University of Chinese Medicine would be accepting students for the following fall. At the time, only two colleges in the entire country accepted blind students; Nanjing was one of them, admitting a small group of blind students once every three years, and only for acupuncture and Chinese massage. Up to that time, only about four hundred blind students had gone to college in China. What were the chances that a blind boy born to a poor farming family would ever attend university?

The possibility that I could apply to Nanjing was immediately intriguing. But I hadn't yet completed my studies at Qingdao, and I knew the school would be displeased if I left early. I was torn: part of me wanted to finish my course work at the school, but I also wanted to start college as soon as possible so I could get a job and become independent. Whatever the obstacles before me, I was convinced that a university education was the only way I could attain the knowledge I was hungry for.

A classmate of mine shared my eagerness to find out what it would take to get into Nanjing, so we agreed to call the university and ask for some details about the requirements, test materials, and tuition. Leaving the school with our canes, we took a bus to a Post and Telegraph Office so we could use the public telephone, which was fairly cheap. After talking with someone at the university, we both felt hopeful, and I started preparing for the entrance test immediately. My one anxiety concerned the tuition and fees, which were exorbitant for a poor family such as mine. It would cost 200 yuan just to apply, and the annual tuition would be 2,800 yuan, which didn't include food, housing, or miscellaneous expenses.

I soon decided that I had to tell my family about this rare opportunity and about my intention to take the admission test—if I missed this chance, I might never get another. I called Second Brother, who now lived in Yinan, and told him that Nanjing offered me the chance to get a real education. I pointed out that a university degree would be much more valuable than the degree I would receive from Qingdao; I was shocked when he flatly objected to this, saying that a university education was meaningless. Besides, he told me, people in Nanjing speak a completely different dialect; what could I possibly learn in class if I couldn't even understand what my teachers were saying? Fourth Brother likewise objected to my plan to apply to university. I knew that one issue was money: my brothers were concerned about the high tuition and fees, a substantial portion of which they would probably end up paying. I also knew that they might be struggling with latent prejudices of their own. None of my brothers had attended college; the idea that I might go to university surely seemed far-fetched and a waste of resources, and their strong opposition wounded me.

I talked over my dilemma with Wang Yongbo, a sighted friend of mine who was already in a medical school and pursuing a degree in Western medicine. She encouraged me to apply, and so, fired by idealism and full of hope for the future, I decided to do everything possible to get into Nanjing University of Chinese Medicine. I didn't care how much difficulty I would have to overcome—my family's resistance, a lack of money—I would go ahead and sign up for the test. Wang Yongbo helped me fill out the form and went with me to the post office to mail the application. I paid the application fee with 200 yuan that an uncle had given me when he'd visited me at school the previous year, a sum so large I hadn't dared spend it.

To take the entrance examination I would have to go to Nanjing and bring some form of identification—"evidence," as they called it—from my hometown. I was uneasy at the prospect of having to produce this, knowing that I would have to face my family's objections yet again. I took a bus home. Second Brother picked me up in Yinan; he still strongly insisted that I not take the test. Finally, back in Dongshigu, I found the validation I needed: my father, hearing my intentions, said simply, "As long as you can pass the test, we should support you."

The next challenge was studying for the test, which, in addition to Chinese medicine, would cover subjects such as Chinese language, math, and politics. There were almost no preparation materials in Braille, so before I left Qingdao, Wang Yongbo began recording herself talking through the course material, so I would have a way to learn. When she got too busy with her own studies to continue, a few friends of hers stepped in and helped complete the work.

Back in the village, the summer days were scorching hot. With only one fan in our house, I found it almost impossible to study during the day, so instead I studied all night and rested after the sun came up. Sometimes the power would go out, which meant that I couldn't listen to my tape recordings. When that happened, I relied on the few Braille books I had.

In late July, it was finally time to prepare for the trip to Nanjing, a city of six million, over three hundred miles to the south. I would be accompanied by my nineteen-year-old nephew, Chen Kegui; at this critical moment, as so often in my life, family members made significant sacrifices for me. My mother knew I'd have to keep up my strength through the days of exams, so she prepared enough *jianbing* to last my nephew and me the whole trip. We also took a great number of cicada larvae, fried in oil and sprinkled with a little salt, a good crispy snack once you've got the taste for it.

The college entrance exam, called the *gaokao*, is an annual rite across all of China, nervously anticipated by everyone, not just the graduating high school students but also their extended families and sometimes whole communities. Our equivalent exam, all in Braille, took place at a different time and was structured and scored a bit differently, but the pressure was the same. The exams were long and challenging. When the *gaokao* was finally over, I was confident that I had done well, but that didn't mean I would make the cut.

After the exams I returned to Dongshigu and began waiting anxiously to hear my results. I worried constantly that the university wouldn't be able to reach me, as my family had no telephone then. At last a notice came in the mail: I had passed my exams and been accepted by the university. I was expected to start in Nanjing the following month.

CHAPTER FOUR

No Turning Back

In September 1998, in the early hours of the morning after a sleepless overnight trip on an un-air-conditioned bus, my father and I arrived in Nanjing. Before the sun was up, we made our way to the city's school for the blind. Despite the fact that I was matriculating at the Nanjing University for Chinese Medicine, my class of blind students would be housed here, and this was where we would study, separate from the rest of the university students. Professors from the university would come to the Nanjing School for the Blind to teach us, except when we attended classes on dissection; then we would be bussed to the university, about half an hour away. As I soon discovered, the prejudice underlying this system of separation was veiled behind a curtain of bureaucracy and official-level excuses.

My father and I made our way to room 102, on the first floor of the dorm, where we found four sets of bunk beds. I chose a top bunk next to the window. The dorm's faculty resident came by to help get me settled and handed me a bundle of supplies: a pillow and bedding, a thermos, two enamel bowls, two spoons, and two basins for washing, each item with a number pasted on top. (Mine was 98018.) The resident told me a bit about how things worked in the dorm, and I was relieved to learn that the cafeteria and a source of drinking water were both close by.

Later that morning my father and I found out that the university would be collecting the full tuition the following day. This news cast a pall over my first hours in Nanjing—just when we should have been excited about my new life as a university student, my father and I felt depressed and lethargic. The financial reality we were facing was all too clear: my father was by then earning a little more than 300 yuan per month from his pension, yet he would somehow have to cover my 2,800 yuan annual tuition bill, plus another 3,000 yuan or so to pay for my textbooks and living expenses. He had brought a total of just 3,000 yuan with him on this trip; he understood that it wasn't enough, but he figured he would find a way to get the rest upon returning to Dongshigu. I knew he had already been everywhere in the village trying to borrow money, but I sensed that he hadn't had much luck. I also noticed that he hadn't been smiling much lately; the pressure he felt was too immense. Knowing the financial burden I was putting on my family, I was feeling intense pressure, too.

After a midday meal of fried doughnuts and fresh soybean milk in my room, I lay down for a nap. That afternoon, a number of other students arrived and began settling into their new accommodations. In the evening, as bedtime approached, I realized I had lost track of my father in the commotion. I found him in the cafeteria, sitting on a small bench and holding his small, worn bag of belongings.

"I have nowhere to sleep," he said, "so I'll just stay here tonight."

"How can that possibly be okay?" I asked.

"This bench will be fine," he replied. "When I get tired I'll just lie down here."

The narrow bench would be almost impossible to sleep on. Did my father, now in his sixties, have to spend the night in a cafeteria? Nine years earlier, when he first brought me to school in Linyi, he had already been showing his age; now he was an old man. He could barely lift his legs when he walked, and his footsteps were slower than ever. I was upset and insisted that he share my bunk bed. He clambered into the top bunk, the whole frame shaking as I helped him up. A swirl of thoughts filled my head—about how bitter my father's fate was, about how life simply had to improve for our family—but my father fell asleep quickly and even started to snore.

The next morning we went downstairs to pay the tuition. Some university staff had come over to the Nanjing School for the Blind to register our incoming class of students, and from them we learned that on top of the tuition due the university, we owed 400 yuan for bedding and sundries purchased for us by the school. Together, the two bills amounted to 3,200 yuan, more money than my father had brought along with him. The university staff agreed to let my father pay 1,800 of the 2,800 yuan tuition now and send the additional 1,000 as soon as he could. After my father paid the 400 yuan we owed the local school, that left about 800 yuan—and the next day I learned that half of that sum would go toward the cost of that semester's textbooks. Over the coming semester, the meager amount that remained would have to cover the cost of food and all the other expenses I would be incurring. Somehow, I would get through the next few months, but once again I would be forced to limit my food consumption to near starvation levels.

The school year began, as it does for all first-year Chinese undergraduates, with two weeks of military training. It was a good time to make friends, some of whom I remained close to throughout my three years in college. There was Geng Yao, who later embraced Christianity and with whom I'm still in touch to this day. There was the brilliant Chen Xianyang, whose family was so wealthy he was able to fly to Nanjing from his home, which at the time was almost unheard of for regular people. We used to have heated discussions about politics, life, and so many other things. Another friend, named He Zhou, was extremely intelligent, but unfortunately he lacked ambition. I loved debating and talking to these friends whenever we were together.

Thrilled to be a university student, I threw myself into my schoolwork. That first semester, I studied anatomy and dissection, diagnostics, acupuncture, and massage; I also took a required course called Basic Marxism. The dissecting room always had a thick formaldehyde taste; a cadaver lay on each table, and we also worked with models that had humanlike tissue. I was not afraid of the bodies; nor was I nervous about dissecting them. My classmates and I came to learn how the bones fit and work together, how the muscles are arranged, and where the veins and arteries are. I found that hands could often do a better job than eyes when determining the precise location of acupoints.

On top of all my other work that fall, I took an elective course on the basic principles of law and medicine, my first and only academic exposure to the topic of law. My interest in the law had grown over the years; I often asked people to read aloud to me from legal materials that came to hand, but, with the exception of the Protection Law, I had never been able to find any legal books or documents in Braille. Not surprisingly, we had no Braille textbook for this course, so I listened carefully and jotted down notes on the lecture afterward. In fact, we had Braille textbooks for only about half of our classes, but after the first semester I couldn't afford to buy them. Instead, I borrowed the textbooks from my friend and deskmate He Zhou, who passed his books to me once he had moved on to something else.

Despite my enthusiasm for school, maintaining my health was still a serious challenge. The pattern by now was all too familiar. The first few days or weeks at school were tolerable. I was never actually full, but at least I wasn't overly hungry, and I could withstand this feeling for some time. In this early period of hunger I often salivated greedily when I caught a whiff of almost any kind of food—even something as common as instant noodles would be enough to make me swoon.

After a month or two, the lack of sufficient food would begin to manifest itself in more painful and troubling ways. Initially, I would find my energy depleted to the point of listlessness, and yet at night I would be unable to sleep. As a child, I had been able to jump and run with agility and speed; I could hang from a tree branch with one hand while I felt for a bird's nest with the other. Now I grew tired just from standing for a while. Even more disturbing, my memory, once nimble and quick, often faltered. At the start of the semester I could memorize texts and school assignments in one reading and be prepared for the next day's class, but as the weeks went on malnutrition slowed down the wheels of my mind and I needed more and more time to memorize even short pieces of writing. I often felt as if my brain were rough and inflexible, that the whole lower half of my skull was thick and lifeless.

Every time I went home for the holidays, my father would be horrified by how emaciated and jaundiced I looked, and he would immediately make me a stew of pork bones and cabbage. By that point, though, it had been so long since I had eaten anything nutritious that my body couldn't accept it. After a few bites I would have no choice but to put my spoon down, my stomach bloated and heavy.

The next day, my abdomen would begin to swell like a great drum—it even made a *dongdongdong* sound when I tapped on it—and it would be another four or five days before I could begin to properly digest food. By the time the winter break was over, I would have barely had the chance to recover my health before I had to go back to school and face near starvation once again. Over summer break I had more time to regain my strength, and I found I slept more soundly and was better able to focus. But once the semester began, the cycle started all over again.

Beyond what I learned from my schoolwork, my awareness of politics and current events continued to deepen, largely thanks to what I heard on the radio. Radio Free Asia, the nonprofit service funded by the U.S. government, was a revelation. The first time I heard it I was lying on my bunk, listening to my roommate's shortwave radio. He had tuned in a program called *Listener Hotline*; anyone could call in and express any opinion or relate any experience. That evening, and on many subsequent nights, we lay on our bunks and listened to the show. I heard the uncensored voices of all kinds of ordinary Chinese people, including those hungry to learn about the wider world, those suffering from discrimination, and even narrow-minded nationalists eager for an opportunity to criticize the United States. This was what impressed me most, in fact—that a station supported by the U.S. government apparently made no attempt to block repeated criticism on its own airwaves. I often borrowed the shortwave when my roommate wasn't using it, sometimes tuning in to RFA, sometimes to Voice of America, listening long into the night when I couldn't fall asleep because I was so hungry.

Some radio programs opened up whole worlds, like *Tiananmen Great Escape*, on RFA, which chronicled, step by step, the stories of people who had fled that brutal crackdown in Beijing in 1989 and made their way to safety in the United States, Hong Kong, Taiwan, and other places. The show was as exciting as a miniseries, except that it told stories about real life. It occurred to me that under other circumstances—if I hadn't been an eighteen-year-old just entering grammar school, just learning to read and write—I, too, might have been in Tiananmen Square in 1989, taking part in the protests, in which hundreds or thousands of students, workers, and ordinary people died.

In fact, not long into my second semester at university, I became deeply involved in a difficult issue involving my friend Chen Xianyang, one that would set me on a collision course with the authorities. One evening I was in bed with a headache when a classmate came bursting into my room. "Xianyang got beaten up!" he cried. We rushed to his room and found him sitting on his bed; his face and arms were badly wounded and bleeding. Deeply shaken, he told us that he'd been talking on the telephone when a teacher from the Nanjing School for the Blind approached him and demanded to use the phone. The man seemed to be drunk, so Xianyang ignored him. Enraged, the teacher attacked Xianyang with some kind of a weapon, then pummeled him and kicked him in the ribs. The assault would be a frightening experience for anyone, but it was particularly traumatic for Xianyang; as a blind person, he'd found it difficult to protect himself from the unseen blows.

After the assault, the teacher ran upstairs, but two people had witnessed the beating. They confirmed Xianyang's story, and we immediately reported the assault to the school principal. After confronting the teacher, the principal reported the incident to the Nanjing Education Bureau and the Jiangsu Provincial Department of Education, but weeks went by and neither gave a response. I was incensed at their delay in dealing with this outrageous attack on a student. We demanded that the teacher pay Xianyang's hospital bills and that the school inform us about the teacher's status, but we got nowhere.

No matter where we turned—the school, the administration of the university, the city agencies responsible for education issues—the result was the same: excuses followed by inaction. At each level we were told to seek help from the next level of authority, but when we hit a ceiling we were told to go back to those directly responsible for the problem. As the end of the school year approached, Xianyang saw that we were getting nowhere and urged that for the time being we should focus on our upcoming exams.

I refused to let the matter rest, however, and advocated contacting the media, as we had heard others do via radio talk shows and as I had done back in Qingdao. I sometimes listened to a well-known local call-in program on Nanjing Traffic Radio, *The Special Line to Get Rid of Your Worries*, hosted by a man named Dong Sheng. The broadcast was devoted to exposing social ills; someone would call in and describe a disturbing incident, and the show's reporters would investigate and then report their findings in a subsequent program. My classmates and I wanted to contact the show, but many students were worried that the school might take revenge on whichever one of us phoned in. In the end, a friend of mine who was visiting from out of town agreed to make the call—using my name—while the rest of us were taking our final exams.

When host Dong Sheng heard about Xianyang's beating on the air, he was livid, and listeners immediately began demanding an investigation, not only of the incident itself but of the school's delay in handling it. After I returned home for summer break, I learned that Dong Sheng himself had gone to the school. The incident caused such an uproar that the Jiangsu Provincial Department of Education finally had to take action. By the time classes started again in the fall, the Nanjing School for the Blind had bowed under media pressure and agreed to our three key demands: that Xianyang be compensated, that his medical bills be paid, and that the teacher apologize publicly. At a school meeting that fall, the teacher apologized in front of all the school's instructors and the twenty-two blind university students. He admitted that he'd been drunk and had beaten Xianyang, and he eventually gave Xianyang 600 yuan as compensation.

The larger lessons of this incident were mixed. On the one hand, we saw that when ordinary Chinese citizens are faced with injustices inflicted on them by those in authority, media exposure is a powerful force, and in this case we had successfully harnessed it. Where Xianyang would otherwise have been wounded, humiliated, and then silenced, he instead experienced a measure of triumph and justice, thanks to our collective efforts. On the other hand, we also saw the extent to which party politics and bureaucratic relationships infect and govern society's unwritten rules. What's more, I had angered and offended the school and a number of education officials by speaking out, and in time they would take their revenge.

The resolution of Chen Xianyang's case coincided with another important event in my life, also relating to media and politics. One day in the fall of 1999, while listening to a program on RFA featuring reports and interviews by a man named Han Dongfang, based in Hong Kong, I dialed the phone number he provided on the air—I remember that number to this day—after he assured his listeners that they could call collect. I got through to him, and we chatted, discussing the massive wave of layoffs then taking place at China's state-owned enterprises, which was impoverishing millions. Dongfang asked about my life, and I described the lot of a struggling student who was unable to buy textbooks or even fill his stomach. "Why don't you tutor to earn some money?" he asked. I admitted that I was blind and explained that finding and undertaking any kind of paying work represented a tremendous challenge. With spontaneous generosity, he offered to help.

At first I resisted, uncomfortable with the idea of taking charity. Finally, I gratefully accepted his offer to send me some money but insisted that, once I was able, I would not fail to repay him. Before sending the funds to me, Dongfang made sure I knew that he had been a labor activist on the mainland before being exiled to Hong Kong; he wanted me to understand the risk of having a traceable connection to him. I said I wasn't afraid and I didn't see any reason why I shouldn't accept his help. In the end, his unconditional support sustained me through my final year and a half in college; during that time, we struck up a warm and lively friendship, one we have maintained to this day. But he'd been right to warn me before providing financial support; his status as "enemy of the state" would have consequences soon enough.

Though the Nanjing School for the Blind had finally capitulated to our demands following Chen Xianyang's assault, the administrators soon made it very clear that they were not pleased about having been exposed by the media in the wake of the incident. At the university's behest, the school would usually arrange a year-long internship for all of its blind students, but in the spring of 2000 the staff made us find our own, explaining that no employer would want us because of the controversy surrounding the Chen Xianyang case. Fortunately, everyone in our class managed to find internships anyway, and we dutifully relayed the necessary information about these positions to the school. The administration's response, however, was to announce that it would be making changes to the placements as it saw fit. Thus, in one fell swoop the administrators took us out of the equation while securing for themselves the unofficial benefits that arise from these institutional connections.

Along with several classmates, I had found a prestigious internship at a hospital in Nanjing. But soon after declaring that they would intervene, the school administrators contacted the hospital to say that they had decided to give me a position in another city. And I wasn't the only one: seven of us, the least "obedient" students in our class, were sent to the Luoyang Massage Hospital, in Henan, which was five hundred miles away, while the more obedient were allowed to remain in Nanjing. We were all furious, but when we confronted the administrators, their completely unsubstantiated excuse ("bad behavior") obviously meant something else: we had disobeyed them. Again I recognized the party's corrupt way of thinking, the idea that, in any situation, people in power can act with impunity and with complete disregard for the well-being of others, much less the truth of the circumstances.

In June 2000, with our classes and exams already ended, the seven blind students singled out by the school—including Xianyang and me—set off for Luoyang, traveling by train. Sweating through our clothing, we sat in the train's cheapest section, known as the "hard seats." All of us were feeling somewhat hopeful about going to Luoyang; we looked forward to experiencing a different culture and gaining new knowledge. Still, after all the years and all the sacrifices we'd made to get an education, our disappointment at the school's deception was acute.

We reached Luoyang at around ten that night and found the third-floor dorm room where we would be staying. The next day we were introduced to our massage instructors, a number of whom were blind as well. In the following days and weeks, I came to see that the hospital offered an interesting yet disturbing vantage point from which to understand society. Many local officials came to the hospital, including the city's vice mayor and the heads of many other bureaus in the city government. While we massaged them or worked on their meridians, these officials spent a lot of time on the telephone, often with a relative who was already at a government office asking for a favor. Sometimes the relative on the other line would simply hand the phone to another employee at the office, who would then get the order to provide the favor directly from the person I was working on. This kind of back-channel interaction allowed me to witness firsthand how corruption works in China.

Sometimes one of these officials would engage me in conversation. While I was working on his back or his legs, he might say to me, "Ah, I've been playing too much mah-jongg, I've been playing too much poker—even in the daytime we keep at it. My vertebrae and my shoulders have problems." Why, I couldn't help wonder, was I helping to heal these officials—just so they could play more mah-jongg? As time went on, I decided that I simply couldn't accept this sort of situation, particularly when so many people in China couldn't afford to purchase even basic medicine. Yes, I could make money doing this work, but what was the point? A hospital should be dedicated to curing people and saving lives, but in Luoyang that mission was nowhere evident.

Our working conditions, meanwhile, were terrible. My classmates and I were treated as the hospital's private property, and our bosses expected us to work seven days a week with no compensation. Eventually we decided to complain: we met with one of the hospital's directors and informed him that the hospital was violating Chinese labor law, which mandates a maximum forty-hour workweek. Never having been confronted with such a specific complaint, he and the other managers at Luoyang were not pleased. In the end, they grudgingly agreed to give us Saturdays off. It was clear to all of us, however, that they were very unhappy with us and would not let the issue go.

Even as I began my internship at Luoyang, I was preoccupied with thoughts of home. An issue that had been brewing in my village for a long time was finally coming to a head.

The year before my internship began, I had returned to Dongshigu during the winter break. Passing by the gate to the first house in the village, I heard a greeting.

"Oh, so you're back now?" a woman's voice said.

The voice belonged to a villager named Su Zhilan, and behind its warmth I heard something else. "I'm back," I said simply. "How are things with you?"

Her answer was grave: her brother had recently collapsed while out at a market. They had rushed him to the hospital, but the doctors had been unable to save him. The cause of his death was unknown.

Because of my immersion in issues of medicine and health at university, I immediately began considering likely diagnoses. But I also found myself thinking about a topic that was already very much on my mind, one that had lately been the talk of the village: the pollution in our drinking water.

For the past decade or so, China had experienced extraordinary economic growth; some even called it an economic miracle. But growth had come at a very high cost—vast swaths of environmental degradation and debilitating pollution of the air and water—and once again the common people were paying the price. Almost a decade earlier, just after I'd left for school, a large paper mill had been built in the town of Duozhuang on the banks of the Meng River, a few miles upstream from Dongshigu. Ever since, the mill had been dumping its untreated wastewater into the river, turning it the color of soy sauce and causing masses of foaming bubbles to appear. Soon our village started feeling the effects. Fish began dying in large numbers; before long, the river supported only loaches, frogs, and toads, and later not even these animals could survive in the water. Many villagers had continued to use the water to irrigate their crops, but their watermelons had died on the vine. No one went swimming in the water anymore, fearful of developing rashes and hives. Once a clean and beautiful river, a mainstay of village life, the Meng was now filled with poison.

Our village had no deep wells; our only source of drinking water was a shallow well, just seven or eight feet deep, close by the river. Our well water was really just water from the river that had been filtered through soil and sediment deposits. That posed no problems when the river ran clean, but now everything had changed. In recent years Dongshigu had seen a whole host of illnesses emerge; many of them were undoubtedly caused by our polluted drinking water.

All this flashed through my mind as I listened to Su Zhilan describe her brother's death. Who knew how many others might be affected, how deep the damage might go? I resolved then and there to raise the issue with the village leaders. It was obvious what Dongshigu needed: a deep well whose water could be piped into people's homes. Only then could the people of our village "eat" clean water, as we say in the countryside.

For the past several years the villagers had tried to attack the river's pollution at its source, demanding that the mill be shut down or at least cease dumping chemicals into the river. None of their protests had gone anywhere. Official visits to the mill by the Environmental Protection Bureau usually ended in great quantities of liquor being consumed and wads of money being stuffed into pockets. Someday, I thought, we would have to get to the bottom of the mill's troubles, but for now we needed to focus on solving our urgent drinking water problem with a new well.

Back at school in Nanjing after the Chinese New Year holiday in 2000 I was speaking with Han Dongfang on the phone one day, thanking him for the money he'd sent me, and I happened to mention my recent visit to Dongshigu. I couldn't get my mind off Su Zhilan's brother, I said, and the dangers posed by the pollution in our river. For years my father and others had tried to get running water for the village, but local officials had always hemmed and hawed and said there was no money. Dongfang heard me out and assured me that something could be done, that someone in the international community, some charity, would support a new well for the village. I barely knew what he meant by "the international community," but I was excited: if we could find funding, officials in Dongshigu would have no recourse but to act. Talk to people back in the village, Dongfang said; draw up a budget for what you need and send it to me.

I immediately called the one phone in Dongshigu, which had finally been installed in 1996, and asked for Du Dexiang, the village mayor. A neighbor of ours and a former primary school teacher, Mayor Du had just been elected, the first time a genuinely popular candidate had beaten out the party hacks in our village.

"Big brother," I said into the phone, using the familiar term of address, "this is Little Five."

"Ah, Old Five!" he replied cheerfully, using the respectful term of address "old," though in fact he was older than I was. "What's going on?"

I asked if there had been any progress in the effort to find a new source of drinking water. All the efforts had fizzled out, he said with a groan. "We always hear from the higher-ups when they want money from us, but it's a waste of time to ask for anything from them."

I asked him if he could draw up a budget for drilling a well and delivering running water to the village, adding that I had a possible funding source. He readily agreed to work on this, thanking me and making it clear that he trusted me—no small thing, since blind people would usually not get involved in such a complex project. In short order I had a budget to send to Han Dongfang, who, in turn, started looking for a possible benefactor. Several months later, he had one: the first secretary of the British embassy in Beijing.

I came to know the secretary by her Chinese name, Wu Ruolan, but her English name is Caroline Elizabeth Wilson. The first time I spoke to Ms. Wilson on the telephone, I was struck by her tone of respect and consideration; as a disabled person, I had rarely been treated this way. Where was the capitalist cunning and single-minded focus on money-making that the party had told us so much about? Instead, after listening to my story about Dongshigu's polluted river and the urgent need for a well, Ms. Wilson told me that the British government had funds to support projects like ours and that our budget of 205,000 yuan (then around $26,000) was well within range. Her government would almost certainly be inclined to approve the funding, she added, but she and others would like to meet the mayor and me in Beijing and then visit Dongshigu so they could verify the existence of the problem firsthand and ensure that the well would meet basic environmental standards.

Grateful and optimistic, Mayor Du and I started preparing for the trip to Beijing, scheduled for later in the summer. By then, resistance to the paper mill and its pollution of the river was growing rapidly. People in two nearby villages had already begun organizing, but the protest soon expanded. Approximately forty thousand people in forty-three different villages were affected, and as popular anger mounted, village committees affixed their seals in support of the demand that the mill be shut down. Yet we still received no response from the powers that be.

Brave villagers armed with video cameras secretly visited the paper mill at night, filming the filthy discharge as it turned the river red and then black. They took their footage to Linyi and made DVDs to show government environmental officials, to no avail. They showed the DVDs to several journalists, all of whom said they didn't dare report it. If an article somehow did make it past a newspaper's editor, the local propaganda bureau would clamp down; if it got by the local censors, the national Central Propaganda Department would do the same, and those reporting the story could easily wind up in serious trouble. In those days, approaching a journalist from a foreign country was not an option; until 2008 foreign reporters were prohibited from traveling around the country to interview people, and in any case it was dangerous for ordinary citizens to have contact with a foreign journalist.

Not long before Mayor Du and I were due to travel to Beijing to meet with Ms. Wilson, several of those organizing the protest against the mill got in touch with me. Knowing that I had once petitioned in Beijing and had an interest in the law, they asked me what they should do. I thought long and hard about how to answer them. Given that the local environmental protection officers couldn't care less, I said, we would have to go over their heads, first to the national-level Environmental Protection Bureau in Beijing. At the same time, I added, we should contact the State Bureau for Letters and Visits, the "petition office." I didn't think anything would come from petitioning, but at the time I didn't know what else to do. I also thought we should send a formal letter to both the Environmental Protection Bureau and the relevant judicial offices, signaling our willingness to consider filing a lawsuit if they didn't resolve the issue. Everyone agreed that these steps made sense, and we decided that a delegation should visit the relevant ministries in Beijing when the mayor and I went to see Ms. Wilson.

In mid-August 2000 a small group of petitioners rented a cheap van, made a wide detour to Luoyang to pick me up from my internship, and then drove to Beijing. Elder Brother came with us, and we all stayed the night at a small hotel near the Beijing TV station. The next day I waited with my brother for Ms. Wilson, who would be taking me to dinner. I can still hear what she said to me and how clearly she spoke. "Excuse me," she asked, "are you Mr. Chen? Are you willing to go with us in our car?" Never in my life had I heard such a sentence before, with its exquisite politeness, its manifest respect for personal autonomy and choice.

We drove to a small, elegant restaurant where the smell of flowers rose up from every table. I can't remember exactly what we ate—one dish had lilies, another had eggplant—but the meal was delicious. We talked until after midnight, more than six hours in all, discussing everything on our minds: the drinking water project, rural education, living standards in the countryside, the status of the disabled in China—even guide dogs for the blind, which are unknown in China. Why don't you have them? asked Ms. Wilson. I explained that most people had never heard of guide dogs, and what's more, many blind people in China are dependent on others and would hardly be able to care for a working dog.

Talking and being with Ms. Wilson gave me a new and wonderful feeling. She seemed entirely at home with me; I wasn't used to that. As we drove through the streets of Beijing on the way to the restaurant, she pointed out and described much of what we passed: such and such building is on our left, she would say; this landmark is coming up on the right. She also knew exactly how to guide me: she took my hand or my arm as if nothing could be more natural. I was used to people pinching my shirt with two fingers, as though trying to stay as far away from me as possible. Ms. Wilson showed me the deepest kind of respect. Thinking about it later, I realized that it was the first time I'd ever felt like a full-fledged human being. Even with my family I didn't feel this way.

Over the course of that memorable evening, I struggled to comprehend the gulf between my circumstances and Ms. Wilson's. I was twenty-nine years old, a college student in his final year at university with an uncertain future. Just one year older than me, Ms. Wilson was already an accomplished senior diplomat. We'd been on this earth for almost the same amount of time—why this difference? How much of it came from the social and cultural advantages of growing up in the

West? How much had to do with China's shortcomings, or my own, or my disability? These were unanswerable questions, but I was moved by the force of her intelligence and shamed into redoubling my efforts to make my way in the world.

"What can I do for you?" she asked me that first night, and I answered as I have countless times since then: "Introduce me to your friends." She promised to do so and was as good as her word. The next night, for instance, we had dinner with a lawyer who was a friend of hers, an evening that seemed like something out of a dream.

I will always remember the way that second night ended. As we walked through a wide, beautifully furnished hall, Ms. Wilson described our surroundings to me. Then we stopped, and she led my hands to something tall and large and round. "Feel this," she said. I rested my hand on the object, but I restrained myself. Since childhood I have relied on my hands and fingers to understand new things. I flutter my fingers over an object, feeling for contours and holes and grooves and notches in the sides of things, my fingers like rovers exploring the surfaces of an undescribed planet. But I had learned from long experience that this behavior makes sighted people uncomfortable; they learn with their eyes, and it's hard for them to watch someone who learns with his hands.

Yet at that particular moment, Ms. Wilson seemed to know exactly what I wanted. "Don't worry," she said. "Go ahead and touch it, get to know the whole thing—give it a really good look." I started touching it, feeling more and more natural and unashamed, as if no one were watching, as if my way of knowing and experiencing were completely normal. My hands moved up the object's slender curving neck, palming its smooth, cold surface, reaching its delicate lips at their fluted opening: before me stood a huge vase, a remarkable artifact that was taller than I was.

That night Ms. Wilson gave me a simple but extraordinary gift: she stood with me, encouraging me and waiting for me. She made certain that I saw every inch of that gorgeous vase with my own eyes.

Shortly before Caroline Wilson came to see us in Dongshigu in September 2000, local officials flew into a panic. As soon as we told the township's party secretary about Ms. Wilson's impending visit, he rushed off to tell the county head, the county's International Relations Department, and then the county party secretary. Stern phone calls were made: We must not mention water pollution to the foreign guests! There are no problems in our county! One of our fellow petitioners was specifically told not to show his face during Ms. Wilson's visit. Securing a little money to build a village well was one thing, but a major environmental and public health scandal would be quite another.

On the day of Ms. Wilson's arrival, Elder Brother and I went to Linyi airport to meet her and Zhang Lijia, a reporter for the British newspaper the *Independent*. Also greeting the two women were several local officials; before going with us to Dongshigu, Ms. Wilson and Zhang Lijia had to endure classic *jiedai*, the overbearing wining-and-dining style of Chinese officialdom. We all drove to a hotel in the county capital of Yinan, and, sitting around a table heaped high with stir-fried silkworms and crispy scorpions and bottles of hard liquor, the officials puffed up clouds of cigarette smoke and bragged at length about all the foreign countries they had visited and their overseas shopping trips. Offering toast after toast, they clearly planned to get everyone drunk, in the hope that the visitors would forget about the work at hand. It was an exorbitant waste of time.

Ms. Wilson and Zhang Lijia were anxious to get to our village to see my home and our life there, but as the dinner went on, I realized that the local officials would actively resist this plan. To the officials, embalmed in the Communist mind-set, any foreigner was an enemy, a threat. The officials were particularly frightened of Zhang Lijia, since she was a reporter. The day before, they had warned my brother and me that we shouldn't see her or Ms. Wilson privately, but I'd angrily insisted that both women had the right to work and stay where they liked.

When the dinner finally ended, the officials informed everyone that they had arranged for Ms. Wilson and Lijia to stay at the hotel where we were dining. Ms. Wilson, who wasn't pleased with this turn of events, went outside to escape the cigarette smoke; after she left the room, I overheard the officials saying among themselves, "What will happen to our plans?" I didn't know what they meant until later, but in the end they had no choice but to relent and allow the two women to travel with my brother and me to our village.

When Ms. Wilson and Zhang Lijia arrived in Dongshigu that evening, I took them to meet our village's barefoot doctor, who described the conditions and diseases we had been experiencing because of the polluted water. I also introduced them to our fellow petitioners, and later, carrying flashlights, we went to see the Meng River. "Look how much higher the river is!" my brother exclaimed, pointing at the dark waters. Someone had tried to clear up the river's water but had bungled the job. Some sections of the Meng looked relatively clean, while others still ran the usual garish red and black; not all the polluted water had washed away. This was the plan the officials had mentioned earlier: apparently someone had arranged for an infusion of clean water from a man-made reservoir upstream, a pathetic trick intended to fool our visitors.

Knowing that the British embassy would approve the project once Ms. Wilson had been able to personally verify the conditions in our village, we had already hired a team of local workers and had planned to begin drilling immediately. Before Ms. Wilson left for Beijing, we held a ceremony to mark the start of the drilling. Nearly all the villagers were there, and listened as the village party secretary spoke excitedly about the project. Then the village mayor called me up—"You say a few words, Old Five"—and I uttered just a single sentence: "I hope we can all achieve a better standard of living!" With the speeches done, we set off firecrackers, turned on the equipment, and began to drill.

Drilling the well proved to be more complicated than expected, and soon I became immersed in every detail of the project, even while continuing my internship in Luoyang. I knew we had to dig deep enough to find water that was free of both river pollution and the nitrates that naturally linger in the soil to a depth of 130 feet; we also needed the well to deliver enough water to serve the whole village, around 350 cubic feet per hour. But the deepening hole remained mostly dry, and I began to suspect that our team was either less than motivated or none too competent. Wary of the approach of winter, when colder temperatures would render drilling impossible, we became so frustrated with the lack of progress that we decided to hire a new drilling company.

A little more than a month later, the new drilling team hit water. We cheered each time they found water at a new level: 130 feet, 260 feet, eventually all the way down to 530 feet, the ultimate depth of the well. That December, I witnessed the thrilling moment when the well started pumping for the first time, the water coming up out of the ground with tremendous force. Many people from the village were there that day, and a great cheer rose up when clear, fresh water began pouring out of the well.

Soon we were ready to lay the pipes. I insisted that we spend a little more money to get top-quality pipes from the Beijing Light Snowflake Electric Company, considered the best in the business. (Many other villages had chosen to skimp on their pipes, and after just five or six years the pipes began leaking, which not only wasted water but dramatically increased the villagers' electricity bills.) Many villagers volunteered to dig the trenches, and each home in Dongshigu got a single hookup to the system. Soon after the Chinese New Year's festival, we were all eating clean water.

While serving my internship in the fall of 2000, I decided to make an effort to pursue the connections I had started to form through Ms. Wilson. I enjoyed Chinese medicine, but I was beginning to see that practicing it was not what I wanted to do long-term. During the process of procuring clean water for my village, I had experienced a surge of optimism about my future: I felt a growing excitement about the possibility of improving people's lives and helping to spark real social change.

On three or four occasions during that academic year, I arranged to go to Beijing for long weekends. Before each trip, I would ask a friend or someone I'd recently met to introduce me to some of their friends or colleagues so I could broaden my network. I always traveled on my own, taking the train from Luoyang to Beijing West Railway Station, finding my way with my cane and forgoing meals en route to save money.

When planning my first trip to Beijing, I decided to spend the weekend at the hotel where I had stayed when I had originally met Ms. Wilson, but I discovered that it was too far from the train station. From then on, I stayed in a basement room at a cheap hotel near the station. Once I had finished all my meetings for the weekend, I would take the overnight train back to Luoyang, arriving at the station in the morning just as the sun was coming up. I would be back at the hospital in time for breakfast, just before the workday began.

I always returned from these trips to Beijing full of energy and new plans. But in April 2001 I received a rude awakening when one teacher from the university and a teacher and a vice president of the Nanjing School for the Blind arrived in Luoyang. They called a meeting of the seven university interns and informed us that staff at the Luoyang hospital had been in touch with them and complained; in particular, the hospital had expressed grave concerns about my behavior and that of a classmate. The little delegation from Nanjing informed the two of us that we would not be permitted to continue our internship there; we had to go back to Nanjing. (Our five classmates were allowed to remain.) They refused to say anything specific about what we had done to deserve this termination, but we knew it was because we had protested the conditions of the internship.

Furious, we packed our bags and left for Nanjing. Once there, the two of us had a discussion with the principal of the Nanjing School for the Blind. "Your behavior there wasn't good," he told us. "You didn't comply with your supervisors."

"What was bad about our behavior?" I asked. "We took care of seven or eight patients each day, which is a lot. What's bad about that?"

Two days later, the vice principal of the school found me in the morning and said, "The leaders want to talk to you." "All right," I replied, wondering exactly which leaders he meant.

The vice principal brought me to a small meeting room on the first floor of the building at the school where our classes were held, and then quickly disappeared. I found myself sitting across from two men; their voices suggested that one was in his forties and the other in his twenties. What followed was a chilling series of events, a vivid display of the absurd lengths to which the Chinese police state will go to prevent ordinary citizens from having contact with people outside the country's borders.

"We're from the Ministry of State Security," said the older of the two. "Do you know what we do?" he asked, clearly trying to frighten me.

"I don't know—do you make missiles or something?" I replied, punning off the similar sounds of the words "missile" and "mischief" in Chinese.

"No, that's not it," the older man said. He seemed deflated—why wasn't I trembling and groveling before them? With much condescension in his voice, he explained that his ministry handled external affairs in the same way that the Public Security Bureau, another state organ, handled domestic affairs. Then he said, "We have received a report saying that you've been in contact with people living abroad. Is that the case?"

At first I couldn't imagine what they were talking about, but then I remembered my exchanges with Han Dongfang, whose radio show was based in Hong Kong. As the interrogation continued, I learned that the school for the blind in Nanjing had written a letter to the university claiming that I had overseas contacts. Clearly an administrator had somehow found out that I'd been in touch with Han Dongfang; undoubtedly someone had informed on me, saying that I often discussed social problems in our Medical Ethics, Socialist Morality, and Marxist Principles classes. The university hadn't paid much attention, but now the school for the blind had complained to the Ministry of State Security. It was obvious to me that the school was determined to exact revenge for my role in the controversy surrounding Chen Xianyang's assault.

Bearing down, the older man said, "Did someone give you money?"

I didn't deny it.

"Who gave it to you?"

"Han Dongfang gave me some money that enabled me to eat," I replied.

"How do you know him?"

I told them about how I had initially gotten in touch with him and that he had offered to send money to me. The two men were clearly not satisfied with my answer.

While the officers were interrogating me that morning, other officials got access to my dorm room and searched through my things.

They took whatever they pleased: my list of contacts, my bank card, and all of my money, including the funds Han Dongfang had given me.

That afternoon, the two men took me to a hotel. There they pressed me for more details about Han Dongfang's money.

"Do you know what Han Dongfang does?"

"No. All I know is that he's involved in the labor movement. Why do you ask? Even if he is associated with the Nationalists, I don't see any problem with someone helping the disabled."

"You're so naïve. If someone calls you up and wants to give you money, isn't that just too easy?"

They interrogated me for several days. They questioned me for hours on end, asking me about every name on my list of contacts. Whenever I asked them to read the National Security Law aloud so I could understand the legal basis for their actions, they refused to do so, saying the law was only for internal use. "What?" I asked, astounded. "Are there two sets of laws in China, one for internal use and one for external use? Amazing!"

"We have internal regulations," they said. "We can't talk about it."

As the interrogation went on, they threatened me, saying that their decision to hold me was a state secret and I was not to tell anyone. I was furious that the state could wield power so brazenly and shamelessly.

After a total of five days, the two officers finally admitted that I hadn't done anything wrong. They brought me back to the school and took me to the dorm. The older man said, "We have the notifications that you were under residential surveillance and then released from residential surveillance. You are allowed to ask for them if you want."

"What do you mean, I'm allowed to ask for them if I want?" I countered. "You have to do what the law says."

In the end, they gave me one piece of paper saying that I had been under residential surveillance and another saying that I had been released since I wasn't suspected of any wrongdoing. Even then, they continued to spin their lies, claiming that we had spent three days in the hotel instead of five.

A day or two after the interrogation ended, the staff of the Nanjing School for the Blind told me that I was to finish my internship in my hometown. A few weeks after I got back, several local State Security officers called and told me they would be taking me in to the police station in Shuanghou. Once there I complained angrily about my extended interrogation and the decision to send me back to Dongshigu. Later, at home, I found myself having imaginary conversations with the two security officers. I would see myself shouting at them: *You, the Communist Party, let a blind student nearly starve to death at school, only to pounce the moment one kind individual offered him desperately needed help. Then you accused this person of being hostile to the government, threatened to have him expelled from the university, and grabbed the money for yourselves. The only state secret is that you kept me locked up and took money that was given to me.*

I thought I had seen the last of State Security, but I was wrong. Two months later, when I was back at school to participate in the graduation ceremony and collect my diploma, the two security officers turned up again and took me to the meeting room where they had first interrogated me. They immediately declared that they would not return Han Dongfang's money to me. When I asked why, they told me that he was "an enemy of the state." I said, "Even if that were the case, why would it be a problem if he decided to help a disabled student?"

Then they switched tactics, demanding that I memorize and record on video a prepared statement saying I had given the money to them willingly.

"If you agree to do this, we'll wrap up the case today," the older man said.

When I refused, they resorted to blackmail: they told me that unless I recorded the statement, they would inform the university that I wouldn't get my diploma.

By this point I was enraged. The party's evil was boundless—was there nothing its officials wouldn't do to get what they wanted? I had long understood that the party controlled all levels of society and the government, but now I saw evidence of their influence firsthand. The corrupt behavior of these officials was obviously condoned or accepted by higher-ups in the party; I had no doubt that the two men would carry out their threat, and they knew how vulnerable I was. I held out for as long as I could, but with my diploma at risk I finally had no choice: I agreed to let them keep the money and to record the statement they handed me. My thinking was that if I could just be awarded my diploma, I could later decide how to get the money back and reveal the injustice that had been done to me.

Never in my life had I felt more humiliated and powerless. My graduation stood as the symbol of everything I had worked and struggled and fought for over the past twelve years. And until this point in my life, I had always maintained my principles against any trials and harm that might follow as a result; now, not only were they threatening to prevent me from graduating, they were forcing me to go against what I knew to be right and true.

With a searing pain in my gut, I recorded their statement: "Of my free will I am giving the money Han Dongfang gave me to the Ministry of State Security." Afterward the two men grew concerned, declaring that I should also write the statement in Braille. Knowing they couldn't actually read my words, I wrote a note next to the statement, saying that I was being forced to sign their document against my will. My hope was that if I could ever persuade someone to investigate this egregious case of blackmail, they would learn the truth.

This was my first direct encounter with the Chinese security state; obviously the agents' aim was to terrify me. But instead of being scared, I was seething with anger. From this point on, I was dead set against the party, convinced of its inherent inhumanity and corruption. And I vowed that I would never give in.

I finally graduated from the Nanjing University of Chinese Medicine in July 2001. Following policy at the time, the Chinese government guaranteed that I would be given a job in my field, just as it did for all university graduates. After obtaining our degrees, we were supposed to bring our graduation materials, including our diploma, transcript, and political dossier, to our local office of personnel management, where officials would make a decision about where we would go for work. New graduates were often given jobs far away from home and family, but since I was not enthusiastic about this prospect, I didn't bother to make the required visit to the personnel management office. As the summer went on, though, my father began to get anxious; he felt I wasn't earning my keep. I couldn't really blame him: I was in fact racking up large phone bills while continuing my advocacy work and keeping up with friends. Eventually I filed my paperwork so that I would be given an official work unit, but I did so knowing that I would never become a practicing doctor.

By now, a few weeks shy of my thirtieth birthday, I was sure that medicine was not for me. For one thing, I didn't relish the idea of spending eight hours a day in a hospital, where the majority of the fees I could charge for seeing patients would have to be given right back to the institution. For another, I didn't believe that medicine could satisfy my hunger to help improve people's lives. I found traditional Chinese medicine fascinating, but I didn't see how a doctor could work on the kinds of fundamental social and political problems confronting China. I wanted to do something that truly mattered to me, that would allow me to have a positive impact on society. I often thought of a wise saying I had read somewhere: "Good doctors cure illnesses and great doctors cure people, but the greatest doctors heal the nation." Though I didn't know where this new path would take me, I wanted to follow it to the horizon and beyond.

CHAPTER FIVE

Defending Our Rights

If I hadn't been at home that May, forced to finish my internship in Dongshigu. If I hadn't decided to lie down at that particular moment, listening to the radio and resting from the midday heat. If she hadn't called the radio station on that particular day, after months of just listening.

"What can we do for you?" asked the radio show's host, sounding clipped and professional.

I heard a long pause on the other end. "I guess . . . I guess I'm looking for work," a young woman finally replied.

"Well, what kind of work?"

"I don't know, I just . . . I mean, maybe teaching or something?"

"In that case, tell us what you studied, what skills you have."

"I studied—I was studying English. At the Qingdao Institute of Chemical Industry."

"Okay, then. Do you want to leave a phone number, in case someone wants to contact you—someone like a potential employer?"

Another pause, after which the woman carefully enunciated her number—6450567.

"Good luck, and thanks for calling in today!" And then she was gone, off the air. The host moved on to the next caller, who was already describing other hopes and worries, another universe packed into a few public moments. Broadcast live from Linyi, the program—a kind of classifieds on the air—was popular, mainly because it revolved around a hotline open to anyone in need of help or advice. I didn't tune in to it much, but sometimes I liked to hear the voices and stories, to listen to regular people talking about their lives.

That day, I heard something intriguing behind the nervous replies. I could tell from her voice that the caller was a woman in her early twenties; I was also certain that she'd grown up in the countryside but, as she'd mentioned, had studied English in the city, which was no ordinary thing. But why had she sounded so hopeless? What could be holding her back?

Somehow the young woman's telephone number stayed fixed in my memory. A couple of days after hearing her conversation with the radio host, I dialed her number. Though a perfect stranger, with no job to offer, I wanted to encourage her. We spoke Standard Mandarin, the marker of a good education, though her village was just sixty miles from Dongshigu and her dialect was similar to mine.

During that first phone call, she was remarkably candid about failing the college entrance exam, about the resulting blow to her self-esteem, and about feeling ashamed and unworthy after graduating. She did not have a job: since she had not tested into college but had had to pay her own way, she was not entitled to government-issued employment. As a consequence, she'd spent the whole previous year at home; much of the time she stayed alone in her room, listening to the radio. Unsure about how to find work, unwilling to face anyone, she hardly ever went out.

How could this be? I asked. You should have confidence. You're clearly a person of real ability. Few people in the countryside have studied English, and you have learned it well, which means you are very intelligent. How else could you have gone to the city and continued your education? Many schools will be looking for English teachers, so you should go out and try for a job.

"You speak so well," she said. "Can I call you again if I need advice?"

"Of course," I said. I gave her my number.

She told me her name was Yuan Weijing, and she called many times in the month following that first telephone conversation, usually just to talk about whatever was on her mind. Before long I realized that nothing in the world seemed more natural than the way we talked with each other.

"Can I come see you?" she asked one day. She wanted to know what sort of man had helped her become more confident just by talking with her on the telephone.

I responded by repeating something I'd said to her once before, but this time with emphasis: "You should know that I'm disabled. Please don't come to see me if you don't want to be friends with a disabled person. Save us both the embarrassment."

She didn't miss a beat. "No problem at all," she said. "I'll come visit you soon."

On the day Weijing first came to see me—it was July 21, 2001—I was lying in bed in my little room, enjoying *wushui*, the Chinese siesta, just as when I'd first heard her voice. "Someone's here to see you," my mother called out, and a moment later I felt the silent presence of a young woman in the room, the woman whose life I'd been listening to through the telephone.

I sat bolt upright and put my sunglasses on. She was astonished to see me moving normally; she later told me she had always assumed that "disabled" meant confined to a wheelchair, and in her imagination she had been picturing a paraplegic like Deng Pufang, China's most famous disabled person. Like most people who've grown up in rural China, she had no sense of the different things "disabled" could mean.

Without speaking, she took in the bareness of my room, the shabbiness of its few furnishings, the crude and homely look of the place. She told me later that my family's home reminded her of her grandparents' house—her parents, by contrast, were more prosperous. Then she watched as my feet reached out for the yellow plastic sandals I knew were on the floor, sweeping wide with an awkward, sightless life of their own. Finding them, I stood up; she saw that even though it was summer, I was wearing the heavy, unfashionable nylon pants of a farmer.

Now Weijing began to understand. She saw that the smooth, reasonable voice of the educated man she'd been speaking to on the telephone belonged to a homespun peasant, the blind son of a poor farmer.

"I had never met anyone like you," Weijing told me many years later. "You didn't frighten me, although back then I had prejudices like anyone else. We had a neighbor who was blind—a remarkable, unsung woman who raised three children, cooked for her family, and handled the housework—and she did frighten me. As kids," Weijing said, "we would hide at a distance and watch this woman, curious to see if she would fall down, and if she did, how she would manage to stand up again. Instead we saw the woman feed her pigs and perform many other chores with a completely unexpected precision. This was my first encounter with the world of the blind," Weijing confessed, "but somehow this woman seemed frightening and not fully human, unlike you."

During that first visit, Weijing and I exchanged pleasantries for a few minutes, and then little by little we began really talking, just as we had on the phone. The differences between us faded. We were both innocent and intense, and for the moment it didn't matter what others might think, or what obstacles they might want to put in our way—back then we could hardly fathom that anyone would want to come between us. Nor could we imagine all that would happen to us afterward, separately and together. All we knew was that we wanted to see each other again; we hoped there would be a next time and then a time after that. On that summer afternoon, we took so much delight in each other's company that we just kept on talking—joking and speaking of serious things, advising and encouraging each other, asking and listening and dreaming together.

Then, about a week later, Weijing had a piece of luck: a new private middle school was about to open in the area, and the school needed to hire several English teachers at once. I encouraged Weijing to apply, urging her to believe that she was no less capable than other people, that in fact she could do things that many other people could not. Though she was doubtful about her chances, Weijing applied, and she ended up being the school's top choice and top hire. She moved out of her parents' house and went to live and work at the school. Her voice on the phone turned bright and hopeful. I had been certain she could do it, and now she knew it, too.

As the news about our successful campaign to drill a well for the village began spreading, word was also getting around about my earlier petitioning attempt, and people began coming to Dongshigu to seek me out for advice. Because of my interest in the law and my efforts to understand my own rights under the law, over the years I had had the habit of collecting books and materials on a range of legal topics, which my family would read aloud to me when I was at home. This informal education, combined with my petitioning experience and work on the well, made me an ad hoc "expert" in our region, which, like many rural areas, had perennially suffered from a dearth of professional legal help. When I was off at school, my father and older brother were able to guide and advise people who sought my help, having learned a great deal alongside me. Their knowledge of the law not only helped our visitors understand their rights but would prove indispensable later on, when we began filing cases.

Many of the people who initially came to see me were disabled, and they wanted advice about their rights, illegal tax collection, and the "volunteer labor" and accompanying fees—the same issues I had addressed in my own petitions. Before being phased out in 2006, all the taxes and other fees collected by the local government had to be paid by every resident, regardless of age or ability.

These taxes were not supposed to exceed a certain percentage of the average per capita income, as estimated by the government for that particular township or region. But over time, local governments began to cheat their constituents by dramatically overstating average incomes and then reporting these inflated numbers one level up, to the township government. The township government would then exaggerate still more and pass that number up to the county level, and so on. If a typical farmer was making 500 yuan per year, for instance, officials might end up claiming that his income was as high as 3,000 yuan and then imposing a tax of 5 percent, or 150 yuan, almost a third of the farmer's real income. Moreover, the imaginary income number usually went up at least 10 percent each year, regardless of actual conditions. Adding insult to injury, the tax campaign always ended the same way: the officials who collected the tax would gather for a massive banquet on the evening the campaign was finished, celebrating their success with a night of gluttonous eating and drinking on the backs of the people.

And how did the officials collect? Beginning in the 1980s, village governments were responsible for collecting taxes, but as the reported incomes grew, regular people began to refuse to pay these unfair taxes. The village governments then called on the township to bring in police and officials to intimidate people into paying. After a few years, people got used to the sight of the police and officials at tax time and paid them no heed.

As a response, the local governments would sometimes form "little work teams" composed of some thirty or forty party cadres and hired hands to handle the collection process. In some villages, villagers might head to the "government office" (often just another yard in the village) to pay their fees and collect their receipts. Those who objected to their tax bill might be ordered into a room, where a team of overbearing cadres would be seated in chairs at the back, flanked by men holding clubs. The villager would be consigned to a low bench facing these assembled worthies. "Did you bring what you owe?" the cadres would demand, looming over the villager. If the villager didn't pay the tax, he or she would be beaten and told to return with the money.

And if you tried to evade the cadres by failing to appear at the government tax office? They would come to your home, and if you didn't answer the door they would kick it in, pry it open with a hoe, or knock it down with an ax. After they demanded money, they would surround you and pin you down while they stole anything valuable, including your animals, your wheat, your dried sweet potatoes, your broken old television—anything they thought they could sell the next day for cash, which they would pocket for themselves without a second thought. And if you resisted, they would begin screaming at you, beating you, torturing you. They might throw you in a burlap sack, head to toe, grab a nearby mug of hot water, and dump it onto the sack. Their cruelty knew no bounds.

Despite the danger, some people fought back, even though their acts of resistance would invariably provoke a new, harsher round of punishment. One of these brave souls was Liu Naitang, an unusually intelligent man in his sixties who had gone blind later in life and who made a living as an itinerant storyteller and fortune-teller. He was one of the early ones who sought me out, and over the years we became allies and close friends.

I first met Liu Naitang in late 2000. Having heard that I was back from school on winter break, he made the lengthy trip by bus to find me, skirting the chain of mountains that ran between our villages. Over a meal of boiled turnips, cabbage, and pork bones, Naitang told me and my family that in November 1997 he simply couldn't come up with the money to pay the inflated taxes and work fees demanded of him, so he flat-out refused.

"I'm a blind man who has lost the ability to work," he had explained to the tax collectors. "Just putting food on the table is extremely difficult. It's not fair that I should have to pay extra on top of what I already struggle to give to you."

The village party secretary was furious. "The reason you're as blind as a bat is because your ancestors were louts and now you have to pay for their deeds," he said. "You want the government to give you a break on your taxes, but what have you ever done for the country that you would deserve special treatment? You're completely worthless, and you can't even pay the taxes you owe."

The party secretary then proceeded to curse and threaten Naitang for twenty-seven straight days over the village loudspeaker, taunting him for everyone to hear. "If I held power," he yelled, "I would kill every last blind person in China, or else throw them alive down a well!" When someone told him that it was against the law to use the public loudspeaker in that way, he walked up and down the village streets shouting his invective instead.

Naitang had repeatedly complained in person to the township government about this ongoing abuse, to no avail. Having heard about the Protection Law from a friend, Naitang sought me out for advice. I was away at school the first time he visited our home, but my father was able to explain what he knew of the law, and armed with this information Naitang went back to the government officials. This time they told him that the Protection Law was a national initiative, not something they intended to carry out at the township level. Naitang tried to make his case with the Canlian, which was supposed to represent disabled persons, and other relevant officials, but their response was to insist that he apologize to the village party secretary.

"Where is there a rule that says the victim should apologize to the perpetrator?" Naitang angrily asked the township mayor.

"The village party secretary is your superior," the mayor replied, "and that's why you should apologize."

With no other recourse available to him, Naitang decided to sing about the details of his case at markets, and he began memorizing parts of the Protection Law.

As my father, an old party member, listened to Naitang's experiences, he shook with rage, incensed at the cruelty and greed that had led the party so far from its old ideal of "serving the people," its abiding slogan and its purported mission since its inception.

Later, when Naitang visited Dongshigu again and I heard his story for myself, I, too, responded with anger, but I also felt an immediate sympathy with him as a fellow blind person. I questioned him closely for details, making sure I understood everything about his case and the particulars of the township's tax-collecting campaign. Naitang did not blame officials in Beijing for his troubles—he thought well of the central government, as many people did in those days. Instead, he faulted local officials, telling me he had resolved never to pay illegal taxes again, since, as he put it, this would be "aiding the enemy." Besides, everyone knew that the officials who were bullying him and others pocketed what they could of the people's tax payments for their own use. He also said that he didn't expect additional assistance from the government but simply wanted the abuse to stop.

I told Naitang that it was against the Protection Law as well as other laws and legal statutes for officials to collect this tax from him—indeed, levying any kind of additional material burden from the disabled was illegal. I suggested that we file a lawsuit against the township mayor himself and thus attempt to force the tax collectors to return Naitang's money. With proof of their illegal activities documented in the lawsuit, we could then demand that the village party secretary who had verbally abused Naitang apologize. Naitang was excited by this proposal, but he was concerned about his ability to pay the resulting legal fees. I assured him that I would help in whatever way I could but that he wouldn't be expected to give me any sort of payment.

At the time I had a cell phone that I used only for urgent matters because it was so expensive. But after hearing Naitang's story, I immediately called a Beijing lawyer named Wang Shiqiang, whom I'd met through Ms. Wilson. Wang was a warm and engaging person, and we had often enjoyed debating social issues. While he'd consistently expressed skepticism about the possibility of achieving social progress through small-scale legal cases, I had always argued that there's nothing in the world that can't be changed. If you believe otherwise, I held, either you're not working hard enough or you haven't yet found the right tool or direction. Even a narrowly focused case can have a wide impact down the road.

At one point Wang and I had applied for a grant from the British government to undertake a project on disability rights, and when I called Wang that day I suggested that Naitang's case be the focus of our project and that any legal fees could be drawn from the grant. Wang immediately agreed, saying that he would find a lawyer who would be willing to take on the case.

Liu Naitang was overjoyed to hear this news. "Coming to see you has made me so happy," he said. "Can I touch you?"

"Of course you can," I said. I got up and stood in front of him. Starting from the top of my head, his fingers fluttered over my entire body, taking in my height, my face, my stature. "Now I know how tall you are!" he said. I stood still while he looked at me in his way, and then we said good-bye.

Soon thereafter, Wang found a licensed attorney named Sun Ting who was willing to represent Naitang in court. In July 2001, around the time I graduated from Nanjing, we were finally able to file Liu Naitang's case, which we aimed directly at the township mayor. When the township officials received notice of our impending lawsuit about the tax campaign, they became very worried. "We made a mistake," they told Naitang, promising to return his money if he would drop the suit.

Naitang asked me what he should do. "The officials will admit they were in the wrong," I told him, "but only after you drop the suit. But if you drop the case now, do you really think they will return your money? And if they don't, what recourse will you have?" Naitang took my advice and refused to drop the suit, at which point the township officials began pressuring his relatives.

On the scheduled court date, August 10, no one representing the township or the mayor appeared. Nonetheless, Sun Ting went ahead and presented the facts of the case: a blind man was being illegally taxed and was suffering abuse and harassment at the orders of the mayor. A few days later, the defendant was offered another chance to appear in court, but when the mayor again failed to attend, the court made its decision: the defendant should cease his behavior with regard to the plaintiff Liu Naitang and should return the tax money illegally collected from him. And with that, we won the suit.

As an itinerant storyteller and fortune-teller, Naitang took the opportunity to hand out copies of his court judgment wherever he went, to whomever was interested. Our success with Naitang's case was an inspiration to many peasants and disabled people in the countryside, but unfortunately it didn't bring an end to illegal tax collection and unlawful treatment of the disabled. In fact, even after the court had announced its verdict, the township "little work team" returned to Naitang's village to "take care of debts." Fortunately, Naitang was not in, but the officials rammed down the door to his home, demanding the money from his family. Facing threats of bodily harm, his family had no choice but to borrow the 300 yuan demanded by the officials. Even after our initial legal victory, this kind of abuse continued, and it would later become the grounds for Liu Naitang's inclusion in our large class-action suit.

Soon after our first meeting in the summer of 2001, Weijing and I began spending a lot of time together. Weijing would come to Dongshigu, and after we finished dinner we would go down to the river, walking among the trees holding hands, no distance between us. Most people in the village had long gone to sleep, but we stayed out. The breeze rustled the leaves, and the river flowed quietly by; in the distance, we heard the night sounds from the village.

Weijing and I talked about many things during those long evenings by the river. Early on she told me that she was unaccustomed to thinking about lives beyond her own; she had never spent much time considering politics or other people's suffering. But the work I did and the way we talked—questioning the underlying problems of society and the issues facing China and the world—opened her eyes. The political ideas and feelings that arose out of our many conversations were altogether new to her.

Early on I noticed that Weijing was miraculously free of that common, inexplicable dread of the disabled, and before long there were even signs and stirrings of love. At first I pretended not to notice; my own feelings for her were growing more intense, but I couldn't bear the thought of being hurt. I knew the depth of prejudice she would face for loving me, a disabled person, and understood that it would put pressures on her that she might not be able to withstand. In my view of love, the tiniest insincerity, the faintest false note, is unacceptable; no compromise is possible. And commitment is everything: if we started down this road, we would have to persevere to the end.

For her part, Weijing didn't dare tell her parents about us. But in the fall of 2001 she called me from school one day and said, "My head is full of nothing but you, don't you know that?"

My heart swelled. I had never in my life heard such tender words before, and I had never expected to have this kind of relationship with another person, so deep was my sense of society's prejudice. What able-bodied person would love me, would marry me? I feared being wounded, but I also worried about how our relationship might affect Weijing's future. Still, her heartfelt words that afternoon changed everything, and after that I called her almost every day, eager to share my feelings with her. We often spoke for hours.

But love never follows a straight road, and one night Weijing called from home, sounding worried. Someone was trying to set her up with a potential partner; she tipped the telephone's receiver so I could hear two men talking on the other side of the room. I knew it was common in the countryside to use matchmakers to bring together people from similar backgrounds and families, but I hadn't imagined that Weijing's parents would choose to do this. I was in Beijing at the time, and I told her I would leave the city in a few days to see her. The remainder of my time there seemed endless.

As soon as I returned from Beijing I traveled to Linshu, Weijing's hometown. An old teacher of mine from Linyi was now working at the county's school for the deaf; I went to visit him and spent that night in the school's dorm. I was hardly able to contain my anticipation at seeing Weijing the following day.

The next morning I stood in the hallway, waiting for her. Suddenly I heard the sound of a bicycle pulling up. "She's here!" I thought, my heart quickening.

I heard Weijing exchange a few words with the man at the door and then run toward the stairwell. Next came the sound of her footsteps bounding up the stairs, a plastic bag rustling in her hand. I rushed to the top of the stairs and took her in my arms. She was a little shy, though, and quickly pushed me away. I took her hand, and we went into my room.

"What do you have in the bag?" I asked.

"Something for you," she replied.

She handed me the bag, and I pulled out a set of new long underwear. Never in my life had I put on this kind of clothing; most of my clothes were hand-me-downs from my brothers. For so many years I had been away at school and living on my own, only going home occasionally; rarely had I been the object of anyone's special concern. But Little Yuan, as I called her, had bought these clothes especially for me. My heart filled with an overwhelming sweetness. I pulled her to me and kissed her.

Later that day, we made ready to head to my home together, speaking of everything that had happened since we had last seen each other. We boarded a bus bound for Dongshigu and before long got off along National Route 205, which runs just outside the village. We walked toward the Meng River, over the bridge, and through the little riverside forest, hand in hand the entire way. My parents, who were out working our little plot of land, saw us coming from afar. I already knew they liked Weijing, and now they called out, "We can see you holding hands from here! We're so happy for you!"

From that day forward, I allowed myself to hope that Weijing and I could find a way to be together always.

There were numerous cases like Naitang's, and we spoke with many people who had experienced similar injustices. One of the most striking cases involved an able-bodied couple who had to care for their two severely disabled children as well as the husband's blind parents. The tax burden was destroying them. One day Weijing and I traveled to the destitute mountainous area where the couple lived to meet the wife and the four disabled members of their family. The husband had taken a job far away to support the family and pay the household tax. He could come home only a few times a year, so the day-to-day work of caring for four disabled people, as well as tending their crops and all the other chores in their remote dwelling, fell squarely on the shoulders of this poor woman.

Weijing marveled at how the woman supported and took care of these four disabled loved ones, day after day, with no chance of relief. "Where do you find the hope to go on?" Weijing asked her directly.

"Well, if you put it like that," the woman replied unexpectedly, "I'd have to say I don't have anything to hope for, actually. In truth, on many days I simply don't want to go on living. But if I took my own life, who would care for my children, neither of whom can even walk? I owe it to them to be here. I have a responsibility to raise them. If I am not willing to care for them, how can I expect someone else to want to? That's why I go on."

From that day on, Weijing felt a new dedication to the work we were doing, which eventually inspired her to quit her job. She later said that she figured other people could teach English, as she had been doing, but she wasn't sure others would be willing to fight for the rights of the disabled, as we were. She also wanted to work alongside me.

Toward the end of 2001, Weijing and I decided to combine a few of the cases we had investigated and build a class-action lawsuit, hoping to inform the widest possible audience about the brutal tax-collection practices. By July 2002, after months of gathering material, we were at last ready to file a suit that covered three cases: Liu Naitang's ongoing abuse post-trial; the crushing tax burden suffered by the family of six;

and the case of a man named Yin Xiangping, who had suffered brain damage as a result of an accident. The common thread was tax collection levied illegally against the disabled by the government and enforced by violence. From the start, we knew we would have to pursue this case on our own, as there were no funds for a licensed attorney.

At that time, as now, there were almost no lawyers in the countryside; there were only farmers who had taught themselves the law out of a powerful desire to fight for justice on their own behalf. These determined farmers became known as "barefoot lawyers," a modern version of a term used during the Cultural Revolution, when the government enabled some rural farmers to get basic medical training so they could treat people in their area. Because these peasants spent much of their time out in the fields, they often went shoeless and were thus nicknamed "barefoot doctors." They didn't receive a salary from the government, but rather earned "points" for their labor that they could later exchange for grain or cash, just like everyone else in the communes.

More recently, people had started using the term "barefoot lawyer" to refer to those who had gained some knowledge of the law and served themselves and others in a legal capacity. The crucial difference, however, is that the government has never supported barefoot lawyers; in fact, it actively persecutes them. Moreover, it is illegal for self-taught farmers to collect fees "in the name of a lawyer"; doing so can lead to the serious accusation of profiteering by practicing the law without a license. A barefoot lawyer's work is not much different from that practiced by a licensed attorney, however: we investigate and collect evidence on cases, write up findings, and prepare briefs and legal documents to present to the courts. Sometimes we even defend our clients in court (though I myself did not do this). In short, we do nearly everything a licensed lawyer would be expected to do, and for which an attorney would usually expect an appropriate fee.

Most of the clients served by barefoot lawyers can spare little or no money for fees, but I never felt comfortable asking for money in any case. People often tried to help me in whatever way they could—someone driving a tractor would pick me up on my way to the courthouse, for instance, or pay for a taxi so I could visit a person needing my help. Later I began applying for grants from organizations to help cover expenses related to my cases, but in the early days I simply did my best to help people in need of legal assistance.

Most practicing lawyers aren't willing to take on cases involving the disabled and the indigent, partly because they will never be sufficiently compensated for their efforts. And since these cases often involve instances of the government infringing on people's rights, pursuing them is risky; wary of angering the government and provoking a backlash, most lawyers choose to keep their distance. Their concerns are understandable: it is widely known that many lawyers who take on these kinds of civil rights cases suffer political reprisals, ranging from losing their work licenses to physical abuse and detention. Even now, I continue to follow the cases of many brave friends and associates who, as civil rights lawyers, have been jailed, beaten, and harassed. Simply because they insist on standing up for the rights of those who are not able to defend themselves, they suffer terribly at the hands of the government.

As we prepared to bring our class-action lawsuit to court, I contacted Li Zhizeng, another self-trained lawyer from the region, and asked him to work on the case with us. We gathered our evidence and drew up our documents and other materials with extreme care, making sure to present our case in strict accordance with legal procedures. I knew from the outset that media coverage would be crucial, so I invited two experienced journalists from Beijing, hoping to set a precedent and bring wide attention to the rights of the disabled.

On July 29, the day the case came to trial, the courthouse was packed—everyone seemed to be there but the defendants, who'd refused to come. We spotted a few administrators, party members whose curiosity had been piqued by the news of a disabled person suing a government representative. But another group of spectators provided the real surprise: the room was full of blind and disabled people from far and wide, most with no direct connection to the case we had filed.

It was a remarkable gathering and show of support: for a moment, the disabled community was made real. For roughly two thousand years, the blind in the Chinese countryside have handled their own affairs and claimed their rights in particular ways, organizing themselves into informal guilds. They set prices for activities such as story-telling and fortune-telling, stood up for those being treated unfairly, and punished those who undercut the group or behaved in ways that sullied the reputation of other disabled people. Messages were delivered by passing a sorghum stalk with a chicken feather stuck in it; the stalk carried different meanings depending on how the feather was inserted. Traditionally, these messages were relayed between villages by sighted people, though in recent years blind people have begun using cell phones.

Now, here in the courtroom, I took stock of public opinion among the disabled, talking to everyone I could. In 99 percent of situations, people told me, the laws meant to protect them were not enforced. Everyone agreed that lawsuits like ours might bring progress, but many were skeptical of getting a fair hearing. At each level of the government, the party held the levers of the power, controlling the outcome of these cases through the political and legislative affairs committees. As people in the courtroom were quick to say, "They are the ones who tell the courts what to do!" I couldn't help but agree: I knew that by bringing this case we were pushing the limits of the law and entering the realm of politics, but I saw no other choice.

Though the township mayor—the ever-absent defendant—should have forfeited the case, he had a useful advocate on his side: the judge. After the trial, we were notified that our carefully tabulated evidence was deemed insufficient, and our case was called "inappropriate." The court did admit that these taxes had been levied in error, but it didn't demand that the taxes be returned. We appealed the case to the intermediate-level city courts, hoping that a city court would be a little less beholden to the local county government and give us more of a chance to be heard. The resulting decision was indeed the victory we hoped for: no more illegal taxes and the mayor's actions must stop.

Despite the many obstacles we faced while bringing these cases to court, I felt invigorated by the possibility of transforming people's lives in tangible ways. In time, I realized that if I could help my clients achieve even a sliver of justice by pursuing their cases through the legal system and the courts, it would be tremendously satisfying.

As more and more people came to me for help, I found I gave little thought to which cases I took on. It was a completely natural process, guided simply by my ideas about right and wrong, my sense of justice, and my understanding of the law. If someone presented me with a situation that seemed worthy of investigation, my only criterion was whether the story I'd heard showed evidence of unlawful behavior that had resulted in the persecution or harassment of the person who had sought me out. When these instances of blatant injustice presented themselves to me, I couldn't help but react, to try to right the wrongs and stand up for those who couldn't do so for themselves.

Although acutely aware of the struggles of the disabled, I was prepared to help anyone in need whose rights had been violated. I generally took things as they came, fighting the battles that were right in front of me. And since both a legal degree and, hence, a law license exam were denied me as a blind person, I had no degree or law license to take away and, thus, had less to fear—or so I thought.

As time went on, I often found it necessary to travel to Beijing for my work. Sometimes I would make the trip on my own, sometimes Elder Brother or my nephew Chen Hua would accompany me; later, Weijing occasionally came with me. Other activists encouraged me to move to Beijing to be a part of the community there, but I always believed that I was needed in the countryside, that I could provide assistance there that no one else seemed to be able to offer. Besides, my extended family supported me in Dongshigu; if I had become a city dweller, earning money would have been the only way to survive, and I would have been forced to take on cases that didn't interest me. As it was, I remained with my parents in our village, and we made do as we always had—living modestly, eating the food we grew ourselves, and incurring very few expenses.

The work I undertook in those years was based on ideas I maintain to this day. We gave ordinary people a nonviolent outlet for pursuing and resolving their grievances; we tried to make the rule of law a reality in a country that lacks it, under a party that disingenuously claims to embrace it. I felt strongly that people needed to understand their rights under the law, and I wanted to instruct my fellow farmers and peasants and the disabled about what should be available to them, and to encourage them to advocate for themselves and for their rights. I wanted them to know that the only way to make a lasting impact is to band together and speak with one voice.

Through a long series of cases, we began to enhance people's understanding of the law and encourage an awakening of their legal consciousness. One case can have a real impact on the circumstance of a family, and that one family can, in turn, have an influence on more families. If a society is to change, people must unite and demand their rights; justice will never be achieved if people wait for change to come from above.

One day in spring 2002, upon returning to Dongshigu after a trip to Beijing, I stopped at the village entrance, where people often gather informally to talk about recent events or play a game of checkers. Spending time around villagers engaged in these games always provided me with a good opportunity to catch up on the local news and hear candid opinions about politics and other current topics.

I had been away for a while, but I quickly understood which issue was provoking the most heated conversations. Apparently, the village leaders—both the party representatives and so-called elected officials, including the mayor—had entered into a secret deal to sell the sand from a beach along the Meng River. They planned to report the sale on the books at only 4,000 yuan, but they would collect another 40,000 or 50,000 yuan for their own use from the contract. As the discussion became ever more animated, I followed several of the villagers as they wandered down to the bridge to survey the scene—the company had already brought in bulldozers, and men were setting up tents under which to carry out their work.

Standing there on the bridge, I thought about how many thousands of years had been required to make this sand, and how the villagers had always used it with care, taking only a small portion every year to spread over the dirt in their yards or walkways. I had loved swimming here as a young boy; I vividly remembered the feeling of the soft sand under my feet. When the bridge had been built, in 1996, connecting us at last with the outside world, the sand served as part of the substrate to hold the bridge's pilings in place. Now I felt only rage; the thought that greed and avarice were about to remove this necessary resource and destroy the beauty of our precious river disgusted me.

Clearly the other villagers felt the same way, and suddenly they all turned to me and asked, "Old Five! What do you think we should do?"

I immediately knew exactly how to answer. "For the long-term health of the village and the surrounding environment," I said, "we shouldn't sell the sand, and we must prevent them from digging at all costs, even if we have to go down to the riverside to stop them ourselves. If dialogue and reason are not successful, we will resort to legal measures."

Then I outlined a strategy. "To begin," I explained, "we should select new village representatives to notify the village leadership that we don't agree to their plan and demand that they nullify the contract. We should also demand that the leadership address several other festering issues, such as the fact that one of our paths down from the hills was never fixed after a storm. Finally, they should promise that from this point forward the village's finances will be transparent. If they don't agree to these demands or don't carry out these changes, we should inform them that we will initiate a recall election."

The villagers liked what I said, and we started talking about how to make our plans a reality. Then, even as we stood there, the bulldozers' engines started up. With no thought of the consequences, we ran across the bridge and scrambled down to the riverside, surrounding the tents and the machines. With no way to maneuver their equipment, the bulldozer operators cut their engines. For that day, at least, we had made an impact.

Though we made no concerted effort to organize ourselves, over the course of the next few days villagers took turns checking up on the site. As soon as there was any sign of work taking place, everyone would be called out. The next morning, in fact, someone ran to my house to fetch me. By the time I reached the riverbank, I found the bulldozer frozen in mid-motion, its engine stopped. I ran my hand over the machine's arched neck and bucket, its teeth perched gently on the ground.

This standoff continued over the next few days. We knew that the village government and the company hired to remove the sand were having heated conversations—company officials were angry that they couldn't begin their dig, not least because the work stoppage was costing them money. Meanwhile, the villagers kept insisting that local officials cancel the contract and get their deposit back—after all, how could the contract be valid if the people had not consented to it? At last the company had no choice but to leave, though we never did learn whether the deposit was returned.

Even as this battle raged, we were busy preparing our other demands and the recall materials. The process mandated that we first gather signatures from at least one-fifth of the villagers of voting age, then notify the Shuanghou township government of the complaint against the village committee and our intent to initiate a recall election. By doing this, we would begin the recall process, and the township government would be required to organize a new election and reply to our filing within a certain period of time. Meanwhile, we would make our recall effort fully public by posting a document on the village announcement board that explained both our position and our intended action.

Throughout this process, we carefully complied with the law, following all the relevant rules closely in order to avoid unnecessary obstacles and delays. But in this we were unsuccessful: though we had done everything by the book and should have been able to proceed with our recall election, the township stonewalled us by simply refusing to respond to our demands. In the end, there was no practical way to carry out a new election. For months, we made no progress at all.

One day in the fall of 2002, I was working in our yard when I heard an announcement come over the village sound system. (Several loudspeakers were scattered throughout the village, attached to tall poles or trees.) The township government declared for all to hear that the village party secretary—the most powerful person in the village, appointed by the party itself, with no term limit—was resigning. Since the party secretary was not elected and therefore could not be recalled, his resignation was not directly related to our recall effort, but the message was clear. For the party, when officials like our village party secretary face extreme criticism from their constituents, they are no longer useful, so getting rid of them is the most expedient thing to do. The fact that our party secretary was resigning, instead of being removed by the party, was immaterial: the higher-ups were merely allowing him to save face, since everyone knows that a failure to resign would eventually mean dismissal from the party, a serious blow to any official's future prospects.

At least for the time being, the sand and the river had been saved. Just as important, the people of Dongshigu had asserted themselves as never before—and they had proven that they could work together to change their lives for the better.

What happened in Dongshigu was not an isolated incident: elsewhere in China's countryside, instances of legal revolt were increasing in frequency. In early 2002, the international edition of *Newsweek* had published a cover story carrying the headline "Barefoot Lawyers," and my work on Liu Naitang's case and on pollution in the Meng River had been highlighted. Too sensitive for most Chinese media to mention, our efforts had now been given global recognition and a recognizable name.

I was in a motel in Beijing with Elder Brother when he saw the photograph of me on the cover of *Newsweek*. He described it to me excitedly: with our village's *chunlian*—the decorative couplet we hang on our door frame at New Year's—in the background marking the traditional Chinese scene, I was pictured in a black jacket, wearing my dark sunglasses. My friendship with Zhang Lijia—the journalist who'd come to Dongshigu with Ms. Wilson—had made the story happen. This was a turning point for me. International recognition of my efforts made me realize that I might be starting to have a significant impact. I continued traveling to Beijing whenever it was necessary for my work, and to deepen my involvement in the struggle for human rights. I met everyone I could, with each friend soon introducing me to several others. I had met Zhang Lijia thanks to Ms. Wilson, and now Ms. Wilson also introduced me to Nick Young, whose *China Development Brief* was a crucial source of information about new developments in Chinese civil society and the international aid community. Through Zhang Lijia I'd met the photographer Li Wei, who'd taken my photo for *Newsweek*. Through Li Wei I met a cultural officer at the U.S. embassy in Beijing who later invited me to participate in the International Visitor

Leadership Program run by the U.S. State Department, which promotes mutual understanding through professional exchange. America, on the other side of the world, began to seem just a little bit closer.

When possible, I attended meetings and conferences, broadening my network of friends and my political consciousness. Promising projects of all sorts were under discussion and, in some cases, under way. One conference brought disability activists from all over the world to Beijing to share strategies and experiences, giving me the feeling that someday we might get beyond the Canlian's official monopoly on those issues. I also became aware of a surge of legal-aid activity, with major centers at the Peking and Wuhan University law schools, both of which I had a chance to visit. Some of the conferences I attended taught me about issues that were entirely new to me, such as feminism and environmentalism, neither of which I could have learned about in school or in the village. I became experienced at giving interviews to the press, getting more attention for my work from both international media organizations, like the BBC, and progressive domestic publications, such as *Caijing* (Finance and Economy), a magazine that was then pushing the boundaries of what you could print inside China.

Poor though I was, I gradually began getting a better sense for the big, wide world that lay far beyond my experience as a blind man from rural China. One evening, Li Wei picked me up at the hotel where I was staying in Beijing. He took Weijing and me out for pizza and a trip to McDonald's, giving me an introduction to foreign food. I had my first experience of going to a real party, one that was hosted by Lijia at her house in Beijing. The food, like the crowd, was about half Western and half Chinese. At a similar gathering of Chinese people, one would wait to eat and observe specific rules of etiquette; here, everything was casual and easy. Diplomats and journalists and political types floated in and out of conversations, saying whatever was on their minds, talking about their work and hearing about the work of others, all the while with a drink or a small snack in hand. And I liked the way Lijia's friends treated me: they didn't look down on me as a disabled person; nor were they overly respectful or deferential. I felt surprisingly at ease.

My overriding goal in those days, as I told everyone I met, was to start a nonprofit organization that would support the rights of disabled people across China. Some people cautioned me about how difficult this would be. Li Wei, for instance, told me that it would probably take about ten years for my organization to begin to have an impact. These sorts of comments didn't discourage me, though, and much of what I did on my visits to Beijing was directed toward finding a way to establish and fund such an organization. Nonprofits were relatively new in China, and other people shared my optimistic belief that civil society would bring about real political change, that progress was inevitable.

I worked hard to register my hoped-for organization, but the resistance we met foreshadowed the problems I would encounter later. The number one priority of the party is to prevent the development of any independent power base and to thwart any individual or organization not directly beholden to it and not under its direct control. Before you can even register any kind of organization—a sometimes lengthy and expensive process, necessary for even the tiniest group—you have to find a *guakao danwei*, a "work unit to be attached to." That such a work unit is an established organization means that it is ultimately an official organ of the state or the party or is attached to such an organ—for example, the way universities are. Nor is this affiliation merely a loose or nominal one: you can't operate without it, so in the end you are still a subsidiary, a disposable part of a larger whole that is controlled by the party. Simply put, in China you cannot be truly independent and still be legal.

As it turned out, no *guakao danwei* would touch me—none would take on the responsibility. And since no work unit would agree to support me, I couldn't register my organization. (At the time, I suspected that the Canlian, which in theory might have served as a logical partner, must have sensed a rival.) With no official support, funding became a difficult matter, since potential sources of funding—large international foundations, Western embassies, human rights groups overseas—were reluctant to assist a lone individual without official status. This problem remains unresolved: many foreign foundations, NGOs, and nonprofits hope to aid the effort to ameliorate social injustices, but since they are only able to invest their capital in programs or organizations that have a close connection to the Chinese government, they can't help change Chinese society without being transformed by the country's power inequities. Even today, the international-aid community provides almost no support for ordinary people involved in the real grassroots struggles of the Chinese people, so instead the money flows inexorably to bureaucrats, creatures of the state, and those with the right connections.

I spent many restless nights in Beijing around this time; sometimes I simply had to get out of the cramped little place where I was staying. Late in the evening I would go for long walks, letting my mind wander as I felt my remembered way among the masses of people and cars, meanwhile reckoning with fundamental questions and digging into the deepest parts of myself. Slowly I was coming to grips with an important truth: however much an organization or an official platform might help, I would have to act as an individual. Project by project, what mattered now was simply doing something.

Besides, I didn't feel entirely alone, mainly because I knew that others were as serious as I was about demanding that the government make a genuine commitment to the rule of law and social justice. Looking back, it's clear that we barefoot lawyers were part of the larger Weiquan movement then taking shape across China. *Weiquan* means "defending rights," and that was always the foundation: we were defending the civil rights of ordinary people under the law. We took the party's legal reforms of the 1980s at face value, seeking to address through the courts such issues as human rights, environmental problems, and the basic freedoms of speech and religion and the press. Political reform had long stalled, economic changes seemed unstoppable, and the government's brutal response to Tiananmen Square had made clear the limits and dangers of popular protest. The Weiquan movement was an attempt to find another way of resisting China's repressive regime. We had no leaders or central organization—the movement was simply a disparate collection of dedicated activists, lawyers, scholars, and others who were committed to using legal means, both domestic and international, as a tool to force the Communist Party to respect the law, both the statutes the party itself had written and those it had agreed to in international forums.

But as we challenged the party to make good on its promises, its true nature began to emerge from behind its rhetoric. By pursuing justice and demanding that the party respect the law, we represented a threat, and party officials saw us as their enemies. Soon enough, I would discover that in order to protect their power they were prepared to do anything to crush us.

CHAPTER SIX

New Roots

After reveling in the early euphoria of our love for each other, Weijing and I had eventually come to realize that we were stuck. Because of my blindness, her family remained strongly opposed to any prospect of our getting married. In a sense it wasn't personal—they hadn't even met me yet—but simply their belief that my disability was a stigma that could never be erased, no matter how independent I might be or what work I might undertake. Particularly obstinate was Weijing's mother, who was just then recovering from a cerebral hemorrhage. "If we went ahead with the marriage now and something were to happen to her," Weijing said to me, "would I ever be able to forgive myself?"

Her parents became stricter and more repressive by the day. One day I asked her whether she had truly considered the possibility that her family would never accept our being together.

"I thought I had, but I guess I haven't, not really deeply," she admitted.

"You'd better go back and think on it some more," I said. "If you believe you can overcome this, we'll move forward." I knew I would be devastated if Weijing ended our relationship, but I didn't want to continue it if we had no chance at a future together. I also knew I would not be able to accept a marriage arranged by my parents through a matchmaker. Unless born to wealth, the majority of disabled people in China marry other disabled people, if they marry at all.

Weijing and I still talked all the time, and that fall she occasionally came to see me in Dongshigu, but the final months of 2001 passed slowly. Sometimes the hours we spent together were enchanted; sometimes we were both too sad to talk. She had come to visit during the Lantern Festival in early 2002, as the staggered sounds of fireworks rippled across the village. Weijing didn't want to see them—she was too upset about what she had been going through—but I insisted that we go up on the roof for a better view, hoping the fireworks would cheer her. Without saying a word she followed me up to the roof. I knew that hothouse flowers were exploding above us, lighting up the heavens with their soaring color, but I stood there in sadness under that invisible sky. Weijing had become another way of seeing for me. Now not only was the radiant world closed to me, but the woman I loved—who might have described it all, who might have brought it to life—had fallen silent next to me.

Despite all the difficulties, Weijing refused to end our relationship. One day that spring, her father, who knew that we remained serious about each other, decided to come to my parents' house to assess the situation for himself. Accompanied by one of Weijing's sisters, he visited us in Dongshigu. I had hoped that our conversation would change his mind; instead, he later told Weijing that he was more opposed than ever to the marriage. Now he had seen with his own eyes just how disadvantageous the match was: not only was I blind, but I lived in a desperately poor, remote village, in a run-down house far away from her family, who, like most families in the countryside, owned no car.

Soon after her father's visit, the phone call I'd been dreading came. "We have to break up," Weijing said, the tears still plain in her voice. Her entire family objected; meanwhile, her friends, classmates, and colleagues were bombarding her with hurtful arguments and rationales, all of them urging her to cut off the relationship. Be realistic, they said. How can a disabled man make money? Of all the men in the world, you have to choose a blind one? What will people think of your child if his father is disabled? You have a good job, a good family; you could find a good match in any field or job. He is so poor—how are you going to live? Her friends thought she had gone mad. It didn't help that Weijing was one of three sisters—having no male children made her mother and father deeply anxious about their old age, given that women usually marry "away" and thus won't be there to take care of their elderly parents.

As time went on, her family even persuaded the school where she worked to limit her contact with me. When I found out about this, I was livid and wounded; finally, I had a friend drive me to the school, where I stole Weijing away for a painful conversation. I urged her to try harder to be strong in the face of the pressure. Whatever we were up against, I told her, we could overcome it together. At home over a long weekend in early April, she was under virtual house arrest—the phone removed from her room, her parents monitoring the line. "You have to leave there," I told her when she was back at school. "You have to decide for yourself." I knew the pressure on her was intense. She was in love with me and didn't want to leave me. At the same time, she loved her family and didn't want to hurt them, especially since her mother's health was so fragile. She also didn't want to leave her students, to whom she was deeply attached.

In the meantime, her family was trying yet another tack. They had found her a suitable match: a handsome soldier from a good family. One afternoon he took her on a motorcycle ride up into the hills, after which she had three days to give a response. Much to her parents' dismay, she said no. The only reason she had even agreed to meet with the soldier was that she thought it would help her family understand that no matter what potential match they proposed, she would reject each in kind.

The following months were excruciating for our relationship, but I continued to focus on my disability work and the effort to establish my NGO. I had been preparing an application for a grant from a Canadian foundation, and Weijing had been helping me assemble a lot of the necessary materials. With the deadline for the application approaching, I persuaded her to come away to Beijing with me, both to escape the unbearable pressures at home and to finish our work. We set out on April 21 and rented a room in the apartment of a working a family, sharing their kitchen and bathroom. Not long after we arrived, Weijing decided to leave her job, despite her fondness for her students. Together, we wrote a letter to her father, full of plainspoken feeling, and Weijing also called her mother to tell her everything. Her mother cried and cried.

Her family's response to the choices she'd made left her in agony, and Weijing decided to return to Shandong after just a few days. I accompanied her, but after only a short time in Dongshigu, I went back to Beijing with my nephew Chen Hua. When not pursuing my work in the city I called Weijing by phone, and she at last agreed to join me again in Beijing. Our circumstances were difficult: after paying our rent, we had nothing left over for food, let alone anything else. We would buy watermelons in the market because we knew we could eat the rind as well as the fruit—that's how poor we were. After two months, we were completely out of money and had to return to Donshigu for the summer.

The Mid-Autumn Festival—which takes place during the eighth month of the lunar calendar—is devoted to family. My family proposed traveling to Linshu to meet Weijing's family, as is a custom for families of couples in courtship, but Weijing decided instead to head home on her own. By this point I was preparing myself mentally for the end of our relationship—I was no longer confident that Weijing could withstand her family's pressure. But I still cared deeply for her, so one day, together with my father and my elder brother, I traveled to Weijing's village bearing a live rooster and meat and mooncakes.

Weijing and her mother met us by their front gate. By now her mother had recovered her health, but it was the first time I'd met her, and my nerves stood on end.

"This is my mother," said Weijing.

"Ma, I'm Guangcheng," I said simply.

Then we all went inside and ate together—we had stir-fried chicken with garlic sprouts. Her father was civil and inviting, but the visit resolved nothing. No matter how hard Weijing and I tried, her family remained coldly unconvinced that we belonged together. Our relationship had come to a full stop.

Fall turned to winter, and then one day in late 2002 Weijing suddenly appeared at our home without calling beforehand. I knew how hard this situation was for her, but I was resigned to whatever might come. She began by telling me how her mother had always doted on her; for her,

Weijing's continuing involvement with me was particularly painful. Her mother responded by taking out her anger directly on Weijing: cursing her, arguing with her, trying to extract from her a promise that she would never contact me again. Weijing felt extremely guilty that she kept turning her back on the love her family had shown her, and as a consequence she swung violently back and forth between the opposite pulls of romantic love and familial love. Her emotions were so intense that at one point she decided to put an end to her pain and the torment of those she loved by taking her own life. Fortunately, her father was able to stop her before it was too late.

But by then Weijing had finally had enough. "I was determined to come find you and figure out a way," she told me that winter day. "Whatever we do, we will do it together. You could call it a gamble, but it's a gamble I'm ready to take."

My heart skipped a beat. I knew I couldn't guarantee the outcome of this gamble, but I was hopeful about our future. I held her, and kissed her, and then, for the first time, we began talking about how to spend the rest of our lives together.

By this point we did have one consolation: we had finally gained her father's tacit support, and he was even willing to help us get married. To make the marriage official, we both had to provide our household registration documents and a form of proof from our respective local governments. We asked Weijing's father to secretly pass along her documents and arrange for the needed registration in her family's village.

Once all the documents were in order, Weijing returned to her village to collect them. Her mother, who had no idea Weijing was coming to Linshu, started berating her as soon as she saw her. "You don't want your mother?" she wailed over and over, chasing Weijing almost the entire two miles to the bus station. "How can you be so cruel? I raised you, and yet you won't give me the least bit of consideration?"

Weijing was distraught, but she felt she had to make her mother understand that she had made a choice. Weijing explained that if she left me, she would be heartbroken, and she felt sure her mother didn't wish that for her. "I told you," she said to her mother, "but you wouldn't support us." Weijing left her mother on the roadside with bitter tears in her eyes.

But the abuse didn't stop. Finally, we realized that we had to go away again to get beyond the reach of her mother, so we went to stay with my brother in Yinan. That first night in Fourth Brother's house, Weijing was very upset—she cried for hours and didn't sleep a bit. She blamed herself, almost crazy with guilt at being such an unfilial daughter. Lying beside her, I wanted so much to comfort her, to ease her pain and sorrow, but the most I could do was to wipe away her tears.

Then, just after the year turned and with my brother's help, we went to the Civil Affairs Bureau in Yinan County to complete the paperwork. On January 3, 2003, we came out with a marriage certificate.

"And so at last I'm a married person," said Weijing, her voice breaking with emotion.

"It's true," I said. This should have been the happiest moment of our lives, but I could tell Weijing was weighed down with a heavy heart.

We took photos and then gave sweets to the bureau's staff. Our year-long struggle was finally over.

My friend Liu Naitang, being well versed in such matters, chose the eighth day of the first lunar month—February 8, 2003—for our traditional village wedding. A wedding in the Chinese countryside is marriage ritual, family reunion, village banquet, and moving-in ceremony all rolled into one. Our "new house," built some years earlier by Second Brother and standing empty ever since, was in the southern part of the village, not far from my parents. We weren't destined to live there long as newlyweds, and in a hideous twist of fate it was later reclaimed by the authorities and turned into our own private prison. But that was years in the future; now, this was where our wedding would take place.

Before the wedding day, Weijing and I tidied and cleaned our new home. We had no money for furniture, but my brothers—none of whom had much cash to spare—saved us by raising 6,000 yuan between them, at my father's behest. With their help, Weijing and I were able to purchase the bare necessities for married life. Though custom dictates that a newly wed couple must have their own new marriage bed, much to my shame we couldn't afford a new bed and had to make do with the one my father had used long ago at the Communist Party school. To prepare it, we bought a simple mattress of packed straw, as well as new quilts, sheets, and pillows. We also bought a sofa set and a tea table, plus a washing machine and a television.

A few days before the wedding, cooks arrived at my parents' home to build a mud-brick stove in their yard. They also started chopping up the ingredients they would need, storing everything perishable in a room where food would stay cold. My father and brothers, all skilled hands in the kitchen, pitched in. Our relatives began arriving in droves, and though we were overjoyed to see them, their red envelopes would not cover our costs, as those gifts of cash are generally meant to do. This would be a threadbare wedding, partly because we would get no help from Weijing's family, who didn't even know we were getting married. There would be no customary third day of celebrations hosted by the bride's family, so the traditional three-day wedding would now take place in two. By this point, Weijing and I were anguished but resigned. Her family had done so much to thwart us, and we knew they simply wouldn't agree to join in the celebration of our marriage.

Our "wedding car" was a Santana 2000, almost every inch of it covered in flowers. We found it deeply upsetting that we couldn't leave from the house of Weijing's parents, as was the custom; instead, we set off from Fourth Brother's house. Weijing wrapped small-change bills in lucky red paper and, following tradition, tossed them out the window every time we crossed a bridge. We entered Dongshigu in slow motion, greeted by triumphal explosions, the whole road into the village lined with bursting fireworks. Completing our little caravan, two cars followed behind us, carrying a colleague of Fourth Brother's and Second Sister-in-Law (with her relatives), who stood in for Weijing's absent family. No fewer than six cars were parked in the village for the celebrations.

One of those attending the wedding was Wang Shiqiang, the lawyer from Beijing whom Ms. Wilson had introduced me to; he brought along his wife and a friend of his from China Central Television, the state-owned network. Their first stop had been the Linyi branch of the Canlian, where officials had at first gravely tried to warn them away from the wedding by telling them that I was being watched by the local branch of the Ministry of State Security, the same political police organization that had interrogated me in Nanjing. When a phone call to the ministry seemed to quash this rumor, Canlian officials changed their minds and in fact joined Wang and came to the wedding; they even presented us with a bedspread. Meanwhile, Wang's CCTV friend had notified Linyi Television and brought along a team of reporters and cameramen. They felt that the village wedding of a blind man and a sighted woman was worth reporting, and I heard that many were deeply moved when footage of the ceremony aired the next day. The Canlian officials would half-drag Wang away before the wedding lunch even started, but not until he had a chance to present us with a very generous gift of 2,000 yuan, which would help us significantly in the months to come.

Once we arrived at our new house, we stepped out of the wedding car, the sun on our faces. I wore a flower on my chest; standing tall, I felt newly made. Weijing and I exchanged two silk flowers and stood in the courtyard, about to cross the threshold and walk into our bridal chamber—with this, we would be married. Despite a shadow of sadness caused by all the obstacles we had faced, my heart was brimming with joy. And though Weijing later told me how sad she felt that her family wasn't there to accompany her, she also said that this was the happiest day of her life.

The courtyard bustled with dozens of family members and friends. I will always remember how proud my father seemed just then: he'd never thought he would live to see this day, and yet there he was, a happy witness to our nuptials. We answered questions from the journalists from Linyi TV, and I even spoke openly about my human rights work. A neighbor's son was getting married that same day, so the entire village was alive with joy and chaos, everyone joining in as the music started and the feasting began back at my parents' house.

As the banquet wound down, we retired to our new home to enjoy ourselves, a large crowd of villagers and friends squeezing in along with us. We handed out the customary candy and cigarettes; on our walls hung red paper cutouts of the "double happiness" character *shuangxi*, symbolizing happiness in marriage. A few people sang karaoke with a borrowed stereo system and microphone, and we served our friends water in little disposable cups. That night, our friends and several of the younger family members stayed up playing wedding games. My nephews tied an apple to a string, and as it swung in the air Weijing and I each had to take a bite without using our hands, everyone laughing as it was suddenly pulled up out of our reach or we happened to kiss inadvertently, which of course was what they all wanted. In the countryside we don't let other people see us kissing, so at a wedding the crowd loves watching the bride and groom squirm with embarrassment.

The next day we rose early for the moving of the marriage bed into what would become its normal position for us as newlyweds. As is the custom, my niece performed the ritual of "worshipping shoes" on our behalf, going around to the homes of our relatives and neighbors and presenting them with newly bought shoes and packets of sweets. The shoes have a double significance: the word *xie*, meaning "shoe," is homophonous with the word for "thank you," and the shoes also acknowledge the hard work everyone has put in to help prepare for the wedding, perhaps even wearing out their shoes in the process. In turn, our neighbors and relatives expressed their thanks by placing little red-wrapped bundles of money on my niece's tray.

After lunch we prepared a few offerings and went "visiting the happiness grave," as we call it, paying our respects to my family's ancestors, the tops of whose graves we covered in red paper to express the joy of the departed for their descendants. We laid out cakes and vegetables and tea at the grave of my paternal grandfather, poured alcohol on it, burned a little paper money, performed the kowtow, and left. In that heightened state, reflecting on past visits to the happiness grave when my brothers were married, I had the palpable sense that there might exist another, more mysterious world, somewhere between heaven and earth.

The months following our wedding were bittersweet. First we endured a painful epilogue to our exultant celebration: Weijing called her parents, who had learned of our wedding while watching Linyi TV, and her conversation with them was pure agony. We were also preparing for a trip that still seemed an impossible dream: having learned about my work from the *Newsweek* article, the U.S. State Department had invited me to participate in a month-long international visiting scholars program in the United States. Weijing and I would be leaving in July, so now we began obtaining passports, filling out forms, and discussing our plans with the U.S. embassy in Beijing.

We were also preparing for an even more momentous event: the birth of our first child. Most married women in China are subject to periodic regular physical exams by family planning doctors to check for pregnancy, but doctors don't check unmarried women and no one could tell that Weijing was pregnant before our marriage, so we were ignored by the authorities. We were delirious at the thought of becoming parents and raising a child together; all the trouble that had preceded our marriage now seemed worth it.

On May 3, around eleven at night, Weijing felt some pains in her abdomen, which we at first ascribed to the long walk we had taken earlier in the day. We had prepared for this—she'd been reading out loud to me from a book about pregnancy and birth—but I was overwhelmed when her labor set in, and anxious about how little I was able to help. We quickly dressed and got ready to go to the hospital. She could only squat as the blows of pain hit her, while I stood there holding her in position with my arms. Stopping and starting, we made our way over to my parents' house and dialed the emergency first-aid number, 120; within an hour an ambulance from the nearest maternal and child health hospital arrived.

At the hospital, a doctor reviewed an ultrasound and saw that the baby was in a breech position. She immediately began pressuring Weijing to have a cesarean section, threatening serious consequences if we didn't agree. The hospital wouldn't be responsible if we went ahead with a vaginal birth and anything bad happened, the doctor told us. We were furious: I knew the doctor was in the wrong, and I thought about switching hospitals, but in truth they're all more or less the same, pushing expensive procedures to make extra money, wanting to disavow responsibility with the flick of a signature. In the end, we had no choice but to go ahead with the cesarean.

While Weijing was taken into the operating room, I stood outside talking with Elder Brother, as the hospital didn't allow any family members to be present during the operation. I did my best to talk to my brother and act naturally, but my ears were pricked for the slightest sound from the other room. A little less than an hour later, we heard the cries of a healthy, strong baby ringing out. My brother turned to me. "Is that one yours?" he asked, surprised at the volume of sound. "It sounds like a six-month-old, not like a newborn," I replied.

But the cries were indeed coming from our son. A nurse came out to tell us that mother and child were fine, and I immediately called my father to give him the news. He was thrilled. A few minutes later, the nurse brought out our little son and asked us to care for him, as Weijing needed to get some rest. I was overcome with joy and couldn't hold myself back from placing careful hands on his marvelous little frame, the first time I had ever touched such tiny feet or such exquisitely thin legs—they were like the legs of the frogs I'd caught in the river as a child.

Completely bedridden for five days, Weijing recovered slowly; she was miserable in her joy. Our son, whom we had named Kerui, seemed to cry all the time, and since Weijing couldn't get out of bed to pick up the baby, sometimes I would try to feed him a bottle. I was no good at mixing formula; inevitably I spilled the contents on myself or on Kerui. I struggled to get him to take the bottle, to put the nipple in his mouth, remembering as I did so the difficulty of getting my little goat kids to drink their mother's milk. I wanted so much to care for our son and hold him, but as a first-time parent I found it far from easy, especially since I wasn't able to see.

We went home after seven days. Following the custom, my mother buried the placenta under our house, so that the newborn child would thrive in life and stay deeply rooted. Twelve days after his birth, Kerui had his little head ceremonially shaved. We made him a symbolic bow and arrow from the *latiao* bush and sorghum stalks, tying on a head of garlic and a red cloth to ward off evil and bring good luck. All this we hung on top of the door to our house, so that our little son should be both a fighter and a scholar in future years.

Weijing then "sat the month" of her confinement, not taking a single bath, avoiding the traditional milk-inhibiting foods, and consuming instead the special delicacies my mother prepared: millet gruel with brown sugar, poached eggs, snakehead fish. Little Kerui mostly stayed inside for his first hundred days, courted and doted on by many admiring visitors. Much to our joy, those visitors included Weijing's parents. Thrilled with their grandson, they finally seemed ready to put their past hostilities aside.

The arrival of summer brought yet more change. To be closer to my own parents, we decided to move back in with them, leaving the "new house" vacant again. Here in my childhood home, Weijing and I would raise our family and, ultimately, choose our fate.

In mid-July we left for America, tearing ourselves away from our eleven-week-old Kerui, miserable and fearful about having to wean him at such an early age. We would leave him with my parents, and somehow he would have to get used to drinking formula all the time.

We packed only one small suitcase for the two of us. We hired a taxi for the drive to Linyi, where we would catch a train for Beijing; from there we would take a plane to the United States. Before we left home, I stood stock-still beside my sleeping son, my lips saying, "I have to go now" but my feet refusing to move. A few minutes later, when I had finally almost made it to the car waiting at the village entrance, I suddenly felt an overwhelming regret and turned on my heel, running back through the village to our house until I stood again by my parents' bed, where once more I could say good-bye. "Ruirui," I said, using his nickname, "your father's going on a journey." I bent down over the tiny child swaddled in thin quilts, stroking his entire body and kissing his small mouth, taking his clammy and tender little hands in mine, until my heart could almost not bear it. I must have lingered too long or brushed him with my mustache, for he began to stir then, making the gentlest, faintest sound. But I coaxed him back to sleep, closed the door, and ran to the car.

The trip to America gave me the chance to fly in an airplane for the first time in my life. I was intensely curious about the plane, touching everything around my seat, including the fold-out tray and the buttons on the armrest. As we taxied down the runway for takeoff, Weijing and I held hands, our grip getting tighter as we climbed into the air. She nervously described to me how everything on the ground below us kept getting smaller and smaller. Slowly I started to relax, and soon I found myself wondering what America would be like. What would I learn and feel while I was there? A series of questions and conjectures started forming in my mind as the plane's flying smoothed out, the heavy sound of the motor now almost soothing, the captain beginning to speak to us about the flight.

Many hours later, we at last arrived in Washington, D.C. Despite having studied English, Weijing felt out of practice and strained to understand what people were saying to her. Everything felt completely new. Fortunately, Annie Wang, a translator arranged by the State Department, was there to greet us and get us settled into the Hilton. As I began exploring our room, I noticed all the little differences: an iron in the closet (something I'd never seen at the cheap Beijing hotels where I'd stayed before), the strange Fahrenheit system for temperature, milk that was far too cold to drink, windows that would barely open (liability issues, I was told), and the remarkable quiet that could hang over a city as large as Washington. Weijing told me that the city's buildings were all low, not high and crowded together as in Beijing.

When the State Department had first raised the idea of inviting us to come to the United States, I'd said we wanted to focus on understanding disability law and disability rights in America, especially the role of civil society in upholding those rights. How did disabled people actually live in the United States, particularly in rural areas? What lessons could I learn that would be useful when setting up an organization for the disabled in China?

The State Department arranged our itinerary to highlight some answers to these questions, and in less than a month we visited seven different places—Washington, New York, Vermont, Cincinnati, Austin, Washington State, and San Francisco—and met with countless groups, organizations, and individuals working for social change. We came away from it all with a vastly enlarged sense of possibility—and at every turn, the differences between China and the United States were staggering.

While in Vermont, I realized that the countryside here was completely different from the countryside in China. Back home, the rural life is synonymous with poverty and backwardness; here, the landscape was more beautiful than the cities, and everything you might need—any supplies, any material goods—was completely available.

As the trip progressed, we met with people at a variety of organizations—including schools—that were dedicated to the needs of the blind and disabled. I saw firsthand the strength of American civil society at the local level, and I began to understand just how many vital services nonprofit organizations deliver, including poverty alleviation, employment, education, and support for the disabled. We learned about the Americans with Disabilities Act, and how disabled people in America had fought for their rights under the law, taking such direct actions as locking their wheelchairs to the Brooklyn Bridge to make their concerns and demands known.

We were also introduced to people at not-for-profit organizations and to academics working on human rights in China. One of these academics was Jerome Cohen, a professor at New York University School of Law and a preeminent expert on Chinese law. Many years later, Professor Cohen told us that at first he was reluctant to meet with me since I wasn't a proper legal student, but luckily we hit it off immediately. Professor Cohen and I could speak directly in Chinese, without a translator, and after talking with him I felt I was finally able to get a better overall understanding of American law, especially with regard to the independence of the judiciary. It was thrilling to have these things explained to me by someone who had not only studied such matters for decades but understood them in a broader global context.

I asked Professor Cohen a lot of questions, but the more we talked, the more he began asking me about all sorts of issues as well. I told him about the situation of the disabled in rural China, issues of law in practice, and the work of barefoot lawyers. We both lost track of the time, and at the end of our conversation, Professor Cohen said we should keep in touch and meet again when he was back in Beijing that fall. I happily agreed, and our meeting in New York turned out to be the beginning of an important friendship.

The honesty, kindness, and fearlessness of those I met in America made a deep impression on me, as did the ways in which policies and institutions reflected these values. In China, for example, the Canlian had shamelessly proclaimed that the employment rate among the disabled had increased from 73 percent in 2002 to 84 percent in 2003. Both of those figures, however, were absurd and obvious lies; the real figure was much lower. The employment rate of disabled Americans, on the other hand, was cited by the U.S. government in 2003 as an unimpressive 25 percent, but at least one can trust this number.

In San Francisco, I was surprised when the head of a local women's rights organization we were visiting criticized the American government at length for its failures to sign on to various international conventions. Counter to what we were accustomed to in China, she seemed to believe that speaking out publicly about those in power was a natural part of her organization's job. I was stunned when she went so far as to praise the socialist system in China. "At least if you criticize your government," I said to her, "you can still leave the country. You're not afraid the government won't give you a passport?"

"Well," she replied matter-of-factly, "I can just go to the post office to get one."

Exchanges like this one helped me understand how vital criticism is for a functioning society, and made clear to me that pluralism was alive and well in America. Nobody likes to hear critical comments, but everyone in the United States has the right to say exactly what he or she thinks, and everyone's voice is important for the health of the nation. In fact, my overriding impression was that America had a small government but a big society—only diplomacy and national defense seemed to be unequivocally the preserve of the government. In direct contrast to China, in the United States the government seemed to have no right to interfere in the everyday lives of its people, except when given explicit permission by the citizenry.

In several of the airports we passed through, I even tried a little experiment to test out the services for the disabled. In each case, I found that when I walked off by myself, an airport employee came to my assistance and brought me where I needed to go. Other travelers seemed happy to lend a hand as well, often going out of their way to endure some inconvenience to help an unassisted, disabled foreigner who couldn't speak their language. In China, if someone falls down on the street, people don't dare to help them up, not because Chinese people are bad but because the system discourages people from acting ethically or out of altruism or empathy. People are also particularly wary of the disabled. But in the United States, someone almost invariably came to my aid.

Of course, that's not to say that I thought everything about the States was superior to China. When we visited New York, for instance, it was raining, and as we came out of the subway I was reminded that the newly constructed subway system in Beijing has spacious glass entry-ways that allow you to open your umbrella before going outside, whereas in New York the water poured directly into the stations through the open stairs. Also, in China blind passengers are allowed to ride public transportation for free—at least according to the law.

Returning from the States in August 2003, I was full of optimism about the future. My first stop in China was the American embassy in Beijing, where I met with diplomats and talked about what I had seen, felt, and experienced on my trip. In the United States, I explained, the broader society understood that basic human rights were at stake when consid-ering how disabled people were treated and how they lived. In China, the burden was almost entirely a private one, borne by disabled people themselves and their families. How, I wondered, could we change that?

Back home in Dongshigu, I was overjoyed to touch and hold Kerui again. Even though we had been away for only a month, I felt little Ruirui had grown so much. Weijing and I were glad to see our extended families again, too. In lieu of real gifts, which we couldn't afford, we brought them some of the giveaways we'd found in American hotels, like mints and soap and bottles of shampoo.

That September, we were due to go to Beijing to visit Professor Cohen. I was eager to continue the conversation we had begun in New York about disability law, conditions in the Chinese countryside, and legal reform. I knew that Professor Cohen had counseled many of Chi-na's leading universities and even met Zhou Enlai and Deng Xiaoping face-to-face; I also knew that he had influence in the States and was the author of many important articles about China. He had played a pivotal role in the formal establishment of U.S.-China relations and in the People's Republic of China's entry into the United Nations. Now I hoped that he might make a third critical contribution: aiding in the struggle for a free, democratic, constitutional China.

The day of our trip, Weijing and I took the train from Linyi to Bei-jing; after arriving in the city, we switched to the subway, heading for the Tsinghua University campus, where Professor Cohen was teaching. Weijing bought her ticket and I held up my disability card, an official form of identification that is meant to work everywhere in China. The subway's ticket collector waved it aside and demanded I buy a ticket. Patiently and for the umpteenth time I explained the Protection Law; I now knew it by heart, and I cited article 44, section 3, which mandated free urban transportation for the disabled. The ticket collector was unimpressed. "You need the Beijing passenger card for the blind," she snapped at me, referring to cards that are only issued and valid in particular cities. This made no sense; the whole point of the Protection Law had been the establishment of a single national standard for the rights of the disabled. "Your company's rule is against the law of the land," I told her, and she replied that I should tell that to her company, not to her.

Since Weijing and I were on a tight schedule, we had no time to argue. I bought a ticket but held on to it, vowing to bring a lawsuit against the Beijing subway system as soon as possible. Since my student days, I had had to explain myself wherever I went and fight for this basic right. I knew I had the strength to fight to my last breath, but how would the typical disabled person, already overburdened and struggling, ever claim his or her rights in the face of so much opposition? What did it say about China that a twelve-year-old national law remained unknown and had yet to be implemented? In a place like Linyi, you could give the excuse that the mountains were high and the emperor far away—to use an ancient Chinese expression—but what about in Beijing, under the very eyes of the emperor?

That same day, after a very useful meeting with Professor Cohen, during which we spoke at length about my recent work and the difficulties I faced, I went looking for a lawyer who would be willing to help me file a suit against the Beijing MTR Corporation, which runs the subway system. After an introduction from a friend, I found Lu Ziming, who agreed to work closely with me on the case and forgo his attorney's fee. By this time I was familiar enough with the process that Lawyer Lu and I could get right down to the details. He wrote up my plea, I signed over power of attorney to him, and then we moved on to the filing itself, which we finished in no time at all.

This encounter on the subway system had been no aberration. After our meeting in his office, Laywer Lu, Weijing, and I headed for the subway accompanied by a friend who brought along a video camera.

Again I attempted to enter the subway, and again I was met with a refusal to recognize my disability card. The video captured the ticket collector physically blocking me from entering the gate, even as Lawyer Lu explained the law to him in the clearest possible terms. "There's nothing we can do," the ticket collector replied. "We just do what our bosses tell us." Then the station manager came out and reiterated, on film, that I would have to buy a ticket. Two minutes of our footage would later be used on a China Central Television program called *Traffic Light*. Meanwhile, armed with my voice recorder, I continued doing test rides day after day, and I invited others to do the same and record what happened to them.

When we filed our suit in court, we avoided the usual fee by arguing that the case could play an important role in spreading awareness about the rights of the disabled, given that the Beijing subway is the most visible and best-known urban mass transit system in China. Miraculously, the court workers were not only helpful and enthusiastic but even notified the media by sending out a statement carrying the headline "Blind Man from Shandong Files a Lawsuit in Xicheng District Court over Riding the Subway." The Beijing City Propaganda Department wasted little time in censoring this news, but the word had already gotten out, and we knew that many people supported us.

Not long after Weijing and I returned to Dongshigu, we heard from our lawyer that Beijing MTR had received our complaint and wanted to settle as soon as possible, promising material compensation. I soon received a call from Cui Junfeng, deputy manager of the Beijing subway, who told me in a polished, professional voice that the judge wanted us to resolve this suit outside of court and that money wouldn't be a problem. After all, the subway was taking in over five million yuan in fares every day, not counting revenue from advertising. But money was not the heart of the matter, and we refused to take a single cent from the corporation. Far better that millions of disabled people should enjoy their legal rights in perpetuity than a single person receive a onetime payoff. Refusing to settle, I reasoned that media attention would pressure the powers that be into allowing domestic media to cover the case. Without media attention, any victory would be hollow—only popular awareness and pressure would lead to an actual change in policy. When a friend from the BBC called me for an in-depth interview, I knew we had begun to have an impact.

The initial hearing took place later that fall, and at first Judge Zhang pressed for a settlement. If I agreed to settle, he said, he and the court would supervise Beijing MTR and make sure it followed the Protection Law. Again I was adamant that the court should decide my case in accordance with the law, knowing that only then would Beijing MTR truly be legally bound to change its policies. Any settlement would risk leaving the status quo in place. At one point I heard Cui Junfeng whispering to the judge, asking if there was still time to negotiate and settle the case quietly. Judge Zhang responded forthrightly that the plaintiff did not wish to settle, that he—the judge—knew the handicapped faced serious challenges in society, and that he would rule as best he could. Was this judge's exemplary integrity due to the fact that he worked in Beijing? For once I seemed to have found a fair and impartial court, and I decided that I would accept with equanimity whatever decision the judge handed down.

At the hearing, Judge Zhang set a trial date of December 10, 2003. The morning of the trial, I was accompanied to the court by Weijing and my friend Li Wei, the photographer; we arrived at the courthouse at precisely eight forty-eight. Weijing told me there were already dozens of Chinese journalists on the scene, including a number from official central news outlets. Apparently, once the party had realized that the story couldn't be contained, the reporting ban had been lifted. Besides, lawsuits in China were not yet the everyday phenomenon they had become in many Western countries, and the fact that a blind man was standing up for his rights by bringing a lawsuit against a corporate monolith—in this case, the Beijing MTR Corporation—had become front-page news.

As we climbed the steps to the court, I heard the voice of a well-known CCTV host yell out, "He's here! He's here!" A moment later, journalists were swarming all around me. After answering a few of their questions, I entered the courtroom and sat down between Weijing and Lawyer Lu, my tape recorder turned on, a Braille copy of the Protection Law set out in front of me.

By the time Judge Zhang called the court to order, more than forty people had crowded into the room, and the shutters of cameras were constantly whirring and clicking. I could hear Cui Junfeng's sighs of frustration: he could hardly believe how badly things were going for his side. When called upon by the judge, Cui Junfeng argued that Beijing MTR had simply been following a policy laid down jointly by the Beijing city government, the city's Party Committee, the Beijing Public Transport Corporation, the Civil Affairs Bureau, and the Beijing Canlian. That may have been true, but I presented a strong counterargument: "You should go find whoever led you to your wrongful implementation of the law, because it resulted in the violation of my rights. You should take responsibility."

When Lawyer Lu summarized our arguments as the trial came to a close, he was so eloquent that some of those listening began to clap, before remembering that this wasn't appropriate behavior in a courtroom. When the trial ended, the journalists crowded around me once again, and I read the Protection Law out loud and answered their questions about the specifics of the case.

A few days later Judge Zhang returned with his decision, affirming that our position was completely in line with the law but awarding only a portion of the money we had requested as compensation for travel and other expenses related to the case. I told the press that I reserved my right to appeal if the Beijing subway didn't change its ways. If they didn't believe me, I said, they should simply follow me into a subway station. And so underground we went, and the reporters captured it all on camera as the pattern repeated itself: refusal from the ticket collector, the same stubborn replies from the station manager, the demand that we not film the encounter even though it was a public space.

In the days that followed, the judge's decision was read out loud to me several times. Analyzing it, I felt a growing dissatisfaction. A straightforward case should have resulted in a straightforward decision, but somehow it seemed as if I had won without Beijing MTR really losing. I wanted clear language that would push the transit operator to change its policy once and for all, setting a standard for the entire country, and so I started giving serious consideration to an appeal. I felt strongly that the injustice had to be changed on the ground, that blind people must be able to claim their right to free transportation without hassle; to accomplish this, we had to keep the issue in front of the media. Many of my Beijing friends, themselves human rights defenders and intellectuals, were surprised at my response, which made me wonder whether their standards might ultimately be lower and more open to compromise than mine.

When I called Lawyer Lu about a potential appeal, he seemed unsupportive. So instead of appealing, I decided to take another tack: I would speak out. In every way possible, I would enhance the force and visibility of the precedent we had set and, hopefully, thus achieve its ultimate effectiveness. I kept up the pressure, holding extensive interviews with trusted outlets like Beijing Television, frequently doing test rides and meticulously documenting them over several months, even calling the judge to tell him that ticket collectors were still stopping me on the subway and not following the law. To my disappointment, the judge seemed not to care that his decision was being ignored. He even told me to let it go—this from the man who had offered to supervise Beijing MTR! His response reaffirmed my earlier resolution not to settle and my skepticism about putting all my faith in the court.

It didn't happen overnight, but after a while my frequent test rides and the steady drumbeat of media reports seemed to have an effect. The ticket collectors in the subway stopped blocking me. Clearly the word had finally come down from on high: not only did Beijing MTR finally begin honoring the national disability card, in accordance with the law, it even started allowing a disabled person's companion to ride for free. In this respect, the Beijing subway could now be held up as a model for mass transit systems around the world.

The relentless pressure had finally paid off. As word of our victory spread, requests for help started pouring in from all over the country. This work, I realized, is the kind that never ends.

Even as I battled the Beijing subway system, I continued taking on a variety of cases involving the infringement of civil rights at the hands of the government. I also began planning and executing a program that would allow sighted people to experience simulated blindness by covering their eyes with a blindfold and going through everyday activities, such as finding their way to the subway station on their own.

My work benefited greatly from my continued contact with Professor Cohen. With his help I acquired my first computer, a high-quality IBM, fulfilling a dream dating back to that first training session with Professor Mao. I learned as much as I could about the computer, and with Weijing's help I was soon able to communicate with Professor Cohen via e-mail, not just by phone. Professor Cohen also understood that I needed more books and materials on the law, and he helped me purchase a collection of much-needed legal texts on a wide range of topics. Weijing read these aloud to me, which proved very useful, given the increasing number of cases coming my way.

In the spring of 2004, my father started having problems swallowing his food. Overcoming his stoic objections, the rest of the family eventually convinced him to visit the hospital for a checkup, and the doctors discovered a growth in his thyroid gland. Though it was apparently benign, they nonetheless recommended surgery, and we decided to go ahead with the operation. In advance of the surgery, my father had to stay in the hospital for several days, and we all gathered anxiously around him.

The operation went well, and a few days later my father was released. He still complained of some discomfort while eating, but he was adamant that he wouldn't return for another checkup. I remained very nervous about his health, however, and in September 2004 we took him back to the hospital for an endoscopy, which revealed a tumor. The doctors told him he had cancer of the stomach, and a second hospital confirmed the diagnosis.

We all felt as if the sun had been blotted out. I sought the help of a famous master of Chinese medicine, but no traditional cure was likely to work quickly enough, and after the treatment we noticed no immediate improvement in my father's condition. I was deeply conflicted: although I advocated continuing the traditional Chinese medicine treatment, my brothers opposed me, insisting on surgery to excise the tumor as soon as possible. In the end, I reluctantly gave in, and, after scraping together the money for the operation and his stay in the ward, we brought my father to the hospital in Linyi.

When my father came home after the surgery, he wasn't the same. I hoped for the best, of course, and one day I was much encouraged when

I saw how pleased he was by the sight of Kerui jumping up and down in the yard. He also displayed a great appetite for sweets, especially the traditional mooncakes left over from the recent holidays. I chastised him for his sweet tooth, and for this I still feel a lasting remorse, just as I do for arguing against lighting the coal stove when my father complained of the cold in early autumn. When we were children, he had done everything he could for us; now, when he felt a chill that none of us could feel, how was it that we were unable to perceive *his* needs?

All of us could see that he was beginning to slip away, but I still thought he had a chance of surviving if we could try some traditional Chinese medicine cures. Following the folk wisdom that declares that preparing for the worst can actually make things better, we also sewed him special clothes. And even as he lay in bed hardly able to move, we tried to make him as comfortable as possible.

In November, his condition seemed to stabilize. Soon after giving him some herbal medicine, I traveled to Beijing to run a series of workshops; supported by the National Endowment for Democracy, an American nonprofit, I would be training seventy or eighty disabled people on how to fight for their disability rights. Weijing came with me, and one morning not long after we arrived in the city, my father tried to call me. Apparently, he had put on his ancient reading glasses, now held together by a bit of string, and begun searching for my cell phone number in his little notebook.

"I'm calling Guangcheng so he'll come back as soon as he can," my father explained to Elder Brother.

"Why?" my brother asked. "He just got there!"

"My stomach doesn't feel well," my father replied. "I'm not sure I'll see him if he doesn't come back now."

Elder Brother called to tell me about this conversation; in the afternoon he called again to say that my father's condition was deteriorating rapidly. Weijing and I caught the next bus bound for Linyi, beginning a headlong rush for home. I was afraid to answer the phone I was carrying, knowing in my heart that my father was dying.

Terrified, I kept repeating the ancient phrase "a thousand miles for the funeral rites," which speaks to the responsibility one has to drop everything and rush to the last rites of a loved one. In the middle of the night, sometime after three a.m., the bus driver let us off on the side of the highway near Dongshigu. We made our way along a ditch by the side of the road toward a rough underpass that cut beneath the highway and led to the village. The ditch was muddy after a heavy rain, and as we struggled forward we clutched the wire fence that ran alongside. At the same moment, both Weijing and I slipped and fell, a terrible omen so close to home. I don't consider myself superstitious, but I said to Weijing, "Our father's dead," and she knew it in her heart as well.

Stumbling into Dongshigu, we came upon Elder Brother's place. It was now around four in the morning; I pushed at the gate but it was locked. I knew at once that the whole family must be over at my parents' house. Just then Elder Brother, who was aware that we would soon be arriving, walked up to us, and I understood from his first hoarse words that he had been weeping for a long time, that our father had already left the world. He had died a few hours earlier, at about ten p.m., my brother told us.

By the traditional reckoning, my father, Chen Gengkui, had been almost seventy years old. None of us were ready to let him go; at my parents' house in the dark of night we wept. Only little Kerui was asleep, understanding nothing; later he woke and called out, "Grandpa!" I battled waves of guilt: was this work of mine worth it if I couldn't even sit with my father at his deathbed? He had always taken special care of me, always nursed a special pride in what I had been able to accomplish, yet I'd been unable to help him in return. More generally, I found myself wondering whether I should continue my efforts to defend people's rights if I couldn't look after my own family. Often the fight I had taken on reminded me of stories I had read about the experience of war: once you cross a certain line on a battlefield, it is impossible to turn back.

Following tradition, we set out a small table with my father's name written on it. On the table we placed a memorial tablet, a goblet filled with alcohol, and a bowl holding grains and incense. At home we boiled water for the "soup" we would repeatedly bring to my father's corpse in homage. Our neighbors helped us in all of this. Everyone in the family wore white on our heads and went barefoot—you shouldn't be even a little bit comfortable at a parent's funeral. We carried funeral sticks of a particular length, made only from the wood of willow trees, wrapped in hemp and with paper for burning tied around the tops. Cremation was now required by law; even so, we brought my father's body to the grave site in a coffin, then took it out and placed it on a hearse, which bore it to the fire. It was unbearable to think of the flames overtaking the body I knew so well, to imagine those gently wrinkled arms of his turning to ash. While his body had lain at home, I had touched his face several times, wanting to remember it as well as I could. I hoped that one day I would regain my sight and so have the chance to look upon a photograph of my father. Otherwise, he was now closed to me, gone forever.

The night after his funeral, I waited up late with all of my brothers for the cremated remains; once they arrived, we put the ashes into the coffin and took them to his grave site. Later all of us ate dinner together at home, bearing large amounts of paper money "to pay the fare" at the table we'd set out, thus ensuring that our father had what he needed to get to the place to which he now must go. The next day we followed the custom of walking around the grave, all the relatives circling the site where he rested, each step we took reminding us of our pain. My brothers and I laid out straw by our father's deathbed in the traditional way, and we slept there together for seven nights, as custom requires.

Over the following weeks, we visited his grave every night to light a fire and keep watch for a few hours. After some twenty meatless days, we observed the custom of the "five-week grave": all our relatives came to our house, along with many villagers and old party comrades of my father's, everyone bearing gifts and offerings and wreaths to honor him. He was a man of great prestige who had done much for many, and they had come to see him off.

CHAPTER SEVEN

Evil Unmasked

Though the pain of my father's death was still fresh in my mind, I was anxious to continue my work, hoping to find a way to help those in need. In early 2005, Weijing and I went back to Beijing for some legal training sessions on disability issues. One day during our time there, my distant cousin Chen Guangdong called, asking if the country's family planning laws had been revised. "Why, what's going on?" I asked. He said the authorities seemed to be cracking down in the surrounding villages and counties, forcing women who should have been permitted to have a child to abort and sterilizing parents if they already had two children. Worried, a number of families had gathered to discuss their options, and Guangdong had offered to call me. "Do you know if there are any legal measures people can take to protect themselves?" he asked. I said I wasn't sure but that I would look into it. Judging from the few details he'd shared and what I knew of past enforcement campaigns, however, I told him that officials were likely acting in violation of the law.

The call from my cousin brought to mind an enforcement campaign in 1992, when more than three dozen officials from different branches of the township government descended on Dongshigu. They unleashed a torrent of violence against the population: women pregnant with a second child were dragged out of their homes for abortions, and both men and women were sterilized against their will. If someone who was targeted tried to flee, officials would threaten the extended family, often appearing in the middle of the night to take parents or siblings into detention; sometimes they would even tear down the house of someone who was "in violation" of the policy.

In addition, these heartless officials would demand enormous sums of money—around 4,000 yuan if a couple already had a second child, and even more for a third—amounting to approximately eight to ten times a farmer's annual take-home income. Those unable or unwilling to pay were beaten up or made to undergo cruelties such as sitting in ice-cold puddles of water in the middle of winter or being forced to hold a pile of bricks for an absurd length of time. If they dropped the bricks, they would be beaten.

Our family suffered during that campaign, too. My oldest brother's wife had given birth to her third child in 1988, and because of this "violation" my mother had to borrow money from relatives miles away to cover the 4,800 yuan fine. Both my brother and his wife were forcibly sterilized, and my brother was not allowed to continue his teaching job, which he had held for nearly twenty years, thus costing his family a crucial source of income.

Although the 1992 crackdown was particularly fierce, these types of coercive, inhumane campaigns were in fact going on all the time; indeed, the recent family planning campaigns were in many respects simply the continuation of a cycle of fickle and often violent political and social movements that the government had inflicted on the nation almost since its inception, in 1949. With respect to population issues, for instance, the government during the Mao era originally encouraged people to have as many children as possible, citing "strength in numbers" as a way to bolster socialism and take on the capitalist threat. Then, in 1978, the government abruptly attempted to put the brakes on the China's exploding population by introducing the Family Planning Policy, which mandated that every couple have only one child.

The One-Child Policy, as it became known in the West, was accompanied by browbeating propaganda. In its milder form, this led to warnings such as "Our nation has limited resources, and more people means everyone gets an increasingly smaller piece of the pie." The government never mentioned the more complex reality that in a thriving society, ten more people might in fact create one hundred more pies. But after years of education and propaganda, many people came to accept the government's statements about the importance of population control; at the same time, people were so frightened of state-sponsored violence that those who were brutalized during these campaigns rarely chose to fight their aggressors. Instead, they suffered alone or sometimes even took their own lives, a fact the government seemed to care little about. One slogan from late 1980s even said: "If you have a bottle of poison, we won't take it from you." Another went: "If you have a noose, we won't loosen the knot." By the late 1990s, the slogans on banners and village walls had become yet more disturbing: "If you need a bottle of poison, we'll give it to you; if you need a rope, we can supply it." And: "Better a river of blood than one more person." The long-term government propaganda and aggressive enforcement worked, and they took a devastating toll.

Now, hearing from Chen Guangdong that the government was again raising the specter of a violent family planning policy campaign, I couldn't help but respond with intense anger. I strongly believed in the fundamental right to control one's own body and one's own fertility, and I knew how much this issue mattered to people in China. Indeed, the principles of the policy have always clashed harshly with traditional Chinese values regarding families. In rural China, for instance, having multiple children is still seen by many as not only a long-standing cultural and economic imperative but also a basic right. Within that tradition, boys are coveted; sons are expected to remain in the village to care for their aging parents, and they are prized for their physical strength in agricultural labor. Moreover, it is widely understood that in a society lacking a solid legal structure, boys are particularly valuable because they can, if necessary, settle disputes with brute force.

Daughters, on the other hand, are perceived to offer none of these protections and are customarily "married out" of the home—a concept embedded in our very language. When this traditional bias against girls meets the One-Child Policy head-on, the result is a wildly skewed gender imbalance. Boys now far outnumber girls, though on paper the law doesn't allow for birth selection based on the sex of the baby. This imbalance has far-reaching implications for social stability in the future and will not easily be mitigated.

My conversation with Chen Guangdong left me determined to do something to help, and Weijing and I decided to head home immediately to look into the situation. Word got around quickly that we were back in the village, and no sooner had we sat down for breakfast than people began showing up at our door, hoping for advice on how to protect themselves.

Listening to their stories over the next few days and weeks, we began piecing things together, and before long we realized that this crackdown was a near replica of past campaigns. The township-level party committee was sending groups of a dozen or more thugs to round up all the women who had already given birth to two or more children to undergo forced sterilizations; those who had borne only one child were made to wear an intrauterine device, though legally speaking the government had no right to insist on a particular form of contraception. Those currently pregnant and deemed by authorities to be in "violation" were dragged to the township-level family planning office and then sent on to one of the maternal and child health hospitals for an abortion and tubal ligation. Any hospital could be pressed into service; the doctors feared for their jobs if they didn't follow orders, and they knew that other doctors could easily be found to replace them.

The abortion methods used by the authorities were typical procedures used to end first and second trimester pregnancies, with the glaring difference that in these cases the authorities were forcing women to terminate their pregnancies against their will. The mental and physical health of the mother was ignored entirely, and postoperative care was nonexistent. In the later months of pregnancy a toxic poison was often injected into the fetus's head, after which labor would be induced with drugs. In the few instances when the baby was born alive, I was told the doctors or nurses would wring the baby's neck or submerge the infant in water until he or she drowned.

These unspeakable evils, carried out with unwritten party approval, were blatant violations of the Constitution of the People's Republic of

China, of our criminal law, and even of the Population and Family Planning Law itself, which calls for implementation "chiefly by means of . . . safe, effective, and appropriate contraceptive methods." The law further specifies that victims can hold family planning officials criminally liable for "infringing on a citizen's personal rights, property rights or other legitimate rights and interests." In other words, it is clearly unlawful for officials to abuse their power by kidnapping one or both parents, seizing money or property, or harassing family members.

With so many people asking me what to do, I consulted with a few friends of mine in Beijing who were attorneys. At first several of them found it difficult to believe that this brazenly criminal behavior could be taking place—city dwellers often have little idea about what happens in the countryside—and on such a large scale. When I mentioned that I wanted to bring a lawsuit on behalf of the victims, one friend in particular counseled me to wait. The stories and anecdotes about people who had been terrorized by family planning officials weren't enough, he said; I should wait until I came across a victim who had suffered direct injury, which would allow me to present a straightforward, undeniable case.

It didn't help that the media were silent about this new enforcement campaign. Apparently the press still adhered to the ban on all reporting regarding family planning campaigns that had been issued by the Central Propaganda Department in 1992. For the moment, then, I could only seethe and do my best to get to the bottom of this burgeoning crisis, all the while looking out for someone courageous enough to stand up to the authorities and demand his or her rights.

The government campaign continued to escalate, and the cases of brutality and terror continued to mount. Just after dawn on April 18, 2005, in the nearby village of Yinghou, nine family planning officials went looking for a young woman named Liu Qinghua, whom they planned to sterilize with a tubal ligation. Like a number of young women across the prefecture, she was in hiding, leaving only her father, fifty-nine-year-old Liu Yuancheng, to keep watch over her house. Storming in, the officials searched everywhere for Qinghua and her husband; not finding them, they dragged Yuancheng out of the house and pushed him into a car bound for the family planning office in the town of Shuanghou. They detained him for two days and one night, refused to give him food, and tortured him. They demanded that he disclose the whereabouts of his daughter, but he insisted he didn't know. They beat him until he passed out, at which point the officials left him by the side of a bridge next to the village of Xiaobu, where he lay unconscious and covered in blood. Eventually he was found by some villagers; with his family's help, he was able to get medical attention. An older woman who had been abducted at the same time and held in the same room as Yuancheng had seen the officials beat him; though terribly fearful of the consequences, she would later corroborate his account of what had happened.

After Yuancheng had recovered enough to travel, he came to my house to ask if we could help him and his family. I believed that their case was unequivocal: the authorities had clearly violated the law when they broke into Qinghua's house without a warrant, and they had unlawfully restricted Yuancheng's freedom of movement by detaining him. I suggested that we should pursue the case by legal means, and Liu Yuancheng and his family readily agreed.

Dictating to Weijing, I began writing up a complaint. We all knew that the real perpetrators were the party committees—everyone was aware that they were directing the campaign—but for all practical purposes it is impossible to bring a lawsuit against the Communist Party in China. Our other option was to file suit against a government official—the head of the Yinan County Family Planning Commission, for example—for implementing unlawful orders from the party.

In this instance, I suggested we bring the suit against the Shuanghou township mayor, since he was directly responsible for sending the thugs out to Qinghua's house. If we were successful with our lawsuit, I hoped that we could establish a crucial de facto precedent. By now we knew that similar campaigns were unfolding throughout the province and, indeed, across the country, and I urgently wanted the people to reclaim their voice in the matter. Just because we were taking on the inhumane One-Child Policy didn't mean people shouldn't speak up for themselves and fight back.

In late April I traveled with members of the Liu family and several other victims of the family planning campaign to the Yinan County

People's Court, where we formally filed the suit. Ordinarily, we should have been able to drop off our complaint materials at the court and promptly receive documentation verifying receipt of the case file; within a week of filing, we could expect to receive a notice informing us whether our proposed lawsuit met the requirements to go to trial. In this case, though, we had to marshal every possible argument just to get someone at the courthouse to deliver our documents to the proper office, and then we were refused any verification that it had been received.

Having anticipated just this sort of bureaucratic runaround, I had packed my voice recorder, and I was now fastidiously recording the proceedings. I knew that we needed to obtain some sort of written proof that we had filed a legal complaint, whether it was the "notification of acceptance" we had hoped for or a "refusal to accept the case." Having the first document would mean that our case had a chance of going forward; having the second would at least allow us to bring the case to a higher court. Leaving empty-handed, however, would mean that our case was almost certainly destined for a bureaucratic black hole from which it would never emerge.

We were told to wait in a small lounge for the proper authority to come out to speak with us—oddly, the lounge was decorated with handcuffs and police truncheons. Before long, the head of the court's administrative docket, a man named Liu Changwei, came out. "Why don't you just go home," he said. "We can't accept the case at this time. We'll talk about it and get back to you."

"Which law specifies this action?" I asked him.

He didn't respond directly, saying only that the tribunal had never had a case like this before.

"You may never have seen a case like this before," I said, "but here it is now. If you only take cases that you have already passed judgment on, then how can you ever have anything to prosecute?"

Liu Changwei then tried another tack, saying that we hadn't shown him a signed letter affirming that we had hired a qualified attorney to represent us.

"According to Chinese Administrative Procedure Law," I replied, "it's not necessary to hire an attorney before bringing a case to court, and for the moment I am acting as the plaintiff's representative."

"Do you think *you* can represent Chinese law?" he asked me haughtily.

I responded by reminding him that if the court refused a case, it was legally required to issue an explanation in writing.

Liu Changwei left in a huff. I told two people in our group to follow him upstairs to the court offices to make sure he gave us one document or the other; they did so, which infuriated him. At last, however, he gave us a notice verifying that our case file had been received.

On the same day we paid a visit to the court, we approached the Yinan County People's Procuratorate; this department is responsible for prosecuting illegal government action, and investigations can be activated by the filing of citizen grievances accusing government officials of misconduct. An officer at the procuratorate recorded our complaint, admitting that he had lately received many others like it. But he made it clear that for the moment he could do nothing; he would have to contact the county leadership and ask for further instructions. I was at my wit's end. What was the use of this office, ostensibly charged with supervision of the law, if it, too, lacked independence and reported things straight to the party?

By early summer, we still had no word on a trial date for Yuancheng's case. Originally, I had hoped that the trial would bring media attention to the enforcement campaign currently under way and would help curb the violence; now, attempting to take matters into my own hands, I traveled to Shanghai and Beijing in an effort to drum up support among friends, lawyers, and journalists. When I realized that the domestic media still weren't willing to cover any aspect of the family planning campaign, I sought out foreign journalists. First I made contact with the *New York Times*, but it showed little interest in pursuing the story. In early July, I got in touch with Philip Pan, a reporter from the *Washington Post,* who told me he would write a story, though he wouldn't be able to come to Shandong until later that month. By this point, I had also met with human rights lawyers Teng Biao, Jiang Tianyong, and Tu Bisheng, as well as the writer and scholar Guo Yushan. All of them had agreed to help, but unfortunately none were able to come to Dongshigu right away.

As time went on, I grew increasingly anxious. I knew Yuancheng's case was straightforward from a legal point of view, but I wasn't sure that this would make a difference in court. When it came to family planning, the laws apparently didn't matter: officials could act with complete impunity, and the whole system seemed rigged, or at least off-kilter. No one—whether doctors, nurses, officials, or judges—was willing to step forward and put a stop to what everyone knew were atrocities.

Meanwhile, our filing seemed to have spurred county authorities to intensify their enforcement campaign. Now, for example, instead of sending two carloads of cadres into the villages, our township was sending four. Instead of seeking out a few young women each day, the authorities began bringing more than one hundred people into the Yinan County Maternal and Infant Health Station or other hospitals for tubal ligations or abortions every single day. Over the next several months I was repeatedly cajoled and threatened by township officials; they would come to my house to berate me or to try to bribe me with enviable positions and financial rewards if only I would drop the case and stop the investigation. Fourth Brother, as a party member and teacher at the party school, was dragooned into monitoring me.

As the long wait for a trial date went on, the horrors continued, often very close to home. My cousin Chen Guangdong, who had originally alerted me to the new enforcement campaign, became a target, along with his wife. The couple had two daughters, and one day a team of a dozen local cadres appeared in their house when Guangdong's wife was at home alone. She pleaded with them, informing them that her doctor had said she shouldn't have surgery because of a thyroid condition. Ignoring her, they threw her in the back of a van and took her to a hospital for a sterilization procedure, a major surgery requiring anesthesia via epidural injection. By the time we knew anything about this, she had already been sent home. Weijing went to see her, and Guangdong's wife cried as she described what had happened.

Other neighbors and villagers were also targeted—arbitrarily, wantonly. A woman named Du Dehong, from a nearby village, had obtained official permission for her two children, but the cadres chased her husband up into the mountains and then forced Dehong to undergo sterilization; the couple's infant child was left at home alone, and her lips were blue from cold by the time her parents were allowed home. Chen Gengjiang, a neighbor just behind us, was able to fend off an onslaught of cadres by wielding a pickax. Eventually he fled to our house, locking the cadres inside his house but leaving his terrified child behind, screaming.

At this point, my overriding goal had become to stop this brutal movement in its tracks, and to stop the persecution of these untold numbers of victims. Unfortunately, by this time it was clear that the law alone was not enough—after all the law cannot ameliorate past suffering, and while we waited for a trial date the violence continued unabated.

But without the media and their ability to spread the word, all the cases and all the evidence in the world would be of no use. What I hoped for was a story that would encompass the entire reach of this huge campaign; spread far and wide by the press, it would spark a public outcry that the authorities could not ignore. With so many people coming to me for help and advice, I decided to gather as much firsthand testimony as possible from around the prefecture, thinking that an investigation with a broader reach would provide the shocking evidence needed to spur the media into action.

Beginning in the spring of 2005, I was in constant motion, my emotions sometimes running high because of all the horrifying stories I heard. I relied on friends, relatives, and the families of victims for rides—in their cars or on their motorcycles—and for meals in their restaurants or homes. Often there was no other means of transport; at those times, Weijing and I walked to nearby villages to meet with victims of the government's campaign.

In May, Li Jian, a citizen journalist who ran a website called the Civil Rights Defense Net, took a trip with me to gather evidence, focusing on the three counties closest to ours. We met victims and heard their stories, then answered their questions and wrote up their complaints. I usually recorded the victims' stories myself and organized the material into written form with the help of others. Li Jian and I listened as people described fractured spines and being beaten with brooms, rubber clubs, and the soles of shoes; we saw skin that had turned eggplant purple from so many beatings.

Where campaigns were still under way, Weijing and I did everything possible to stop family planning officials from carrying out their mandate. Sometimes we tried to help victims by going directly to the villages where the abuses were happening; once Weijing and I even forded the Meng River at night in our hurry to get to a family in need. Since the officials feared exposure, we often found that our presence was enough to put a damper on their activities. Meanwhile, we wrote letters to family planning officials in both Shandong and Beijing, alerting them to the situation and urging the party to address these problems in accordance with the law—all to no avail.

Later we learned the source of the directive to step things up in our region. An official document had been issued by the party secretary for Linyi, who was feeling pressure to meet population-control targets—often precise caps on births—from his provincial bosses. The paper instructed officials and cadres not to overestimate people's legal consciousness and to adopt the tough "traditional" methods used in 1992. They said it was better to slaughter a hundred innocent people by mistake than let one person who had violated the law get away. After we discovered the existence of this paper and some of the contents, the party recalled all the copies and had them destroyed.

By then, however, the damage had already been done. The vicious enforcement program had been rolled out across a vast prefecture that is home to more than ten million people. In 2005, nine counties and three other jurisdictions, all within Linyi, were included in these centrally orchestrated campaigns, which relied on raids, detention, and torture and lasted from early winter into the fall. According to my later estimate, as many as 520,000 people would ultimately be harassed, fined, detained, or tortured over the course of the campaign, and up to 130,000 people would be subjected to forced abortions or sterilizations.

As it happened, something very personal was at stake in this fight: Weijing was pregnant again. We knew the family planning law, of course, but we considered it a violation of our rights and an assault on human nature. We wanted another child; why should the Communist Party have any right to stop us? Weijing had gotten pregnant before we even knew about the family planning campaign spreading across Linyi, and she fearlessly traveled and worked with me during much of her third trimester. We responded to what was directly in front of us and what we knew to be right, blocking out the politics as much as we could, despite the dangers.

Weijing and I worked tirelessly until she began to feel her labor pains, at which point I brought her directly to her mother's house. On July 21, 2005, exactly four years to the day from Weijing's first visit with me in Dongshigu, she gave birth by cesarean to our daughter, Kesi. As I cradled my beautiful new baby in my arms, I thought about how many terrifying abuses were taking place even then—and each one because of a sweet child, like this one.

By August 2005, we had assembled our full investigative team. Our first step was to broaden the scope of our investigation, and our first stop was a village in Fei County, which abuts our own. A number of victims had gathered in the village so we could interview them all at once. One woman, named Fang Zhongxia, told us the following story.

> Some time ago, Family Planning officials inserted an intra-
> uterine device in me, following the birth of my second
> daughter. When I became pregnant again by accident, the
> officials went after my mother and forced her to pay one
> thousand yuan, after which she hid in terror. Two months
> later, they came for my mother-in-law, smashing her belong-
> ings and seizing her on several different occasions; then they
> did the same with my elder brother's wife and my elder sis-
> ter's husband, whom they detained for a week and beat on
> twenty-seven separate occasions. My uncle's wife, who was
> beaten and stomped on during the drive to the family plan-
> ning office, lost consciousness three times and suffered such
> serious kidney damage that she was no longer able to work.
> Then they went for my nephew, his wife and child, and my
> husband's younger sister—in short, every relative of mine
> they could find, twenty-two in total. Already seven months
> pregnant, I was forced to turn myself in and then injected

with an oxytocic drug against my will. The child was aborted the next day, and I was made to have a tubal ligation; only then were all my relatives set free.

Over the next few months, we continued our investigation, listening to and recording dozens of stories. At the Fei County People's Hospital, we spoke to Pei Jinglan, who was resting in a recovery room. She related her story.

My younger brother had overbirthed, and the family planning committee burst into my house and started shoving me around. They swore at me and dragged me to their office. Four men undid my shirt and put a sack over my head and beat me for almost an hour. They stuck their fingers between my ribs so hard that I cried. They made me crouch on my hands and knees and wouldn't let me pick up my head, and one of them pushed my head down and squeezed my neck, while another one kicked me while saying they would kick me to death. There were thirty other people locked in the room with me, and there was nowhere to go to the bathroom. There was an old woman there who had to pee in a rice bowl.

Song Huahou, a sixty-year-old resident of the village of Maxiagou, in Fei County, Liangqiu township, told us what had happened to her.

My son's wife had a son and was not allowed to have a second child. But she got pregnant again, and they dragged me to the family planning office. They beat me with a rubber club and beat my face with their fists. My teeth were bleeding. I was held for twenty-six days, during which time a number of other relatives were also detained and beaten for the same reason. Some of them paid a lot of money and were able to go home. My brother was detained as well, and they used the same kind of rubber club to beat him, too. Then they told me I had to beat him. And then that he had to beat me. They complained that we weren't rough enough, not up to their standards, so they showed us how to do it. They kept my brother for eighteen days, and when he finally got home he found his peanut harvest and his goats had been stolen, and he was now out three thousand yuan. My brother now hates me and says if I don't give him three thousand yuan to cover his losses he will never speak to me again.

Xia Jingshan of Xiajiagou Village, in Liangqiu township, Fei County, told us:

> Seven people from the family planning bureau broke into our house, threw my wife and me in a van, and ordered me to give them directions to a house where they wanted to grab people. When I said I didn't know where this house was, they beat me with a club and swore at me. I had no choice but to take them from house to house, and in the end they grabbed people from more than ten different families and beat them. After that, my neighbors and relatives all blamed me for bringing the family planning people to their houses, and they all despise me now.

Chen Baigao from Lanshan District said:

> I was locked up in the family planning "study group." Every night we were beaten, and after being beaten we would be forced to pay fifty yuan for "study" fees. There were more than sixty people together in one room, men and women together, and we had to relieve ourselves in a bucket in the corner, one for men and one for women. By night there was nowhere to lie down since the buckets had overflowed and there was piss everywhere.

Xiao Ruibin, forty-four years old, told his story:

> The family planning people turned over a chair and made me lie on top of the legs. One person pushed my head down

while another beat me with a rubber club. They said if they beat me to death they might give twenty thousand yuan in compensation for the burial. They beat me until I fainted, then threw cold water on me to wake me up so they could start beating me again.

We also visited the family members of an elderly man named Shi Mingli, from Tanyi township, who was taken into custody because his son had overbirthed. Shi Mingli was later let go and allowed to return home, but the officials then went after his daughter and son-in-law. His son-in-law escaped, so the family planning people went after his neighbor. The neighbors complained bitterly that Shi Mingli and his family were to blame; finally the old man went to the family planning office and offered to take the punishment on behalf of the neighbors. The officials refused to accept his proposal, and in desperation Shi Mingli took his own life.

All these people were the victims of terrible cruelty and abuse, both physical and emotional. Besides being illegal and inhumane, the enforcement campaigns ripped families apart, destroyed friendships, and made neighbors into enemies. And I am certain that the incidents I was able to investigate and write about provided just one small part of the total picture. For instance, we heard few detailed descriptions of abortion and sterilization surgeries, undoubtedly because the trauma was too devastating and personal to discuss openly.

Listening to the expectant voices of these victims hoping for justice and comfort, I felt their wounds in my own soul. Their stories confirmed my belief that the Cultural Revolution has never ended—it has simply metastasized. It continues whenever the party mounts a campaign against rights defenders, religious believers, practitioners of Falun Gong, or women who have more than one child. Anyone—*anyone*—can become collateral damage in such campaigns.

But the stories we heard also served a crucial purpose, for it was from these interviews that our most detailed and damning report would ultimately emerge. Teng Biao and Guo Yushan wrote up many of the stories we recorded, and I gave interviews about the enforcement campaign's abuses to reporters from the foreign press. This put pressure on the national Family Planning Commission to issue a statement, and eventually the commission declared that there were indeed infractions of the policy taking place within Linyi and that responsible officials had been asked to step down or were being otherwise punished. Despite their response, we continued to file individual cases; moreover, the results of our investigations in Fei County and elsewhere led us to conceive of a large-scale class-action suit against the Family Planning Commission office in Linyi. However slim the chances of success, we all agreed that we had to try.

That summer, the authorities began an aggressive campaign to intimidate my family, and some of the people we had interviewed were threatened as well. I became aware that surveillance teams were monitoring us constantly. Wherever we drove, two or three cars would follow us, accelerating when we did, braking when we did, sometimes openly and other times covertly. As we pulled out of one village after an interview, we were blocked from leaving by a local official. The narrow road ran between crop fields and dropped off steeply on both sides, allowing just enough space for two cars to pass each other without scraping. The official stopped his car and opened his door, making it impossible for us to get by. "Why don't you come back to our office so we can talk?" he said, his tone threatening. He then demanded our IDs but refused to look at our evidence of family planning abuses. A small crowd of villagers quickly gathered and angrily asked him to let us pass. Eventually the official gave in, but not without trying to follow us and later sending us a harassing text message.

On August 11, Teng Biao and Yushan came back to Dongshigu with me to continue the investigation, and we noticed people following us and watching us. When we arrived in a village in Yitang township with the intention of interviewing victims, the mayor was already there with various cadres and officials, ready to stop us with a police car. A chase ensued; having rented the cheapest car we could find, we doubted that we could stay ahead of the police car or those driven by the other cadres. But the driver we'd hired was a local man, and when he saw an opening he suddenly steered us down a dirt road, out of sight of our pursuers.

The night after we were chased by the cadres, our investigative team decided to stay in a hotel in Linyi, having spent the day conducting surveys. We figured we would be safer in the city, but what we didn't realize was that the police could track our position through our cell phones. It was already late and I was lying down in bed when I heard a knock at the door.

"We need to see your IDs," said three policemen who barged in.

"The law says you have to show yours at the same time," I replied.

One of the policemen quickly flashed an ID and put it back in his pocket—they were from Linyi. We asked the others to show their IDs as well. "One is enough," they replied. Then the Linyi policemen promptly escorted two members of our team out of the room. More officials and policemen entered as they left. We later learned that dozens of officials and cadres who had been pursuing us had secured the hotel, some in the guise of guests and staff.

"It seems you have some issues with our family planning work," said one of the intruders. I recognized his voice: it was Liu Wenbin, the vice chair of Yinan's Family Planning Commission.

"Don't you know anything about the actual regulations and laws regarding family planning?" I asked.

Before Liu Wenbin could respond, someone else said, "Why do you insist on trying to put everything on the Internet?" He was clearly referring to the fact that our findings had been posted on Li Jian's Civil Rights Defense Net website. "Why don't you go through the proper channels?"

"I have already gone through all the legal channels," I answered. "Besides, there's no prohibition against putting things online. But is there a law that permits you to beat people up and take them into custody at will? Don't you know about the family planning regulations and the 'seven prohibited items,' including illegal detentions, beatings, humiliation, stealing people's property, and arbitrarily implicating others? If you have any issues with me, you should speak to my lawyer."

I saw there was no reasoning with them, so I made ready to leave, but one of the policemen grabbed me and pushed me back.

"What basis do you have for restricting my freedom?" I demanded.

Touching the policeman's arms as he held me, I realized that these weren't even proper uniformed police—the man was wearing a T-shirt.

Teng Biao, Guo Yushan, and Tu Bisheng were staying in the room next door, and when they heard the commotion they had come over to see what was happening. "These men are illegally restricting my personal freedom," I told them.

Then I turned toward Liu Wenbin. "Who are these people?" I asked angrily, referring to the other intruders.

"How should I know?" he replied. "I just know they're Yinan police."

Disgusted, Teng Biao, Yushan, and I went next door to their room. There we came upon a group of cadres from the Linyi Legal Department, including the head officer of the judiciary, a man named He Fali.

"Are those people who just barged into our room with you?" I asked him.

He Fali took my hand in his and gave it two firm shakes.

"You aren't answering!" I yelled at him.

"This is my answer," he said, shaking my hand again.

I asked him the same question again, and he hesitated, replying that he didn't know and that he had no relationship with them.

The whole scene was pure farce. No one would answer our questions about what was happening. They claimed not to know who the other people were or why they were there. Of course, this was completely laughable and completely untrue. In fact, representatives from four different government agencies had descended on our hotel that night: we were visited by officials from Shuanghou township, the judiciary, the Family Planning Commission, and the police. There is no question in my mind—and no question in the minds of anyone else who was present—that the orders to harass us had ultimately come from the party secretary in Linyi. No one else had the authority to mobilize so many people from so many different branches of government in the middle of the night.

He Fali went downstairs, leaving my friends and me in the room along with a group of Shuanghou township officials. After some debate on their part, the officials announced they would now be taking us home to Dongshigu. We understood that their goal was to prevent us from continuing our investigation; they would bring us home, yet once they did, we knew they probably wouldn't let us out of their sight. What's more, they would surely try to separate us, which could prove dangerous for us all. We said we wouldn't go.

Seeing they weren't getting anywhere with us, the officials went downstairs, which gave us the chance to talk among ourselves. Surrounded by all these officials here, we couldn't possibly continue the survey, and I was worried about losing the material we had already collected. I suggested we head home with what we had and try to get it online as quickly as possible. If they tried to put us in separate cars we wouldn't go. The others agreed, and I notified the officials about our decision and our demand. They agreed to find a minibus, and soon we were in the van, bound for Dongshigu. We arrived at about two in the morning, followed closely by the cadres and officials. An alarming change was immediately pointed out to me: sentries were standing guard at every entrance to the village. Many wore civilian clothes, and though they were township cadres of different levels, they appeared to be working closely with the police.

From that night on, twenty or thirty guards were always watching me and my friends and the family planning victims who were working on the investigation. The guards hardly attempted to hide their presence: each time we went out, we saw them everywhere. They followed us wherever we went; sometimes we followed them as well, and sometimes we tried to get them to tell us what they were doing and what their orders were. They would never reply. What made me especially angry was their refusal to allow anyone to visit me. Not only were we prohibited from traveling to nearby villages; those seeking my help were prevented from reaching me, as well. Our investigation was effectively at an end.

One afternoon in late August I traveled to Weijing's mother's house in Linshu to see Weijing and our daughter, who had been there for the better part of a month. A number of government and party officials followed me, and when I exited my in-laws' house they forced me into their car and took me to the township office, where they held me until late that evening before sending me home to Dongshigu.

Meanwhile, pretending to be inspectors checking the electricity meter, a family planning team barged into Weijing's mother's house, where Weijing was caring for Kesi, then just twenty-eight days old. They discovered the child, quickly reported her, and then waited for orders, squatting on the floor of Weijing's room while they kept an eye on her. When Weijing confronted them, they grew incensed and stood up to hit her—thankfully, Weijing's mother returned just then and found them preparing to beat a new mother and drag her baby girl outside during the child's first month of life. My mother-in-law's angry response prevented them from taking action right away, but the guards remained in the house that whole night. At dawn, they packed my wife and child into an unmarked car and whisked them off to the headquarters of the township government in Shuanghou.

The next day they took me to the township office as well. On the ride over, I started calling my lawyer friends in Beijing, talking loudly so that the officials would hear, explaining clearly that if I didn't call them back within an hour, they should contact the media since it would mean I was being held against my will. When I arrived at the office, I found Kesi wailing from hunger; the experience had made Weijing so anxious that her milk had suddenly stopped. A few minutes later, I announced that we were leaving, tugging on Weijing's arm and not betraying the slightest hesitation. A notorious female official named Zhang Tingju tried to block our way, but I pulled Weijing and Kesi with me and we walked right out the door.

Sometime later, several family planning officials came to our house in Dongshigu and demanded that I pay tens of thousands of yuan, declaring that this was the requisite fine for having a second child. I readily agreed but said I would need to leave the house in order to borrow the money. Not wanting to let me out of their sight, they were stymied, and eventually they left. Once again we had escaped harm, but soon enough our troubles would grow much more serious.

Despite all the harassment, I still had work to do, and it required that I get out into the world. I wasn't going to allow my captors to keep me isolated. I refused to waste away at home as long as our work remained unfinished.

On the night of August 25, I managed to slip away. Earlier, Weijing and I had left the house a number of times so that the guards would become used to our moving around. That day, we visited various neighbors and relatives in the village, always followed by a crowd of guards. That evening, my nephew Chen Hua came over and we decided on our plan. First, he would return home to make the guards around his house think everything was normal; later, he would sneak out and go to a rendezvous point in the village.

Around ten that night, after the children were asleep, Weijing and I headed out carrying flashlights. The guards immediately gathered behind us, a wavering black mass of people in our wake. When they came too close, we threw sand at them to keep them back.

When we reached the rendezvous, Chen Hua hissed at me from the darkness and then pulled me into a field planted with crops. Luckily, the darkness hid my movements from the guards, and they continued to follow Weijing as she led them on a wild-goose chase throughout the village, eventually winding up at the cottage where we had lived when we first got married, climbing over the wall of the yard. She threw stones over the wall at the guards and pretended to talk to me as though I were there with her. After an hour or so, they got the key to the yard from my older brother and found Weijing there alone. She shrugged in response to their questions. "I think he went home," she said. "Didn't you see him?" They were furious, and they scoured the village and the surrounding fields into the wee hours of the night.

While Weijing was busy distracting the guards, Chen Hua and I ran together through orchards and peanut fields, often backtracking and purposely taking the less-traveled way toward our destination, the neighboring village of Huangying. It was a difficult journey through the night: steering clear of the roads, we found ourselves scrambling over a mountain and wading barefoot through streams. Soaked and covered in mud, we at last reached Huangying and hid under a bridge.

We spent a number of hours calling every number we could remember; eventually we located a taxi driver who was willing to pick us up and take us to a bus station outside Linyi jurisdiction some 120 miles away, where we boarded a bus for Nanjing. From there, we caught another bus bound for Shanghai. After arriving in Shanghai at about seven that evening, we were famished; we had eaten nothing for over twenty-four hours. We found some food, and then made our way to my final destination: an important conference on the rule of law and human rights. Here, I surmised, I would be safe for a short while, sharing experiences with and learning from many of China's most brilliant and committed activists.

During my time in Shanghai, our findings at last began making it out into the wider world. The government had been blocking the Internet sites that had posted our investigation results, but on August 27 the *Washington Post* ran a story by Philip Pan under the headline "Who Controls the Family?" The article had an immediate impact. Even the national Family Planning Commission was forced to admit that the "local" abuses in Shandong seemed to be against law. Officials claimed they would be launching an investigation, though of course nothing came of it beyond a brief notice in the official media.

A few days after the article appeared, I took a train from Shanghai to Beijing to meet with Professor Cohen and discuss further strategies with our team of lawyers and activists. Before leaving Shanghai, I had made several calls to a reporter from *Time* magazine, arranging for him to visit Shandong and report in more depth on family planning abuses. I had also had Weijing call the U.S. embassy to talk about funding a small civil society project. These conversations were probably a serious mistake; I realized later that my phone was being tapped and that I was only giving the party new reasons to consider me dangerous.

From the moment I arrived in Beijing, my pursuers were after me. Jiang Tianyong, the human rights lawyer from Beijing who had become part of our team, had bought a ticket so that he could wait for me on the platform, and he was able to board the train to meet me. He immediately told me that a group of people with Shandong accents was waiting outside. "How do you know they're looking for me?" I asked. "They were watching a passenger who came off the train wearing sunglasses," said Jiang, "and they commented that the man resembled you." As soon as I heard this, we left the train and walked along the far edge of the platform, staying as far as possible from the men from Shandong. Fortunately, we were able to exit the station undetected.

That afternoon we met up with Teng Biao, and we told him about our recent challenges. Teng, who was teaching at China University of

Political Science and Law, said he too was being threatened because of our investigation. The party secretary at the university, who was obviously acting at the direction of the national party, had sought him out on a number of occasions and tried to pressure him into stopping his work.

Worried but refusing to be scared off, I went to the U.S. embassy with Jiang Tianyong to discuss the details of a program on the rule of law that I was trying to fund. As we approached the embassy from the subway station, I heard a car idling at the curb across from us as we walked through the embassy's front door. Sometime later, as we came out, I heard a car idling in the same spot; I told Lawyer Jiang that I thought this car was suspicious and that we'd better keep moving. He sensed it, too—as we hurried toward the subway, he told me he was sure we were being watched.

A few moments later, we turned around and there they were: a large team of officials and cadres and thugs, all of them up from Shandong. Among them were Zhu Hongguo, the township mayor; Zhao Feng, the township vice mayor; Xia Fatian, the township vice secretary of the party; and some other people from the Yinan Public Security Bureau. By now, walking as fast as we could, we were just twenty yards from the subway station, but they quickly caught up to us.

Zhu Hongguo stepped up to me and patted me on the shoulder, saying, "Brother! Let's just go home. You're killing me here, I just can't take it anymore."

I told him I wasn't going home, that I still had work to do. But as we pushed toward the subway entrance, the men from Shandong blocked our way.

"Hold on right there," someone said. "We're from the Public Security Bureau."

"Even police have to abide by the law," I replied.

One of the Shandong team tried to pull Jiang aside, saying he wanted to have a little chat with him; obviously, what they really wanted was to isolate me. Several bystanders were watching this encounter, aware that something was not quite right but unsure of what to do. "Look, they're all from Linyi!" Lawyer Jiang said to them. "They're trying to seize us illegally!"

That seemed to give the men from Shandong pause, and we took the opportunity to push our way into the subway. At least we didn't have to buy our tickets—our earlier work on that issue had been a complete success, and it even gave us a jump on our pursuers. The cadres followed us in, quickly buying their tickets and boarding the same train, sitting on one side of the car while we sat on the other. Lawyer Jiang and I behaved as if we planned to get off at the next stop; when we did, the Shandong team got off to follow us, but we quickly got back on, just as the doors were closing. Most of them couldn't make it back in, and we repeated this process all the way around the Beijing subway system's Circle Line until we reached the Gulou stop, having shaken every one of our pursuers.

Deeply unsettled by this experience, Lawyer Jiang and I went to find Tu Bisheng at his office. I gave him the materials from our investigation, hoping that he and the others from the team could continue the work if I was arrested. We then made contact with Professor Cohen, and he invited us to dinner at a Japanese restaurant near Tsinghua University, where he was teaching at the time. Over dinner, we had a long and very useful conversation about the status of all the different family planning cases we were working on. Professor Cohen expressed much anxiety about my situation, and he was also concerned that many victims of the family planning campaigns might suffer serious repercussions in the wake of our investigation.

We stayed on high alert throughout dinner, but we didn't notice any suspicious activity, nor did we sense that anyone followed us when we left the restaurant. Somewhat relieved, we went back to Jiang Tianyong's apartment and made plans to meet Philip Pan of the *Washington Post* at three o'clock the next afternoon in a small park near the Lido Hotel, not far from Lawyer Jiang's apartment.

The next day—September 6, 2005—Tu Bisheng and I left Lawyer Jiang's apartment, took the elevator down to the lobby, and emerged into the open air, heading for our meeting with Pan.

Tu Bisheng was the first to see them. "Zhu Hongguo!" he shouted.

At that moment, Zhu Hongguo rushed toward me, and it was evident that this time he wasn't going to let me get away. Several others hurried up—Xia Fatian, Zhao Feng, and two or three of the men who had chased us on the subway—and together they shoved me into the backseat of their Santana sedan. When I resisted, they started punching me in the head. One kidnapper grabbed my hair and one grabbed my arm, while another put me in a tight headlock. Another guard pummeled me in the side. I wanted to scream out, but I could hardly breathe.

I felt a small device in one guard's pant pocket, perhaps a phone or a little recorder. Once I had been completely immobilized, the guard reached into his pocket and turned the device on. It played a recorded message: "Only through continuous armed struggle will the proletariat and the party be victorious, and will the revolution be successful!" The speaker's voice was vicious and piercing, reminding me of the public announcements that had been broadcast throughout the country during the Cultural Revolution. "Let him have a good listen to this," said one of the captors in the front seat with an audible smirk.

Enraged by the recording, I struggled with all my might to break free. The sentiments apparent in the message were almost never openly expressed, although a river of party-instigated violence ran beneath Chinese society. Clearly, this recording was the mobilization order that all participating government and party officials had received. As my captors pinned me down to my seat and beat the last wave of resistance out of me, I understood why they were able to act with such confidence and impunity: they had the backing of this voice and, with it, the secret approval of the party to dispense with all scruples, to rely on violence, to retain power at all costs.

I later learned from an inside source that county officials had convened a large meeting after my escape from house arrest and the publication of the *Washington Post* article. It was agreed at the meeting that I was to be captured and detained, which was why approximately two hundred people had been sent after me, including the two teams stationed near the U.S. embassy and Tsinghua University, all authorized to kidnap me, using violence if necessary. Though they came from Shandong Province, these teams clearly had the tacit support of, if not active assistance from, police units and officials in Beijing. Such outsized mobilizations to control individual, nonviolent activists were rare back then, but recently they have become the norm. A stone colliding with an egg, as we say in Chinese.

While the Shandong guards were busy subduing me in the backseat of the Santana, Tu Bisheng persuaded the security guard to close the gate to the drive leading from Jiang Tianyong's apartment building, preventing the abductors' car from speeding off, and then he called the police. When the Beijing police arrived, the Shandong cadres told them I had violated the Population and Family Planning Law by "overbirthing"; the compliant police merely looked over the Shandong security detail's paperwork. Then the Beijing police made the security guard open the gate, and the Santana started moving.

Philip Pan had just arrived for our meeting, and now he witnessed what was happening; at the same moment, Teng Biao pulled up in his car and immediately tried to stop the Shandong team. But the Santana drove off, zigzagging through the Beijing streets in an attempt to shake Teng Biao, whose car was in close pursuit. As the Santana raced through the city, the men on either side of me held my arms from behind and twisted them painfully, making it impossible for me to move.

I was now alone with my enemies, bound for an unknown fate. At one point the Santana pulled over so they could take off the fake license plate they'd been using in Beijing and replace it with the real one: 鲁Q83555, as I was later told. It was a number I knew well from the surveillance we had endured during our survey work. Soon I heard my kidnappers on the police radio calling Linyi, reporting that they had captured me, that I was subdued and in the car. "Where did you find him?" asked the voice on the other end. "At the Lido Hotel," someone replied.

Once we left the city center and got on the highway, the car began moving very fast. I had no idea where my captors were taking me, but one thing was certain: I was fully in their power now.

CHAPTER EIGHT

Kidnapped

As we sped away from Beijing, I heard my captors talking among themselves and gathered that we were heading to Tianjin, about eighty miles southeast of the capital. They continued to pummel me while twisting my arms behind my back and gripping my neck in a painful choke hold, letting up only when we pulled over in Tianjin. When the rest of the Shandong retinue caught up, Zhu Hongguo and another man slipped into our car, replacing the men who had been holding my arms during the trip. Zhu Hongguo motioned his cohort to release my arms, and then began patting me on the back, as if to console me—he apparently regretted this violent, unseemly way of bringing me to heel. Although fully implicated in everything, he was a good man at heart, and in various subtle ways he tried to support and protect me while still following the party's dictates.

Before long we got back on the highway, and by my reckoning we pulled up at our destination soon after midnight. My captors hauled me out of the car and through the lobby of what I later learned was the Victoria Resort in Yinan, an upscale spa hotel where corrupt local government officials went to spend their ill-gotten gains. I was taken to an ordinary guest room on the first floor; it contained two beds, a table, some chairs, and a TV, which no one turned on. I lay back on one of the beds, refusing to interact or cooperate with my kidnappers in any way.

By that time, I could hardly speak, my throat having been wedged in a crushing headlock during the earlier part of trip. My entire body was aching and bruised, and when my captors refused my request to see a doctor, I immediately made up my mind to begin a hunger strike, leaving the breakfast they brought to my room untouched.

As morning broke, cadres came and went. At one point Liu Jie, the vice mayor of Linyi and the head of its Public Security Bureau, arrived and ordered everyone out of the room except for two other officials.

"I'm here today to talk about some things," he said.

I made no response.

"We're equals," he added, as though trying to appease me.

You kidnap me, and now you call us equals? I thought to myself, remaining silent.

"You ignore me," he continued, sitting near the window, "but I still have something to say. I believe you can hear me and that you are listening. I brought you back here from Beijing in order to save you. You were surrounded by so many reporters there in Beijing, and you agreed to be interviewed by them. You agreed to an interview with the *Washington Post* and thus were in breach of article 111 of Chinese Criminal Law, illegally providing intelligence to foreigners." Just one interview, he added, would be enough to earn me five years in prison, and two interviews would mean a ten-year sentence.

This was nonsense. According to this line of reasoning, nearly all of China's leaders would be facing life in prison for communicating with foreign journalists. The party simply had no legal basis for detaining me, but it needed to concoct an excuse to legitimize its actions.

Liu Jie went on to say that the Western imperialist countries were obsessed with finding out everything about China and that the interviews I'd given had actively helped the imperialists. "Just because problems exist in our society does not mean that socialism is bad," Liu Jie said, "and just because corruption exists that doesn't mean the party is bad."

I was infuriated by his comments but did not move from the bed, refusing to accord him any sign of respect. He finally left the room, embarrassed that he had been unable to elicit the slightest response from me in front of the other officials.

Meanwhile, Fourth Brother, Elder Brother, and my father-in-law had been summoned to coax me into giving up my work on the class-action suit and to begin eating again. The government instructed Fourth Brother to remove the computer and fax machine from my home to a governmental office, supposedly for "safekeeping." I was given permission to talk with Weijing on the phone, and I immediately told her to tell Professor Cohen what had happened; I was optimistic that his intervention might help.

In the early evening, roughly eighteen hours after arriving at the Victoria Resort, I was in my room with two guards when Zhu Hongguo came in and announced that I was to be sent home as soon as possible. I immediately guessed that Philip Pan had been able to publish an article, and that foreign media coverage of my kidnapping was having an effect on the authorities; I also thought it possible that pressure brought by friends such as Professor Cohen and Teng Biao was having a positive influence on my situation.

Heartened, I said, "I'm not going. On what legal basis did you kidnap me? And on what basis do you now suddenly send me home? I want an explanation, or I'm not going anywhere."

What I hadn't reckoned on was pressure from my extended family. During the afternoon Weijing's father had been upset by what he felt was my disrespectful behavior: while speaking with him I'd continued lying on the bed. After he got off the phone with me, he called Weijing in a fury to complain. With all the guards around, I hadn't been able to explain my thinking to him, and he grew increasingly annoyed that I refused to leave, in part because he, too, wanted to be finished with this business. At last I had no choice but to agree to return to my village.

Once back in Dongshigu, I learned that the authorities were initiating a plan to put me under long-term house arrest, using the false pretense of assisting the poor. Dozens of guards were stationed just outside our main gate; others were taking up positions outside our yard and throughout the village, preparing to man their posts twenty-four hours a day, in shifts. They had tarps for cover from the elements, as well as coal briquettes to keep themselves warm once the cold weather arrived. They'd also transported a TV and a number of beds over to the village government offices, though the majority of the guards would sleep on the ground at their posts.

Within days of bringing me home, the cadres had organized a number of working groups with different responsibilities. There was the "Exit Prevention Group," which was assigned to keep me from getting out of the village, and the "Friends and Relatives Group," which included members of my extended family and colleagues of my fourth brother. Fourth Brother and others droned on dutifully about why I should give up my work and how well I would be rewarded if only I would obey the wishes of the party. I ignored them.

Then there was the "United Front Group." Composed of fifty government and party cadres, its job was to spread propaganda against me, a ridiculously large effort, given the small size of Dongshigu. In teams of two, the cadres visited almost every family in the village, telling my relatives, friends, and neighbors how to interpret the case of native son Chen Guangcheng. Everyone knew that I had traveled to America in my effort to learn more about disabled people's rights and that I had talked with a lot of foreigners over the years. But it was inconceivable that a poor blind boy from the countryside had done all this on his own; the only possible explanation was that I was a spy sent by the United States to expose China's failures, a traitor who had taken American money and had suspicious foreign contacts.

Every villager had to sit and listen to the lies spread by the United Front Group. In 2005, the party was using methods identical to those deployed with such grim success during the Cultural Revolution, which were designed to instill enmity between friends and divide families. But people are not so naïve nowadays, and for the most part the villagers didn't believe what the party cadres told them. Some villagers were intimidated and afraid to have open contact with me, but many would find an excuse to visit us or other close relatives at their homes to let us know what was being said about us.

For a while I was able to take a few calls from the media, but on September 9 the phone line was cut a few yards outside our front gate. Initially I had hoped my cell phone would work, but only one day later it became clear that the cadres were jamming our signal with devices stationed at a neighbor's house. The guards also began refusing to let us leave to buy food; before long, only my mother was allowed out. At several points our food supply grew dangerously low.

Domestically, my case was subject to a media blackout as a result of both official mandate and self-censorship on the part of Chinese journalists, who were understandably afraid to write about me. One young journalist named Yang Ziyun did manage to publish an article in a small magazine affiliated with the Ministry of Justice called *Legal Life*. She suffered immense pressure from having written the piece, we later learned, while the Linyi branch of the party ordered the article removed from the magazine's website and all print copies destroyed. Before its disappearance, however, Third Brother was able to get a copy of the magazine, and he made a few hundred photocopies of the article for us. He and other villagers handed out copies at the market, and also distributed the article to any guards who seemed curious about who we were. Whenever possible, we tried to enhance their understanding of the law and, as a result, some of the guards later quit their jobs.

One day in late September, I was resting in our kitchen building when I heard a crowd swelling into our yard. I barely had time to react before a number of guards locked Weijing inside our main house and hustled me into a car. After taking me to the police station for questioning, they demanded that I confess that I had "leaked state secrets"; they also wanted me to tell them how I had done it. "Put the blame on that lawyer Teng Biao and you'll be fine," said one of the interrogators. They clearly expected that I would betray my friend at the slightest threat.

While I was away being questioned, our house was pillaged. Without even the pretense of a search warrant, a squad of cadres, officials, and policemen rifled through our home, searching everywhere for "evidence" of my crimes. Anything written in English was carted off, although most of it was just brochures and materials from the disability organizations we had visited while in America. Once the cadres had taken everything they wanted, the guards brought me home.

After filing a report with their superiors, the cadres were told that their "evidence" proved nothing and that I didn't appear to have done anything wrong. Soon members of the Relatives Group started coming to me with extravagant offers of hush money, hoping I'd keep quiet about my treatment. The township alone would pay me 300,000 yuan, they said, quickly upping the figure to 500,000 when I remained steadfastly silent. I would also get a million yuan from the county, they added eagerly, as long as I agreed to sign a document saying that I would cease the work I had been doing.

As I told them repeatedly, I was interested in only two things. First, I wanted the cadres and officials who had kidnapped, detained, and tortured me to be held accountable under the law. Second, I insisted that the violent treatment meted out to victims of the family planning campaigns be investigated and prosecuted. Whether anyone ever paid the least bit of attention to my words I will never know.

By now the guards were always with us. Just outside our yard stood the hired thugs, all of them ready to commit violence at any time. Stationed beyond them were the township cadres and officials, sitting on benches and blocking all possible access points to the house. The next layer of surveillance was made up of police and public security officials; they secured the village entry points. Last came the security and traffic police; their job was to take up positions on the main road and keep visitors, journalists, lawyers, and observers of any kind from getting anywhere near us. Consider the absurdity of this sprawling operation: the government had created an entire anti-Guangcheng industry, all with the aim of controlling one blind, nonviolent man.

Despite the blockade and the media blackout, numerous friends and supporters were aware of our situation, and some of them dared to travel to Dongshigu to see us; all of them suffered physical violence as a result. In early October, three of my lawyer friends—Xu Zhiyong, Li Fangping, and Li Subin—came from Beijing to see me, making it as far as the village entrance. With the help of a number of relatives and villagers, I forced my way past the dozen guards outside our yard, and Xu Zhiyong and I were able to exchange a few words before being dragged apart. The guards, grasping at any excuse to get my friends out of the village, told them to go to the Shuanghou township offices to discuss my situation, but when the three attorneys arrived there, they were told that they couldn't intervene because my case now concerned "state secrets." After returning to Dongshigu to again attempt to see me, they were chased by police officers, dressed as thugs, who yelled at them and hit them, trying to get a reaction. A police car followed behind: my friends knew that if they resisted at all they would be grabbed and detained. Eventually they had no choice but to return to Beijing.

This pattern repeated itself ten days later when two activist scholars came down from Beijing, saying they wanted to see Kesi on her one hundredth day. I heard a commotion outside the yard, and the sounds of guards beating people up. When I rushed out to try to help, the hooligans immediately turned their assault on me; someone punched me in the eye, and the fragments from my glasses cut deeply into my face. Then, after knocking me down, the guards kicked me. Two-year-old Kerui, who saw them beating me up, became frightened and started crying.

In late November, on the one-year anniversary of my father's death, my captors allowed me to visit his grave together with my family. As we made our way to the graveyard, we were shocked by the scene: guards and cadres were everywhere, some dotting the landscape along the road, others following us to the grave site and then standing next to us, taunting us and staring. Later we were told that more than five hundred people—including the entire Yinan County People's Court and procuratorate's office, as well as public security, party, and government officials—were involved in this security operation. Clearly, party officials had made careful preparations for the event; fearful that we would try to communicate with friends while outside our home, they made it impossible for anyone to get near us. Their intrusion on our private moment of mourning and remembrance was infuriating.

As autumn rolled into winter, Weijing and I remained captive in our own home, while the village itself was under a kind of siege. Nerves were on edge; the village seemed to be reaching a boiling point, and there were more and more confrontations between villagers and guards. Over Chinese New Year, when family and friends visit respected village elders, hundreds of villagers—nearly 80 percent of the village, we calculated—came to visit our house to honor my septuagenarian mother, despite the obvious danger of doing so. But the crowds were so large that the guards had no choice but to let people in.

During that New Year holiday, my nephew Chen Hua, who lived

adjacent to our home and who had helped with the family planning investigation, became impatient with the guards for piling equipment, including some stoves and several large umbrellas, in front of his door. When he moved the equipment to make it easier for relatives to visit on this important festival, he angered the guards terribly. In recent months, he had already gotten into a series of skirmishes with them, and on February 3 he was detained. No one had any idea where he had gone. The message was clear: anyone who tried to help us would be punished.

Chen Hua's wife, desperate to find out what had happened, came to our house to question the guards stationed outside, but their response was to surround her, threatening violence. I heard her wailing and rushed out, as did a number of our neighbors, and we arrived just in time to prevent their assault. The neighbors and I then headed down to the village government office to demand an explanation for Chen Hua's detention. The guards attempted to block us every step of the way, pushing us and pulling at our clothes, but as more and more villagers joined our ranks we were able to force our way through.

A heavy snow was falling as the sky darkened into night. By now almost the entire village had swarmed out, including Chen Hua's elderly grandmother, who soon collapsed, sick with worry and anger. The villagers asked to use one of the guards' cars to bring her to the hospital, but the guards ignored the request.

Taking advantage of the darkness, the thugs began throwing stones at the villagers, and one person was struck on the head. The villagers erupted. "You've been here for so long, and we haven't lifted a finger," they shouted. "Not only are you not protecting us from anything—as you claim—you're actually hurting us!" A crowd of villagers rushed to the village entrance and overturned two cars used by public security officials, rolling them into a nearby gulch.

In the midst of this melee, and with the help of several villagers, I led Chen Hua's grandmother to the nearby home of my cousin Chen Guangyu, where together we took refuge. Guangyu guarded the door, holding an ax. But the guards never tried to enter the house, and I ended up staying there for nearly a month, despite the infuriating pressure from Guangyu's relatives, who came to the house to "encourage"

Guangyu to pressure me to return to my home. At several points I stopped eating, in solidarity with a hunger strike relay then unfolding across eighteen provinces and major cities in China, led by the activist Gao Zhisheng in protest of the center's use of violence.

As the weeks went on, the work teams continued to vilify me in the most ridiculous terms, telling villagers that I had luxury offices and apartments in Beijing and Shanghai, that they had found nine million yuan in a bank account of mine, and that a further six million yuan was unaccounted for. Even more absurdly, they spoke of a sum of ten million U.S. dollars that was secretly being paid to me—more spy money from America, of course.

On March 11, around seven p.m., Guangyu left his house to buy cigarettes at a small village shop near his home. Four hooded men instantly overtook him and assaulted him with wooden clubs, leaving his face, neck, and arms bloodied and bruised. The police stationed nearby did not intervene, and the thugs quickly ran off and dissolved into the ranks of guards ranged around the house. They knew he had been protecting me, and they were hoping that his beating would force me to leave his home.

Their tactic worked. When I learned what had happened, I couldn't restrain myself and immediately went outside with Guangyu and Third Brother, determined to report these violations of Chinese law to the township and county cadres closest at hand. Weijing came over from our house, carrying little Kesi, and together we headed to the government office in the nearby village of Yinghou, where our captors had moved their base of operations. (The government office in Dongshigu was very close to Guangyu's house, and the authorities had decided to put some distance between us and them so we wouldn't get wind of their planning.) When we got to the Yinghou village office, we saw that it was crammed with a number of beds, which we understood to have been put there to house the people carrying out our illegal detention. Only two men were present, and when we told them what had happened and demanded that they find out who had beaten up Guangyu, they responded with complete indifference. We decided to walk to the road and flag down a bus bound for either Jinan or Beijing. In one of these two cities, we would bring this latest atrocity and my illegal detention to the attention of higher authorities, petitioning for justice much as I had in the past.

Not long after our little band had gathered at a spot on the side of National Route 205, several police cars drove up and blocked the road. We were abruptly surrounded by a crowd of some seventy or eighty people, many of whom had followed us from our village. My mother came up on the side of the road holding Kesi, who was crying for Wei-jing. Moments later, the police grabbed Guangyu, Third Brother, and me; we were separated and hustled into the police cars. They threw my mother and my wife, still holding Kesi, into a roadside ditch.

And then, just like that, we were gone.

Later that same day, I found myself back at the notorious Victoria Resort. The authorities held me there for several weeks under a nearly constant barrage of interrogations and torture sessions. They tied me to a chair and restrained me further with chains. "Tell us everything you've done and don't leave anything out," they demanded. I was kept awake for days at a time in the hope that I would confess something that could be used against me, but for now all they had was the absurd charge of "disturbing traffic." "Why did you cause a traffic jam on a national road?" they asked, referring to the blockade they had created by surrounding us with their parade of vehicles. "I didn't cause that traffic jam," I replied. "That was you!"

Again I went on a hunger strike to protest their illegal actions, this time for three days. A group of doctors from a nearby hospital was brought in to force-feed me, but after my captors agreed to remove my chains I began to eat on my own. Then, a few days later, the guards refused to give me anything but water, and before long I was barely able to move. "You might be resisting, but you're just a little pebble, and we're going crush you into dust," one of the interrogators told me. Another frequently poked a stick deep into my ears, causing excruciating pain.

I was still being held without a formal charge, in contravention of Chinese law. I had no means of contacting anyone, and no one but my captors knew where I was. They lied and claimed ignorance of my whereabouts to my family and my lawyer friends, who, I later learned, were frantically trying to locate me. Toward the end of March, Weijing wrote a letter to President Hu Jintao and Premier Wen Jiabao. "Here in this place," she implored, "a Chinese citizen has been persecuted merely for speaking the truth. Do you know how many people live in a state of fear each day? Or how many people are wronged and suffer in despair? Or how many wives and mothers . . . weep while uneasily awaiting their husbands and children?" The letter was signed, "A Chinese citizen, Chen Guangcheng's wife, Yuan Weijing." She received no reply.

In early April, after three weeks at the Victoria Resort, I was packed into a car once again. "We're taking you to another place," my captors told me, but they wouldn't say where. I was being disappeared into a "police training center," a so-called black jail, an extralegal detention center run by security forces. Such facilities are not uncommon in China these days; ordinary citizens often vanish into thin air, disappearing into zones beyond the law.

I was kept on the second floor in a small room with a single bed and a bathroom. At the time, I seemed to be the only person being held there. More than twenty people watched me; they worked in four groups, all drawn from the Shuanghou government offices and the Yinan County Public Security Bureau. The guards sat in the room with me all day and refused to tell me where we were.

It's difficult to describe to a sighted person how oppressive and terrifying it was to be kept in this kind of isolation. Confined to this small room, watched constantly by guards I could not see or interact with, I had no way to assess my environment beyond the four walls I could feel. I felt completely immobilized—even when I got up to use the bathroom I would be immediately surrounded by the guards, who would rush in front of me and block the room's exit. The windows remained closed, and the stale air grew thicker and mustier by the day. I had no idea how my family was faring or for how long I would be kept in this place—I hoped every moment would bring relief and freedom, but each hour and day dragged on like an eternity, with almost no variation. Though I was not physically tortured while being held here, the psychological stress was nearly unbearable.

I strained my ears to pick up any hint about my surroundings.

Once, I realized that someone had opened a window—just a crack, but it was enough to tell me a great deal about where I was. I got a whiff of fresh air, and it brought the sweet scent of cherry and apricot blossoms a bit past their prime. I heard the muted sounds of life beyond the glass, and they gave me a precise imprint of the environment: there were frogs croaking and birds singing, and for a moment I caught the whooshing sound of a bird in flight, one I recognized. It was the *shagu-liu*, a bird that lives near fresh water and makes its nest in the soft sand of a riverbank. A little while later, I was able to discern the words of an announcement over a distant village loudspeaker, and that's how I figured out that the detention center was just outside a small riverside village called Xiaohe. Soon the window was closed again, but at least I now had a name for where I was.

Sometimes I tried to chat up the guards a bit, since we were together for days on end. I wanted to see what they were about, hoping that at least one of them might be harboring an unspoken sympathy for me. They were all relatively young—one was just a teenager, and the others were in their twenties. I did my best to draw them out, sometimes asking about their lives and how they came to get these jobs. "Just needed work" was the most common reply.

Some of the guards and officials seemed to wonder at the reasonableness of holding me for so long. In mid-May, I overheard a man named Zhang, the head of the group of county officials and police officers in charge of my capture, on his cell phone as he walked down the hall. "It's already been two months," he said to his caller. "You should just send him back. What are you keeping him here for?"

I wanted desperately to find out more about my circumstances. On one occasion, two guards stepped outside for a smoke, leaving two others in the room. On a whim, I asked the younger of the two remaining guards to please go downstairs and see if he could get a tomato—they should be in season, I said. I had a hunch that the remaining guard—somewhat older than the others—was on my side. As soon as the two of us were alone, I moved to stand up, but he immediately instructed me to sit, saying that there were cameras watching us. Then he told me that my family was still the same—still under house arrest—and that the higher-ups were debating what to do with me.

That was as much as he was able to tell me before the other guard came back in, tomato in hand.

The one bit of relief during this otherwise terrifying time came from the television in the room, which the guards left on much of the time. The station they usually turned to happened to be playing episodes from four of China's greatest literary classics: *Journey to the West*, *Romance of the Three Kingdoms*, *The Dream of the Red Chamber*, and *Outlaws of the Marsh*. I had known these masterpieces for ages, ever since my father had read them aloud to me; now, confined and alone, I encountered a strange and unexpected opportunity to drink them in once again and recall the presence of my father by my side.

As time went on, my health deteriorated. The hot peppers the guards put in my food upset my digestive system, and their brittle, dry skins sliced and burned my throat. I developed debilitating diarrhea and demanded a doctor, but my captors ignored me. I grew increasingly angry and agitated. I often couldn't sleep at night, and if I slept at all, I would have bad dreams. Sometimes I complained to the guards about my inhumane treatment; in my mind, I argued with them constantly, yelling at the men who had confined me, who did whatever they wanted, who acted with complete impunity. I rebelled in my very bones at the lawlessness around me.

I often wondered how my family and friends were getting on in my absence. Later I learned that Third Brother and Chen Guangyu, both of whom had been arrested with me in March, were also being held in a detention center, and that several other family planning activists had been sentenced to jail terms, some for as much as seven months. Weijing, meanwhile, continued to live under house arrest, even though I was gone. Every day she went to the gate, hoping to be allowed to go out or at least get word about where I was, but to no avail. In May, Li Jinsong and the other attorneys retained by my family went to the Public Security Bureau to demand that they be allowed to see me. The authorities insisted—straight-faced—that they were not keeping me in custody. Many friends and supporters tried to bring attention to my plight by writing articles and letters, signing petitions, organizing missions to visit Dongshigu, and printing my face on T-shirts. A number of international organizations, governments, and foreign newspapers expressed their ongoing concern.

Finally, on June 10, 2006, after three months in a black jail and seven months of illegal house arrest, formal charges were brought against me. The head of the local criminal police squad, He Yong, came to my room with two others to "announce their decision to detain me," as though my detention were beginning that very day, as though the months of house arrest had never taken place. "Detain me on what basis?" I asked. "Disrupting traffic and destroying public property," he said, reading off the current date.

"And what about the last ten months of arbitrary detention?" I asked.

He hesitated, as though thinking of a response. "I can't do anything about that," he replied. "I just do what I'm told."

"Why don't you try doing fewer bad things?" I asked him. "It would be good for you." They tried to make me sign my name to validate the detention notice, but I refused.

The next day, Yinan County officials at last informed Weijing that they had me in custody and that I was being held under criminal detention, pending trial. Seven or eight cadres came to our home, pounded on the door, and demanded that Weijing sign her name to a detention notice. When she asked where the authorities had been keeping me over the past three months, they waved her off. "Don't worry about that," they said. "Just sign your name and be done with it." "Unless you answer my question," Weijing replied, "I'm not going to sign." Realizing that they wouldn't get anywhere with her, the officials left.

Shortly after being formally charged, I was transferred from unofficial detention in Xiaohe to the very official and very overcrowded Yinan County Detention Center, which had been designed to incarcerate 80 people but was packed with some 270 of us. The guards brought me directly to an interrogation room where they chained and handcuffed me to an iron chair, and where I remained for eight or nine hours as they pounded me with questions. Later that night, three police guards took me to my cell—Room No. 1, which was directly across from the guards' office. As they swung open the iron door and pushed me in, one shouted a warning for my new cellmates to leave me alone and go to sleep, a sure sign that my situation in the detention center was unusual.

Each fourteen-by-eight-foot cell in the detention center normally held at least two dozen detainees, who had to sleep in shifts or face punishment for resting out of turn. But when I arrived, there were only six other prisoners in the room, and they had obviously been hand-picked by the detention center authorities. None of these small-time criminals, thieves, and dethroned corrupt officials said anything to me for days; once again I was surrounded by people but ensconced in a deadening, terrifying silence and could learn nothing about my circumstances. Later, on the few occasions when one of my fellow prisoners would slip me some information on the sly, he would quickly be replaced. We were constantly monitored by surveillance cameras and watched by guards stationed elsewhere in the building.

Stretching the length of the cell and taking up most of the floor space was a raised, concrete sleeping platform covered by a sheet of plywood. Two quilts had been placed on the platform, marking where I was to stay; squeezing between two other inmates, I lay down at once and tried to sleep. Unnervingly, two men stood right next to my head, watching me; I learned later that a security camera had been placed directly above me on the ceiling. As I usually did, I made a mental note of the four points of the compass: my head pointed west, while my feet, resting against the wall, pointed east. Our room was quiet, and I listened to the chatter of the guards across the hall, my mind swirling with complicated emotions.

After a few hours of restless sleep, I got up and made my way around the room, tripping over the shoes at the base of the platform and feeling my way to the far wall. There I found a small window with reinforced steel bars, as well as a little door leading to a fetid toilet; the toilet let to another door, which was locked, and which I later learned opened onto a tiny outdoor area called the "wind space." The space was essentially a cage, with iron bars arching from the wall above our heads to the ground; beyond the bars was a courtyard, but we were never permitted to go there. It would be two or three months before the guards allowed me to enter the wind space, and they rarely let me stay there for any length of time.

Over the course of my first two weeks in the detention center, I was interrogated relentlessly by public security. By Chinese law, public security officials are not supposed to go beyond a prison's "second gate," the gate that leads to the interior of the jail. This law is based on a justified fear that allowing officials to have access to detainees could lead to bribery, extortion, and other evils. But in the Yinan County Detention Center, this law was often violated—officials came to the jail's interior almost every day in a never-ending attempt to extract confessions.

In my case, the officials kept me handcuffed and chained to an iron chair for twelve or thirteen hours at a time, day after day. I found the whole process disgusting, and from the start I decided to keep silent as a form of protest. These sessions verged on farce. For the first three days, my interrogators put on a good show, filming the proceedings and shouting at me with great energy and arrogance. "Don't you know you've become a target for attack by our Communist Party dictatorship," said one of them, "and that your only hope now is to seek clemency?" "Once we're done with you," said another, "we'll go after your wife—don't forget that she's fair game as soon as little Kesi has been weaned." A third interrogator said, "You should know that people die in this detention center all the time."

After a few days of this, their enthusiasm for this pointless exercise started to wane, and they fell in to chatting among themselves, discussing matters such as their personal insurance policies or whether, in keeping with current nationalist sentiments, they should boycott Japanese imports. One day a group of officials came to inspect the detention center, and the guards pumped themselves up again. Slapping the table and shouting themselves hoarse, they acted their part to perfection, but I wasn't the least bit cowed by their aggressive behavior.

The name "detention center" sounds innocent enough, and most detainees are technically "suspects" who have not yet been convicted. But in China, most detention centers, including Yinan's, treat detainees as though they are convicted criminals, and in Yinan officials broke any number of laws on a daily basis, including using prisoners to control and punish other prisoners. They also authorized forced labor, mostly the primitive kind of repetitive manual labor that can be done in a cell.

Some prisoners wove flowers together into wreaths; some plaited twine; others folded and packaged the cheap plastic gloves that are sometimes used in East Asia for eating oily foods such as spare ribs. Those who didn't finish their work would have their food withheld or their hands chained to the bars of the cell window. I refused to work and, given my disability, the guards didn't try to force me. I spent my days lying down or sitting inside the cell.

One of the most flagrant violations of the law involved my own status. One day when I was in the cell with just one other prisoner, he told me that there was a list of prison regulations printed on a poster hanging outside the guards' office. Peering through the small window in our door, he read it aloud: "According to the Official Detention Center Regulations, the following types of people may not be detained: (1) Blind people; (2) Pregnant women," and so on. Such is the hypocrisy of the Communist Party: it can completely ignore its own rules, even when they are posted in plain sight.

In one thing I was fortunate: I had a decent warden, a sympathetic man named Wang Guijin. One day early on he brought me into his office for a "number chat," as such things were called, detainees being the numbers. After closing his door so it was just the two of us, the warden told me that he personally felt no ill will toward me and was, in fact, an admirer of what I had been doing. "I know you haven't done anything wrong," he said, and from the gentle rhythms in the depths of his voice I could tell he meant it. During our conversation, I mentioned that we detainees didn't have enough boiled water to drink and that this was likely a cause of many of our health problems. Soon after our conversation, he purchased several more small coal burners and ordered more shipments of coal briquettes. While we were out in the yard, the work numbers boiled our water on these stoves, providing us with more clean water to drink.

Three of my attorneys did manage to visit me in the detention center a few times, again braving threats and the possibility of bodily harm. Unfortunately, we were never able to discuss anything of import; each time my lawyers visited, the guards said they would end our conversation if I answered even the most basic questions, including where I had been held prior to being taken to the Yinan County Detention Center. Two of my lawyer friends, Teng Biao and Xu Zhiyong, were specifically warned to stay off the case, but they refused to do so. Another lawyer, Li Jinsong, gave me a vital piece of information: according to Chinese law, my trial would not be legitimate if I wasn't being represented by a lawyer of my own choosing. He told me to insist on having my own legal representation, a shrewd piece of advice that later proved valuable.

CHAPTER NINE

Trial and Imprisonment

On August 18, 2006, my first trial began—and quickly ended. I was being tried for two absurd charges: disrupting traffic on March 11, the day the police and the other thugs surrounded us on National Route 205, and destroying public property on February 5, the night the two public security cars were overturned, which they'd decided was my fault.

In order to prevent my friends and supporters from attending the trial, the authorities repeatedly changed the date, and when the Yinan County People's Court finally started the proceedings, neither Weijing nor my lawyers were allowed to attend. I had no idea what was in store for me; I had not yet received any information about the accusations against me, nor had I been allowed to prepare for the trial with my attorneys. I later learned that one of my lawyers, Xu Zhiyong, had been roughed up by some suspicious-looking men in Yinan: they planted a wallet in his bag, accused him of stealing it, then held him in custody for the entire court proceedings. My other attorneys—including Li Jinsong, Li Fangping, and Teng Biao—were not even allowed into the courtroom as auditors. A day before the trial, Gao Zhisheng and dozens of other supporters put on T-shirts emblazoned with an image of my face and gathered around the courthouse, but the shirts were torn from their bodies and destroyed. Many other friends, supporters, and protesters who had come to Yinan were taken into police custody, locked in hotel rooms, or sent home.

I knew nothing of these things as I was led into the courthouse that afternoon, dressed in my detention center–issued clothing with my hands cuffed behind my back. Guards shut me in a small room next to the courtroom, whereupon my two court-appointed lawyers, Lawyer Zhu and Lawyer Li—the two clowns of this kangaroo court—were brought in for a perfunctory introduction. "Excuse me," I said, "I have lawyers, and I don't need you." They laughed sheepishly, replying that my lawyers didn't want to represent me, which by any account was simply a lie.

The trial was a farce. When I demanded that my attorneys be present to represent me, the trial judge, Wang Jun, retorted that my lawyers didn't want to see me. From that point on, I remained largely silent. I refused to participate in a trial where I was denied representation by my own attorneys and that otherwise was unlawful.

As the afternoon progressed, Lawyer Zhu and Lawyer Li offered no defense on my behalf; in response to the accusations made by the court, they simply said that they "had no objections." Judge Wang asked me if I had anything to add, and initially I maintained my silent protest. But when he accused me of tacitly agreeing to the accusations against me, I could barely contain my ire. "You're all a bunch of thugs, a bunch of bandits!" I yelled. The judge ordered that I be removed, and I was led away by two court policemen. That was the end of my so-called trial.

A few days later, before the sentence was officially announced, the deputy warden of the detention center, Wang Zhijun, called me into his office. "The trial was a great miscarriage of justice," he said, "and you have been given a much longer sentence—seven times longer, in fact—than would normally be handed down for the crime of which you have been accused." He didn't specify what the sentence was, but I immediately requested that he tell the court that I demanded to see my lawyers, my real lawyers in Beijing, so we could plan our appeal.

Two days after the deputy warden's visit, I learned the verdict: four years and three months in prison. The two clowns again came to see me and asked if I intended to appeal. "Of course," I replied. Two more days passed, and then the presiding judge, Wang Jun himself, came to see me. He told me that everyone knew my case was a fraud but there was nothing he could do about it. "Sooner or later," he said, striking the table with his hand, "the truth of your case will be revealed to the world. I personally was not against you, but there was nothing I could do." I asked him why in the world he had given me such an inflated sentence; he replied by reminding me that the court had to listen to party orders. He left me with one piece of advice: urging me not to be silent, he told me to speak up for myself during the appeals process, however desperate the odds.

I remained in detention for two more months, awaiting news. Then, on October 30, I was told that the appeals process undertaken on my behalf by my lawyers had led to an acknowledgment by the Linyi Intermediate People's Court that the first trial had been illegitimate. The verdict was canceled, a new judge from within the Yinan County People's Court was assigned, and a retrial date was set. Most likely, party officials were worried that, in the light of the foreign media's scrutiny of my case, their breach of justice had been too egregious to leave standing—this was their opportunity to make it appear that they operated under some semblance of the rule of law. This time they would cross their *t*'s and dot their *i*'s, but I was not the least bit optimistic about the outcome. I prepared myself for another show.

The second trial commenced on November 27. When we arrived at the court, the guards took me to a small side room and handcuffed me to a chair. I could tell that the officials felt a lot of anxiety: people outside the room hurried up and down the hall, sometimes whispering to each other. On the first day of the retrial, Elder Brother and Fourth Brother were allowed to attend, while my mother, Third Brother, and my wife were called in as witnesses. The other forty or fifty people present were all cadres and officials sent by the party.

For this second trial, the court tried its best to make the proceedings look aboveboard. The judge even used a gavel, which was unusual for the local courts; typically, judges would just bang on the table with their fists. Once again, I was charged with two crimes: disrupting traffic and destroying public property. From where I sat in the side room I heard the judge bang the gavel, and then someone yelled out, "Bring in the suspected criminal Chen Guangcheng!" I walked in with my head high: I knew I'd done nothing wrong.

My lawyers, Li Jinsong and Li Fangping, argued powerfully on my behalf, exposing the injustice of the entire process: the ludicrous investigation, the sham evidence, my unlawful detention. I described my house arrest, the interrogation I'd undergone at the Victoria Resort, and the many months during which I'd been held without charges at the so-called police training center. I demanded that an investigation into these brazenly illegal acts be opened.

Not surprisingly, the court declared that no investigation was needed, and then the three prosecutors unleashed a series of charades. They played video footage that purported to show me disturbing traffic on National Route 205 outside Dongshigu. The video was entirely black and contained no sign of my voice or image. Then they presented the fabricated testimony of ambulance personnel, who claimed that we had blocked a pregnant woman who was trying to make her way to the hospital; the woman's mother supposedly even knelt before me and begged me to let them by. They showed a sham video in which Third Brother "admitted" that I had forced him to help me cause a disturbance on the night of February 5, a false confession that I knew had been obtained while he was subjected to torture and abuse. In fact, on the day in question, Third Brother was in Linyi, not in our village.

I was enraged when I heard my brother's testimony, knowing that it had been obtained under torture. "Hooligans!" I yelled out. "You're all a bunch of hooligans!" The judge and everyone else became agitated, declaring that they were acting in accordance with the law and claiming that no one in the courtroom was a hooligan. They had no idea how ridiculous they sounded.

Attorney Li Jinsong walked out in protest, leaving Li Fangping alone with me. The court recessed, and a number of people took a break, leaving primarily party people, who were there to fill the ranks and keep an eye on the proceedings. In a loud voice I quoted a Chinese saying: "If heaven does wrong, it is as it should be; if people do wrong, they will not survive." In other words, you can't do wrong and not expect to be punished. As soon as I uttered these words, a party official standing behind me shouted, "Take him away!" Objecting, I said, "The court is in recess—you can't force me to do anything." The man yelled, "I can make you do anything I want. Take him downstairs." Two bailiffs had to obey but seemed somewhat reluctant.

Once we were downstairs, one of the bailiffs said, "It's cold down here, whereas there is heat up in the courtroom, but you could see we had no choice." I asked the bailiff his name, but he didn't dare tell me. Then I said, "You saw it all, the good and the bad—you can judge for yourself who is right and who is wrong." He said, "We do know, at least a little, but we can't say more—we're just here because we need the work." I asked him what he made per day, and he said, "Not much. We used to be in the army," he added. "When we came home, we couldn't find work, so we got jobs here so we could make a living."

That first day of the retrial ended with our renewed demand that the court immediately conduct an investigation into my illegal detention and all the evidence surrounding my case. Again the court refused. On the second day, Weijing, my mother, and I were allowed to exchange a few words. Our reunion that day was brief, bitter, and thwarted. Weijing wanted to take my hand but was pushed away by the guards. She told me that my brothers had been threatened and that the authorities had sought to compel them to terminate their relationship with me. Then she said that some time ago, my mother had broken a rib and had been lying in bed for months, leaving Weijing to care for both her and Kesi, who was now almost a year and a half old. My mother told me that she had not been able to get out of bed for a long time. She also said that Weijing had held Kesi in one arm while feeding my mother noodles with the other hand. The child was small, my mother said, and if you put her down she would cry; with all that was happening, Weijing couldn't bear to hear her daughter crying. "Weijing," my mother said, "has taken care of me as if she were my own daughter."

Soon two bailiffs dragged me away, and Weijing and my mother were lost to me.

The day after the trial, my lawyers went over the stenographer's notes of the previous day's arguments to make sure they were accurate, and by that afternoon my retrial was officially over. As we were leaving the court, Third Brother stood at the bottom of the stairs holding Kesi out to me. "Hold her as you walk," he said, but the court police pulled me away. Seeing me in handcuffs, Kesi shrank away in fear, buried her face in Third Brother's shoulder, and cried. Then, as I was led away, Teng Biao, whom I hadn't seen in more than a year, came up to me. Blocked from assisting me during the second trial, he had come from Beijing to Linyi anyway. Now he placed a bunch of leaves tied together with a string in my hand, saying, "Your daughter made this bouquet for you—take it, and enjoy it."

My heart overflowed. I held the offering in my hand and thought, One day I will bring this bunch of leaves out of jail with me, when I am free. My fingers counted nine large leaves, and by their shapes I identified them as from a *fatong* tree, a type of plane tree. As two court bailiffs pulled me toward a waiting van, I held Kesi's gift carefully.

The bailiffs tried to keep Teng Biao from saying anything else to me, but just before they pushed me into the van to return to detention, he called out, "Guangcheng, remember, the truth is on your side!"

With the two bailiffs at my arms, I turned my head and replied, "Don't worry, brother, I won't fall. I won't be pushed down—I will only become stronger!"

On December 1, the court pronounced its verdict. Judged guilty as charged, I was again sentenced to four years and three months in prison for "intentionally damaging property and gathering crowds to disturb transport order."

That afternoon, I met with my lawyers. Shaken and discouraged, they apologized to me over and over. I smiled and told them not to worry. "Don't think of me as being locked in jail," I said. "I'll still be fighting for human rights. Besides," I joked, "after having been under house arrest for so long, what's another four years?"

My lawyers told me they would appeal the verdict, but I did not believe the appeal would succeed. As we parted, I said, "Never give up. Never give up the yearning to find goodness in us all or the belief in the strength of the rule of law. Never give up the search for truth and the eternal quest for justice." I also asked them to thank my supporters, both in China and abroad; to thank my wife, who had walked with me unshaken in her commitment through countless hardships; and, lastly, to thank my aging mother.

On December 22, the Linyi Intermediate People's Court dismissed our appeal. Soon after the judge announced the decision, someone quietly told me that my lawyers would come see me in a few days. On December 27, Li Jinsong and Li Fangping again set out on the trip from Beijing to Linyi, traveling by bus. In the middle of the night, as the bus neared Linyi, it was pulled over by two unmarked cars. A group of men boarded the bus and beat the two attorneys with metal clubs. Both attorneys were badly injured, with Li Fangping sustaining a skull fracture. The attorneys repeatedly called the police, but when they arrived on the scene they did nothing, and left soon after. Li Jinsong called the city, provincial, and national level police departments, but none of them did anything either. The message, however, was clear: my attorneys could no longer meet with me safely. The police had effectively chased them out of Shandong.

On February 15, 2007, I was transferred to Linyi Prison, there to remain for forty-three months. The prison complex held about five thousand prisoners and was ringed by a wall over fifteen feet high, with guard posts on every corner. Within the complex were a number of large buildings—factories, really—where the prisoners performed different tasks. Long-term inmates might be responsible for building fire trucks, while those in for less time might make the little paper sacks in which containers of milk are often marketed and sold in China or Christmas lights for export. There was even an ironworks at the prison.

On my first day, I was led into the section set aside for new inmates and given a cursory checkup by inmates who had once been doctors but were now serving time. Soon enough, I learned that in fact the entire prison was run by inmates, called "work numbers." They operated under the supervision of distant overlords—the guards and wardens who were all simply known as cadres and whose separate world lay beyond a yellow line painted on the floor, which no prisoner could cross without permission.

The work numbers patted me down, made me remove my clothes, and took them away. They gave me my prison uniform: a blue-and-white striped nylon shirt and a pair of pants with a white reflective strip running down the length of the outseam, for ease of spotting at night. Here, unlike in the detention center, pants with belt loops and a button closure were allowed. The inmates also gave me a thin jacket and hat and cheap canvas sneakers. All of our clothes were made by prisoners at another jail in Shandong.

As they patted me down, the work numbers saw Kesi's gift. When I had returned to the detention center after the retrial, I had taken a piece of thread out of my blanket and tied it around the bouquet. I was worried that the leaves would dry out and get crushed, so I hung the bouquet on the iron bar running across the top of the windowsill, out of harm's way. Every two weeks the guards would sweep through the cells and turn everything inside out, looking for prohibited items. Each time they did, I would grab the bouquet and hold it in my hand, the only way I could protect it. Now, having carefully preserved Kesi's gift during my final two and a half months in the detention center, I was clutching it tightly.

"What are you doing with that?" the inmates asked roughly.

"My daughter gave me this," I answered.

For a moment they didn't respond. Finally, one said, "Well, if you're willing to hold on to it, go ahead."

Located on the first floor of the prison, my cell was about twenty feet by twenty feet and held thirty-seven inmates, with eleven bunk beds pressed together, only enough for twenty-two of us to sleep at a time. As a newcomer, I was forced to make my bed on the floor, lying down on an empty cement bag and a few rags that some of the other work numbers gave me. Besides the bunk beds, there was a shelf for our plastic washbasins and two large glass windows, which were closed off with iron bars. Outside was a prison walkway; I was sometimes able to speak with people who were coming and going if no one else was around. Facing the interior of the prison, there was a plywood door that opened to the hallway, and a small window in the wall next to it.

Our floor had a dozen or so cells; some were used as work rooms, others housed between one hundred and three hundred prisoners. There was a single bathroom at the end of the hall, with a row of faucets against one wall where we filled our washbasins every morning. The water was dirty and undrinkable, but some of the new arrivals weren't used to the lack of water and the constant thirst that resulted, so they drank it anyway. Behind the wall of faucets was a long open ditch that was used as a toilet.

About two weeks after I arrived, my initial cellmates, having learned the rules, were moved elsewhere to make room for yet more new prisoners. (For some reason, I was kept in the prison block reserved for recent arrivals during the entire length of my sentence.) Now, having no one else to compete with, I quickly claimed a bottom bunk. All the beds were rickety and stank with a smell that burned the nostrils and eyes, but any bed was better than the floor. For a few days I was left alone with the head of the new arrivals block, who lived in the cell indefinitely and whose job it was to instruct the newcomers on the prison regulations. It was clear that he had been instructed to stay away from me, and for a long time he spoke hardly a word in my direction.

Many of the regulations in the prison were illogical and completely unreasonable, designed to instill maximum obedience and fear. For instance, if a prisoner passed a guard on his way to a workroom and was holding a tool of any sort, the prisoner had to immediately throw the tool down and stand at attention, keeping at least fifteen feet from the guard, until the guard had moved on. If a prisoner needed to speak with prison police, he had to squat on the floor in deference. I refused to do any of these things, deciding that I didn't care what they did to me. Why should I follow such absurd rules and allow them further violations of my dignity?

This was the daily routine: at six in the morning we woke up, threw water on our faces, and immediately went to work. The Chinese prison system is called *laogai*, "reform through work," a forced, unpaid labor regime that does nothing but line the pockets of those who run the prisons. The work at the time of my imprisonment was packaging disposable chopsticks, slipping little paper or plastic sleeves over the cheap and splintery wood—up to five thousand pairs in a single day, once a prisoner became proficient. As at the detention center, they didn't know what to do with me. They made me sit next to those who were working, my body confined to a hard wooden bench whose every contour I soon memorized. Even if they had demanded I actually do the work, I would have refused.

At eight a.m. the new prisoner section was given breakfast: two small steamed buns per person, and on good days a bit of corn porridge. For this and all our meals, we were made to squat in two rows, face-to-face in the cement prison yard outside, while other work numbers placed the food before us. We had a few minutes to wolf the food down and clean our bowls before the work began again. Lunch was served only on weekdays, when we worked, and was little more than boiled, half-rotten cabbage, cooked in used, rancid oil with a little salt. Dinner, hardly more substantial than the other meals, came around six-thirty, followed by more work. At around eight p.m., we had twenty or thirty minutes to mill around the small prison yard or smoke or exercise—which was important, given the terrible health problems that resulted from sitting all day at repetitive, mind-numbing tasks. We then had thirty minutes during which the entire floor of prisoners—usually one hundred to two hundred people—had to wash their face and hands and brush their teeth at the row of taps.

Before my transfer from the detention center, my attorneys had written formal complaints to all levels of the court system, arguing that my conviction had been a miscarriage of justice. Once I arrived in prison, I expected to be able to discuss my case with a guard or warden, naïvely assuming that they would be able to help. But the prison hierarchy was fearsome and complicated, and an ordinary prisoner had as much chance of seeing a prison warden as a commoner once had of coming before the emperor.

I waited, but for days at a time I failed to encounter a single warden, let alone one with any authority. I had to use my ears and instincts, or else rely on the eyes of others, constantly asking if a guard was nearby. I soon understood that I would have to break through the prison's tightly organized hierarchy. First there were the "secondary guards," the inmates who ran things at the cadres' behest, beginning, in my case, with our group head. An "old number" responsible for thirty-five or forty new prisoners, he had assigned another prisoner—an "economic criminal" in his fifties—to take care of me, to help me at meals, and to lead me to the bathroom.

After I received my group head's approval, I would need approvals from the leader of my work team, the head of all the work teams, the head prisoner for the whole prison area, and the prisoner guard on duty, who controlled who came and went. Once I got approvals from the right people at all these levels, each one composed of prisoners, I would be given an opportunity to cross the yellow line and speak to an actual cadre. But what could an ordinary cadre—effectively just a guard—actually do for my case? He, in turn, would have to contact the party leader for our particular prison block, who would have to raise the issue with the assistant warden or overall warden at the prison, who might allow some document or a bit of news to be passed down the line. For a "new number," with no connections or relationships, the prospect of trying to break through all these layers was daunting.

During my first few weeks in prison, however, I was determined to get through to someone who mattered: how else would I ever be able to make an appeal to someone higher up? And my persistence, my absolute refusal to allow my case to simply disappear, did finally pay off. After endless delays and difficulties, I was led across the yellow line. I came before the cadre Chen Qingru with two straightforward requests: that I be able to contact my lawyers and that I be granted a meeting with the procuratorate staff here in the prison. The cadre understood that my case was unusual, and he agreed to report my demands to his superiors. He also said that I would have to dictate a letter to my lawyers, but this presented its own challenges since I was responsible for finding the paper to write it on and then locating a work number to draft it for me.

In early March, my mother and Weijing came to see me, with Kerui and Kesi in tow. The guards seemed to think I might have important connections on the outside, so they put us in an individual meeting room with no glass partition, a sofa, and a tea table. Even so, we were entirely surrounded by the same thugs who were keeping Weijing under house arrest back at home. Although no one besides my immediate family should have been let in, Weijing said the prison guards had let the thugs all pass, as though everyone was in cahoots.

Weijing tried to give me a radio, which should have been allowed by law, but the prison guards wouldn't let me keep it. As we adults talked back and forth, three-year-old Kerui was silent, sitting beside me on the couch holding an orange. I wanted nothing more than to take his hand and walk a few steps with him. I hadn't seen my son for over a year, and at my first family visit, my mother had said that he missed me terribly. Suddenly Kerui began pounding the orange against the arm of the sofa, over and over with all his might, his heart full of the formless rage of a child. When the meeting ended, about ten minutes later, I wanted so badly to hold Kesi, my little daughter, in my arms, but the prison guards denied me this, too.

Later that day, I learned that before our meeting had taken place, a call had come into the prison authorities from the Linyi Party Committee. Apparently it had asked about my current situation, and somehow the prison officials mistook this as an indication that I had powerful benefactors and should not be mistreated. As a result, I was relieved of the requirement that I sit every day beside my chopstick-bagging fellow prisoners, and although there weren't many places to go in that part of the prison, now I could at least come and go from my room as I pleased.

It might seem reasonable to believe that many of the prisoners had given up hope, and indeed some people do. But for me, hope remained a tangible thing; I did not yield it lightly, and it helped keep me going. In the worst case, I figured, I would have to serve out my entire sentence. But I also felt certain that there was very little possibility of it being extended. Meanwhile, I tried to learn as much as possible about my fellow inmates, at least those who were willing to talk to me. What were their experiences? Had they been tortured? I wanted to get an understanding of the entire system of lawless repression from the inside.

I was also determined to reestablish contact with the outside world. During those first few months, I fought to be able to get a phone card and use the prison phone to call home, just as other prisoners were able to do. In June, I finally placed a call to a niece who lived next door to us in Dongshigu, since the phone at home was still cut off. My niece called Weijing over, and she and I spoke briefly on what we hoped was an unmonitored line. Only a couple of minutes into the call, I used rudimentary English to tell Weijing, "Remember tell Jerry," referring to my hope that Professor Cohen might somehow help in my case. But with this bit of English, a risky attempt to skirt our auditors, the line was immediately cut. Not for fourteen months would I be allowed to make another call.

Months later, I was still waiting for a response to the letter I had dictated. By then, I had figured out how to reach the cadres' offices on my own, but one day in mid-June, the cadres ordered the work numbers to actively block my way, on the pretense that my hair had grown too long. The guards told me my head would have to be shaved, like those of the other prisoners. I countered that there was no law requiring prisoners to have their heads shaved; what's more, a prisoner's bald head signified guilt, and I had done nothing wrong. Finally they agreed that my hair could be cut shorter without actually being shaved, but once several work numbers started in, they quickly shaved all of the hair on one side of my head. I protested, saying I would go to the cadres and make them stop.

By now the prisoner lackeys were looking for any excuse to beat me up. I held them off, but when I reached the cadres I realized they would do nothing to stop the beating; on the contrary, they were more than willing to authorize it. More than a dozen work numbers grabbed me and dragged me back to the cell, where they vented their evil spirits in a surge of violence. In the lead was a murderer named Li, a vicious criminal, a man full of animal rage. He and six or seven other attackers kicked me and tore at me without mercy as some sixty inmates looked dumbly on; later, I heard that a senior cadre named Xu Weihua watched from a distance. Eventually, Li had the others drag me into another room, where every last hair on my head was shaved. Once they finished, my attackers stomped on my back, my legs, and my arms until I collapsed into a heap.

I will never forget that beating; my entire body was racked by searing pain, and it took me many weeks to recover. I kept some of the dried scabs from those weeks during the entire time I was in jail, imagining that somehow, someday, I could use them as evidence of this further crime that had been committed against me.

* * *

Nothing was ever done about my beating, of course. Not long afterward, Weijing came to visit me again; when she saw my cuts and bruises, she cried. Soon after, she got the news about the assault out to the wider world, and I was finally sent to the inmate doctors for an exam. But when I arrived in the infirmary, I found the murderer Li lurking there, a sure sign that nothing good would come of my visit. A few of my ribs had certainly been broken, but no note of this, or anything else, was made in the physician's report.

In September I was suddenly called into the procuratorate's prison office after months in which its doors had been closed to me. During the meeting, officials from the procuratorate told me that I shouldn't consider them an enemy; they assured me they had had nothing to do with what had happened to me, and they promised to report my case to the party. I was mystified by this sudden turn of events; as it later emerged, I'd been summoned because of a letter sent earlier that month to President Hu Jintao by thirty-four members of the U.S. Congress, protesting my treatment. Though the letter was just a piece of paper, this symbol of international concern, this little bit of pressure, produced a concrete result. Suddenly I was treated by the cadres with something like consideration; my existence was validated. Little do foreigners know how much impact they can have when they exert some of their influence, when they take the time and have the courage to speak up.

Controversy surrounding the Beijing Olympics in August 2008 had a similar effect. That spring, people all over the world were threatening to boycott an Olympics orchestrated by a repressive regime trying to solidify and glorify its own power. The Chinese government was very sensitive to criticism around this time; it feared that a world leader like President George W. Bush would refuse to participate in the games, or that an embarrassing incident would mar this elaborate event.

Knowing how the authorities typically reacted to criticism from around the globe, people began speculating that the party would release me as a way of demonstrating its benevolence. Though this never came to pass, the government responded to the protests in a number of other ways, including by making some welcome changes in the routine at the

Linyi City Prison. That April, the prison built a two-story canteen so that all the prisoners could eat together rather than wait for work numbers to carry slop from the kitchen and deliver it to the yard. The overall food situation became marginally better. The prison normally made a "soup" for its approximately five thousand prisoners with just forty eggs, but now it increased the portion to sixty eggs; as well, they allowed us to eat our fill of steamed buns.

Unfortunately, the improvements in our conditions ended as soon as the movement to boycott the games collapsed. President Bush was among those who undermined the boycott; in early July, he indicated his strong support for the Beijing Olympics and announced his decision to attend. Hearing this news, I was reminded of a day back in the detention center when a group of us, while enjoying a rare moment of television, learned that the United States and China had just signed a trade deal involving billions of dollars. "You see," one of the other prisoners said, "the propaganda about those capitalists is true. All they care about is money; their supposed concern about human rights is just another form of capital." The Chinese government, for its part, cared only about self-perpetuation. Prison officials at Linyi even made us watch the triumphalist ceremonies that opened the Beijing games, that ultimate propaganda show. The real winner, as always, was the party.

In the hell of prison, contact with the outside was the stuff of life. Phone calls, letters, and visits were rare, restricted events, and months could go by without any of these. But in November 2007, I finally got a shortwave radio. A fellow prisoner arranged to procure one for me, hiding it in his pocket and counseling me to keep it entirely secret, since other prisoners wouldn't hesitate to denounce me to curry favor with the cadres. Owning a radio was extremely dangerous; if you were found out, your sentence would almost certainly be extended.

I could listen to the radio only while wrapping my whole body up in my quilt. Pretending to be at rest or asleep, I used headphones and turned the volume as low as possible. I was thrilled to have access to the world again, to know what was going on after so long in the dark. Because I didn't work, I spent much of my day lying in bed, trying to get informa-

tion from the outside. Periodic campaigns in the prison sought to elimi-
nate "contraband," but I managed to avoid these checks and keep the
radio hidden, either in my bed or in an empty milk carton refashioned for
the purpose. When the hole for the headphone jack was somehow dam-
aged, I worked intensively, meticulously, to try to fix it with a small piece
of wire.

Not surprisingly, the radio signal was often terrible. My routine was
to wake up and hear the broadcasts of Radio Free Asia, Radio France
Internationale, the Voice of America, the German station Deutsche
Welle, and several other stations. By the spring of 2008, I was able to pick
up the Sound of Hope, the Falun Gong radio station, which became popular inside China. I heard depressing stories about friends and fellow
human rights defenders who were imprisoned, tortured, or under
house arrest; I heard hopeful stories about ordinary citizens who were
starting to defend themselves against the corrupt and powerful.

The radio could also bring bitter news from home, as when I occasionally heard about the harassment and beatings to which Weijing was being
subjected, especially when she was preparing to visit me. Tragically, her
brother-in-law was killed in a car accident, and when she tried to leave our
house to see her widowed sister she was beaten. Over the radio I could
make out the sound of her tears in the midst of the broadcast report. I
often felt devastated by what I heard, and by what was happening, but I
couldn't show my anger or the prison authorities would know that I somehow had illicit access to information. Only after a rare visit from my family could I seek out the cadres and complain bitterly about what was
happening in Dongshigu.

In time, I fell chronically ill, as so many prisoners did. The food was
awful, and often rotten; many people suffered from food poisoning
and diarrhea. In my case, digestive difficulties worsened into what was
probably gastroenteritis, but even when I had dangerous quantities of
blood in my stool the prison refused my request for medical treatment.
I told my family, hoping that my lawyers would be given permission to
see me. They were not, but they did apply for me to be let out on medical parole. The prison refused this as well.

I harangued the cadres about the poor food and sanitation, and
sometimes I gave acupressure treatment to the other prisoners, using

my medical training to help where I could. Summer was an especially dangerous time: the prison prohibited mosquito nets, supposedly to prevent suicides, but everyone knew the mosquitos could transmit infectious diseases between prisoners. When I first arrived, the prison almost never sprayed the grounds with insecticides, but after numerous protests the spraying became more frequent and more effective. Other prisoners gradually came to see that my relentless demands for better conditions had an effect; when rumors would circulate that I was about to be released, as happened more than once, a number of my fellow inmates had high hopes that I might be able to lobby on their behalf once I was on the outside.

I also continued the fight to clear my name and bring my kidnappers and torturers to justice. Ultimately the cadres allowed me to obtain law books from my family, which other prisoners read aloud to me; my family brought me Braille books as well, but I was never given access to them. My jailers also eventually allowed other prisoners to help me write up materials for my appeal. Whenever I heard that officials from the Shandong Provincial Prison Administration were visiting, I would stand along the path they would take in the jail so I could tell them about my case and various illegal acts by prison authorities. My lawyers and I sent my formal complaint to every local authority, to the National People's Congress, to the Chinese president and premier; I also sent my complaint by registered mail to the Supreme People's Court and the Supreme People's Procuratorate. In every case, all that came back was silence.

During my time in both the detention center and prison, I repeatedly tried to raise my case with officials in the prison's procuratorate office; I even kept track of the number of times I attempted to contact them and the number of meetings I actually secured. Later, I calculated that during my prison term I asked the prison guards more than two thousand times to contact the prison procuratorate's office for me, and these requests resulted in a total of twenty-four meetings.

I looked for every possible way to protest my punishment. In 2009 I started wearing my prison clothes inside out as a constant reminder of my dissent. Some people, thinking that this was because I couldn't see, tried to point out my mistake. Of course I knew full well that my clothes were inside out; I had decided that I simply wouldn't follow the authorities' laws if they themselves ignored them. As I often said to them: "Now the part of my uniform that normally faces the criminal is facing you, because you are the ones with a crime on your hands."

As time passed, I, too, became an "old number," seasoned in the ways of bondage. Like other prisoners, I accumulated "points" for the amount of time served, which would supposedly make me eligible for early release. Eventually I accumulated over fifty of these points, which should have made me eligible for release up to a year early, in addition to as much as six months for my disability. Following the proper procedure, the cadres applied for my early release, but the Shandong Provincial Prison Administration, doubtless heeding orders from on high, rejected the application out of hand. Later, in fact, I learned that the warden was almost fired for submitting my application.

In late 2009, rumors of an early release started up again, and I was told that I would soon be meeting with the prison chief. Then I realized that the authorities still expected me to write and sign a formal admission of my guilt; in addition, they wanted evidence that I had been "transformed" and would mend my ways in the future. I refused to sign a false confession and instead wrote an open letter in which I reviewed the facts of my case. I also decided that I would do everything possible to put even more pressure on the authorities. Twice each day from January through August of 2010, I asked the cadres about my pending request to meet with the prison chief and my prospects for early release. My persistence may not have achieved the desired result, but at the very least it set an example for others: you can never give up.

The months ticked by; at last, with September's arrival, the end of my term approached. In the days leading up to my release, prison officials bought a few items of clothing for me, since my original clothes had long ago been thrown away. A cell phone and a watch came back to me, ghosts of 2006. They weighed me and performed an unusually thorough medical check; against my will, they insisted on drawing blood from me. I am still not certain that this is all they did: that evening I suddenly found that my throat had become so hoarse I could barely talk. The night before my release, I lay quietly in my cell, surrounded, as always, by twenty or thirty new numbers. Turning on my radio under the covers, I had a surreal experience: I listened to the reports of my impending release.

Early the next morning, I gave my radio to another inmate. Just after five a.m. on September 9, 2010, one of the inmates on duty said, "Guangcheng, the two block leaders are here for you." Release time was normally nine in the morning, but I knew they wanted to spirit me away before any journalists had gotten out of bed. I moved slowly, partly because I didn't feel well. Though I had taken some pills the day before, my throat was still swollen and my voice was all but gone.

The head of the block led me forward, and I gripped his arm and walked on while my fellow prisoners called out their good-byes. My jailers banged on the big iron door of the second gate and shouted, *"Release!"* prompting confusion from a guard on the other side, who didn't understand how a release could be happening so early in the day. We went up to a little window to handle the last formalities, and then I was squeezed into the backseat of a car between two block leaders.

At last I had left Linyi City Prison behind, my body ailing but my spirit unbroken. I would soon be turning thirty-nine years old. I had a wife and two young children, but for the past four and a half years I had barely seen them; Weijing had visited me no more than six times during my entire term. Despite parole laws that allow most prisoners outside of the criminally violent to return home after serving half their term, I had served my full sentence, not a day less, starting from the filing of formal charges in June 2006.

Even so, I was not free. My family was not allowed to pick me up that day; I would be driven home by my captors, avoiding any journalists, curtailing any fanfare or commotion in the village. As we drove away from Linyi, our car was preceded by a police car from Shuanghou township and followed by a car from the prison, carrying someone who filmed us the whole time. Together we formed a strange little caravan all the way to Dongshigu.

We stopped at the entrance to the village just after six in the morning, and I discovered that Weijing, Kesi, and Elder Brother were already waiting there, along with a number of guards. Weijing ran over to the car as soon as it stopped, helping me get out. "I've brought the leaves back," I said, my voice still barely more than a whisper. I handed her the bunch of *fatong* leaves from Kesi, dried and curling but clean. "They've been with me all this time."

My strange, hoarse voice cast a pall over my family's joy on seeing me, raising questions about my experience that could not be answered, a reminder of what we had endured and would still have to endure. For Kesi I had become a stranger; not knowing how to respond to me, she ran off to play with her friends.

My jailers handed over the proof of my release, my few effects, and the Braille books the prison had never allowed me to read. The block leaders shook my hand and said, "Guangcheng, we've brought you home now." At the time I had no idea why they would say this, but I later realized they were speaking for the camera behind me, and that every step of this false release was being recorded.

Moments later I heard the sound of feet shuffling and circling all around me. I knew exactly what was happening: when I'd got out of the car, Weijing told me that for the past week dozens of guards and hired thugs had been swarming around the village, preparing for my arrival. Even before my release from Linyi City Prison, I'd begun to wonder if I would just be exchanging one jail for another. I felt all but certain that the authorities wouldn't give me a moment of freedom when I got home.

As we began walking into the village, the guards surrounded us. There could be no more pretending: once again my home would become my prison. And now, more than ever, it seemed I would never escape the prison walls of China.

CHAPTER TEN

House Arrest

When we were nearly home, Weijing told me that my mother had come out of the gate and was walking toward us. As her footsteps drew closer, I could hear her crying. "I'm home from prison, and you're crying?" I said, hoping to comfort her by joking a bit, though the raspy quality of my voice must have alarmed her. I knew my mother had much to be upset about: my hair had more gray in it, and she had probably expected that our troubles would be over now that I was back. Instead, we were surrounded.

Reaching out for her, I felt a bucket in her hand. "What are you doing?" I asked.

"I'm going down to the river to gather sand," she replied. "The yard got muddy from the rain, so I'm putting down sand to dry it out." Able to carry only one pitcher of sand at a time, my seventy-five-year-old mother was making trip after trip to the river so that our life could be a little more comfortable.

Weijing wanted to take me to see the doctor; she was concerned about my voice and the physical injuries I might have suffered in prison. But once we were home, the thugs wouldn't let me out. Weijing was able to leave to get some medicine for me, but she was followed closely, and two days later she, too, was prevented from going out. From then on, only my mother was allowed out, though two or three guards shadowed her wherever she went.

Things had not been easy at home. Weijing, Kesi, and my mother had all been living under house arrest for five years, and the task of caring for the family had fallen largely on Weijing's shoulders. Weijing found it difficult to keep a close watch on Kesi amid the struggles of daily life, and the child often got her own way. My mother—always doubtful about my human rights work—was burdened with worry and work when she should have been enjoying a restful old age. She still had to work in the fields, planting and harvesting the foods that kept us alive.

Kerui, now seven years old, was living with Weijing's parents in their village, both to protect him and to give him a more normal childhood and education. But he had seen too much, and the separation was hard on him. When he was very young, this sweet child had talked and thought and dreamed about violence, having witnessed firsthand the brutality directed at his parents. He often spoke of lifting our siege single-handedly with his little fists, about summoning what he called "super-strong people" to rescue us—heroes who would never arrive. In 2005, when he was just twenty-nine months old, he had witnessed my being beaten by guards. Later, during a meal, Kerui had suddenly said to my brothers and me, "Let's finish eating and go drive off those men at our gate." When none of us replied, he vowed to go do it himself.

During those early days of house arrest, Kerui would often tug at me and say, *Baba*, quick, let's hide, and lead me out to the stone staircase in our yard, the same one I would eventually use to escape. He would pull me down and we would crouch together quietly, as a way of hiding, until my legs grew sore. I knew his real meaning was: Why aren't you running when people beat you? When at last I would tell him we had to go back inside, that we couldn't just sit there anymore, Kerui would quickly grow nervous and try to pull me back. I missed him terribly in prison.

Not long after my release, we celebrated the Mid-Autumn Festival, and my in-laws brought Kerui to see us. Except for one brief visit in prison, I had not seen my son in several years. "Baba!" he called out as soon as he saw me. "Kerui!" I called back. "Did you miss Baba?" I hugged him, and he buried his small head in my chest. "It's okay," I said, "your *baba*'s back now, you won't have to cry anymore." He had grown so much, and it was so wonderful to see him, that I could almost ignore the dozen thugs who had been sent by the government to watch over us during this reunion.

Only now did I learn more about what Kerui's life was like, how he often cried and sought out his grandmother, how he was so scared at school and cried so much that sometimes the kindergarten teacher had to leave him outside in the yard to prevent him from upsetting the other students. I didn't know if the teachers were aware of our family situation, but my in-laws were not likely to have said much, since they were embarrassed that I was in prison. Hearing about Kerui's troubles caused me great pain; wounds inflicted directly on me I could handle, but it made me sick at heart to think about the psychological damage being done to my family.

That evening Kerui spontaneously said he wanted to sleep with me in our bed, so I took him in my arms and carried him into our bedroom. Both children were naked in the still-warm autumn evening; I felt their soft bodies, their legs and bellies and arms, and as the two of them clung to us and slept sweetly, I whispered, "Baba wants to say he's sorry for everything." I lay awake for a long time, listening to the sounds of autumn creatures beyond the window and the noises from the guards in a distant yard. With guilt and regret, I thought about how much our two children had grown up, how I hadn't been there to play with them, and also of how I hadn't been with my wife or my mother as they'd endured these years of bitterness.

The next day, Weijing's parents were ready to depart, taking Kerui with them, but Kerui cried and refused to go. He hid in a spot between our beds; when I found him there, he said he didn't want to leave. I knew how much he had missed us, so we let him stay a few more days before sending him back to his grandparents.

Kesi, meanwhile, was still not accustomed to me. She had no understanding of why we were constantly surrounded by guards; after all, she had really never lived any other way. Her bond with her mother was strong, and I realized it must be confusing for her to now be in the constant presence of this strange person who had been away for so many years. Quite some time passed before she felt comfortable with me around.

A month or so after Kerui returned to Weijing's parents' house, we learned some frightening news about him. Weijing's father had bought him some Play-Doh, which he loved to mold with his hands. Kerui sometimes took out his anger on things around him, and on this occasion he had impetuously grabbed a cleaver from the kitchen to open the package of Play-Doh and had cut his finger, deeply. The bleeding was so bad that Weijing's parents had to take him to the hospital.

Later they came to Dongshigu to tell us about the accident in person, as our phone line had been cut back in 2005, but the guards threatened them and forced them to undergo body searches at the village government offices before allowing them to proceed to our house. Even then they were followed by a group of thugs and officials, who stood close by, almost touching us, some sitting on our bed and ogling us while Weijing's parents related the story of Kerui's injury to us. We were extremely upset and insisted that we be able to go to Kerui to comfort him, but the authorities refused. Weijing was so enraged that she tried to break through the throng of guards outside our yard, but she was no match for the lot of them. She sat on the ground, screaming and wailing at their coldness, at the pain of not being able to console her own child.

That fall, my close friends and family were divided on how to handle my release from prison. I tended to agree with Teng Biao and my other Beijing lawyer friends, who felt we should make a lot of noise, that we couldn't allow the party to spirit me from prison to house arrest even as they were announcing that I was free. Others disagreed, including Weijing and my mother, saying that we ought to lie low. I had served my sentence, they argued; maybe my treatment would improve. Some advised me to give up my human rights work, but this I categorically refused to do: I would speak the truth, whenever I had the chance. I firmly believed—as I still do—that if you bow your head before the Communist Party, it will soon make you get on your hands and knees, and next it will stomp on your crouching body until it destroys you. I felt miserable about the pain my family had suffered for simply being associated with me, but I still felt I had to be resolute.

But the party was resolute, too. Shortly after my release, Zhang Jian, vice secretary of the Shuanghou township party, and Ma Chenglong, head of the Yinan branch of the Public Security Bureau, went to Elder Brother's house to issue threats, undoubtedly expecting that their message would get through to me. One of them told Elder Brother that things had changed since 2005 and 2006. "The party now considers Guangcheng an enemy," the two men said, "a counterrevolutionary, and at any point we could make him go back to prison." Under the Communist dictatorship, once the government brands you a criminal, you cannot escape that label. Even after years in prison, the stigma remains. Elder Brother was allowed a rare visit to my house the next day so he could pass along these threats.

It soon became obvious that the guards weren't going away. As in 2005, I was hemmed in by a large-scale effort to imprison me in my own home. But this campaign was more draconian: it was clearly directed from the highest levels, and those executing it were more professional than anything we'd experienced before. This time, guards conducted twenty-four-hour surveillance and staged a nearly complete takeover of the village. They would stand on the walls of our yard, and if they couldn't see me they would send someone into the house to find out if I was there. Each guard had a direct line of sight to the neighboring posts, making escape all but impossible.

No one was allowed to visit us—whether villagers, outsiders, even most other family members—and whoever tried would be confronted, sometimes with fists. As before, teams of cadres knocked on every door in Dongshigu to vilify me and spread lies about me, making it plain that anyone who helped me or my family would be implicated in our "crimes." Besides mobile phone jammers, the guards installed high-tech security cameras at several points in the village and set up lights all along the perimeter wall of our family compound. These measures were partly directed at preventing a nighttime escape but were also a means of intimidation.

Untold numbers of people were involved in this miniature security economy, from a few dozen when things were slow to hundreds when things were tense. This nightmare seemed to be about us, but it also had a lot to do with the 100 yuan daily salaries paid to the guards, many of them locals who could otherwise expect to earn no more than 50 yuan per day for backbreaking labor. Often as not, these men were less hard-hearted thugs than unemployed people for whom the relatively easy job was simply too enticing to turn down.

Further driving this mini-economy were the fancy equipment and the kickbacks that could be charged to the government. This was graft on a grand scale, the embodiment of much of what we were fighting against. From what a guard once let slip, we learned that a total of at least sixty million yuan was spent on our house arrest, not including the bribes that must have flowed to officials in Beijing whenever permissions or authorizations were needed from the center. In stark contrast, we ourselves had no means of earning a living. Prices were high, inflation was rampant, and we had no source of income whatsoever. Thankfully, we had some savings from kind supporters who had contacted Weijing while I was in prison, and also from a few awards I had been given for my human rights work. Without this aid, I don't know how we would have survived.

Meanwhile, our neighbors and other villagers were scared to help us, fearing for their own safety. But we knew that most secretly supported us. A remarkable thing had taken place while I was in prison: there had been an election for village mayor, and several brave villagers had written my name on their ballots. In Dongshigu, whatever little prestige the party had held on to after the pollution, corruption, and family planning scandals was now entirely forfeited by the crazed ways in which it persecuted me.

That October, Liu Xiaobo was given the Nobel Peace Prize in honor of his long fight for human rights in China, and we celebrated with a little beer that Weijing had bought before I came home. I hadn't tasted any alcohol for years, but I didn't drink much, in part because I remained concerned about my health. Since prison, I had been experiencing bouts of severe diarrhea and bleeding, and by this point I was so weak from loss of blood that I often lay immobile in bed for days at a time. Though we asked for permission to see a doctor many times, our requests were always denied. My captors even circulated the rumor that sooner or later I would probably die from what ailed me. The world might consider the circumstances of my death suspicious, but how would anyone ever learn the truth?

The news about Liu Xiaobo, though, was a faint but welcome whisper suggesting that people in distant places cared for the plight of activists in China. For weeks Weijing and I had been talking about how to connect with sympathetic citizens in China and foreign countries; now our discussions about how to regain the world's attention through the media took on new urgency. We also talked about the possibility of escape. Though I considered it a real option, Weijing was initially firmly against it, and we both knew that my mother would reject the idea out of hand.

In late 2010, we seized upon an audacious idea. Back in 2007, Hu Jia, our invaluable activist friend, had helped Weijing buy a small video camera, but she had never bothered to learn how to use it. Soon after my release, I made a quick study of the machine, learning its functions and capabilities. Now we decided to film a brief video and find a way to get it to the outside world. The act of filming was itself fraught with danger, given how close the guards were at all times; still, we recorded ourselves while tucked inside our kitchen, speaking directly to the camera. We described in detail our painfully circumscribed lives, our difficult conditions at home and the lack of food, our attempts to give Kesi an education. We connected our situation to a broader struggle and appealed to the world to pay attention. Eventually, I found a way to have the footage smuggled out, along with the formal complaint I had written in jail.

The video went online on February 9, 2011, and the reaction was immediate. For many, this footage provided the first authentic account of human rights persecution in China, a shocking look at an ongoing house arrest. When I listened to my shortwave, it seemed that every radio station in the world was broadcasting a report about the video. Just like that, after months of silence, our case was back on people's minds and back on the political agenda.

The party struggled to contain the story, and at first officials clearly didn't know how to react. Supporters in Beijing formed the Chen Guangcheng Citizens Assistance Group, and new online services like

Weibo, the Chinese Twitter, spread the video far faster than the government and its Internet police could delete it. Global public opinion remained important, but now I saw that the Chinese Internet and the activism of its netizens—a newfound, burgeoning force—were paramount in exposing the brutality of the regime and holding the government accountable for its actions.

Nine days after the video aired, we paid the inevitable price for recording it.

The previous two weeks of Chinese New Year celebrations had been a rare and wonderful respite—Kerui had spent the holiday with us, and my brothers and their families had joined us for several hours. As best we could under the circumstances, we observed the holiday and all its customs, eating special foods and ringing in the Year of the Rabbit. Though our family might be trapped and spied upon, at least we were together. I didn't know it then, but this was the last real family reunion we would have.

That holiday two visitors—Zhang Yongpan and Liu Guohui—came to show their support. They had gotten in touch with my family and stayed with my nephew Chen Hua at his house in the hills. Though they weren't able to see me in person, they had my older brother deliver a power of attorney document to me so they could properly hire a lawyer in Beijing, and also had me record images of our house arrest on a tiny video camera small enough to hold in my hand undetected.

Around this time, I had a chance to go through a pile of wonderful letters that my family had received while I was in jail, written by people from all over the world to Amnesty International, then passed on to Hu Jia and, finally, to us. As Weijing read the letters to me, I felt a palpable sense of support: how heartening it was to hear so many messages of solace from so many people who were truly concerned about justice! Those who wrote to me then, and those who have since written other such letters, should know the great value messages like these have for a political prisoner. May they never stop coming.

Around noon on February 18, we were gathering Kerui's things and making ready to send him off. The guards reported that Weijing's sister and mother had arrived to pick up Kerui, but the security people wouldn't let them enter our village. We had no gifts to give our son, no school supplies or special treats, just seventy or eighty eggs carefully placed in empty milk crates. We had been collecting and saving the eggs from our chickens for a number of days.

Just as Weijing and my mother were packing them up, the head of a team of guards started banging on the door to the yard. He shouted that he wanted to see with his own eyes what we were boxing up for Kerui. Weijing refused; she leaned on the door and wouldn't let him in. "Brother, help Mama push on the door and don't let them in!" cried Kesi, the two children screaming and crying as they pushed with all their might beside Weijing. I was inside the kitchen building, surreptitiously documenting everything that was happening with my voice recorder.

A minute or two later, three thugs managed to force the door open. They dragged Weijing out, knocked her to the ground, and began pummeling her. For a moment Kesi and Kerui stood beside her, horrified; then, as Kesi cried wildly, Kerui ran back inside and came out with a large stick. As he raised it to strike the guards, one shouted, "If you hit me, I'll kill you!"

My mother heard Weijing being beaten and the children screaming and crying; running outside, she yelled at the thugs, "What do you think you're doing? It's just some things for the child!" The guards stopped beating Weijing momentarily, and my mother grabbed Kesi and Kerui and ran out to the village entrance.

Listening to all this, I had the wild impulse to grab a knife from the kitchen and stab these criminals. But I also knew that this would be tantamount to suicide, that they were hoping to provoke me into just such an act so they could condemn me to death or put me away forever. Weijing managed to limp back inside the yard, locking the door behind her. She said she had seen a county official lurking outside; this gave her the idea that they might have other plans for us once the children were gone. She was in great pain, and I began attending to her wounds. We both realized that we needed to think seriously about breaking the blockade, about the critical importance of crossing to safety. For the first time, Weijing was persuaded that our situation would only get worse. Our enemies would stop at nothing.

Within minutes we heard another group of people banging at the door. Weijing hurriedly stuffed our video camera into a black plastic bag, then hid it in the bottom of a metal bucket of coal fragments. I was in the outhouse and could hear Zhang Jian, the Shuanghou township party vice secretary, demanding that Weijing open the gate to the compound. She refused, pressing all her weight against it. But more than twenty guards rammed and kicked the iron gate with full force, and it suddenly popped open, the bolt slamming directly into Weijing's eye. Shaking with pain, she staggered back, her eye immediately swelling. As some eighty plainclothes police and cadres poured into the yard, Zhang Jian ordered a dozen of them to subdue Weijing. She screamed in pain and terror as they dragged her onto the ground. Zhang ordered them to pull a quilt off my mother's bed and throw it on top of her; several of them stood on the edges of the quilt to keep her from pushing it off while they kicked and beat her. She couldn't see their faces, and no one but me would hear her muffled cries.

The rest of Zhang Jian's squad began rifling through our meager possessions, then came looking for me. I hid my voice recorder under a plastic jug and a pile of hay and corn stalks just outside the outhouse. The guards started breaking down the doors of all the buildings in our yard; I hesitated briefly, considering the possibility of lying low, but then I rushed out, coming face-to-face with a dozen of them. "So you have something you want to talk about?" I shouted. For a moment they gave way before my charge, but then a heavyset security official grabbed my arms and said, "Sure, let's talk. Don't move."

I heard them surrounding me. Two of them grabbed me by the wrists and twisted my arms, and another kicked my knees from behind, causing me to fall to the ground. I tried to stand up, but someone shoved my head down. Another guard grabbed my collar, choking me, while yet another stuffed a dirty rag from our yard into my mouth. It was clear from their practiced motions that they were well-trained police. I put up what resistance I could, but I was sorely outnumbered.

By now a swarm of guards were turning everything in our house upside down and inside out. Smashing furniture, pocketing whatever they considered valuable, they searched everywhere: in the walls, in the woodpiles, and under rocks in the courtyard. They were particularly eager to find our video camera and a number of guards carried metal detectors that they swept across the yard and throughout our house. Zhang Jian kicked Weijing repeatedly and asked her where the camera was, but by this point neither Weijing nor I was able to speak. Except for Zhang Jian and the man who had grabbed me earlier, no one spoke aloud, using whispers and gestures to communicate, trying to avoid being identified and maybe one day held accountable. They knew I would easily remember their voices.

By the time they were done, roughly six hours later, Weijing lay twitching uncontrollably on the ground, crying out weakly. A few days later, when the swelling around her eye had gone down a bit, we determined that the bone above her eye socket was fractured; she also had several fractured ribs, and we feared for her liver, spleen, and kidneys. She looked so battered lying in the dirt of the yard that even the guards were a little worried, so they sent for the barefoot doctor, whom they trailed closely while he examined Weijing and administered some medicine.

As Zhang Jian prepared to leave, he walked over and kicked Weijing in the leg, saying, "This wasn't our idea—the orders came from way up. You probably knew that anyway." It was true: this beating was unquestionably in retaliation for the video. They had clearly made some changes in personnel in preparation for this assault: the local hired guards had been ordered to stay outside the village, and instead they'd brought in a pack of county-level policemen to do the dirty work. We learned later that the license plates on the assailants' cars had been removed or covered in black cloth.

By the time Zhang Jian and his gang of thugs left, they had seized virtually everything: our radios, cell phones, cameras, tape recorder and tapes, letters, records, tools—and, of course, the video recorder, which they had finally found. Before they left the yard, a few guards seemed to take pity on us. First they carried me into the house and heaved me onto the bed; they hauled Weijing in after me and left her on the cement floor just inside the door. Neither of us could move; neither of us could speak.

While the thugs were terrorizing us at home, my mother brought Kerui and Kesi out to the main road to meet Weijing's mother and sister. The guards seized Kerui and made him strip completely naked in their car while my mother stood outside; incensed and humiliated, Kerui demanded that they tell him what they were looking for. Finding no messages or other incriminating evidence hidden in his clothes or on his body, they allowed him to leave with his grandmother and his aunt. Soon thereafter, my mother and Kesi were taken to the village government office. They were prevented from returning home until word came down that the public security officials had finished with Weijing and me.

When my mother and Kesi entered the house and saw Weijing lying on the cement floor, her face bruised black, they both cried out in horror, and Kesi began sobbing uncontrollably. Neither of us could speak or make any response. Turning to the guards, my mother screamed, "You wouldn't let us back inside, and you've killed my children!" Weijing said weakly, "They beat us really badly, Mama. First go take a look at Guangcheng." Weijing had seen the thugs beat me, but she had no idea if I was still alive.

Still crying, Kesi walked over to me. I was only half-conscious, but I felt her put her little hand lightly to my nose. "Grandma, Grandma, my *baba*'s not dead, he's still breathing!" she shouted excitedly. My mother ran to get a doctor, but she quickly discovered that the door to the yard was now locked from the outside, and the guards wouldn't let her leave. Crying, she came back in. Beyond comforting us, there was little she and Kesi could do.

Sometime later, I began to come to full consciousness. Fighting the pain, I helped my mother get Weijing over to the bed. Neither of us slept that night; we were both in so much pain we could hardly move. I had the wild idea that this would be the ideal time to escape, as our captors would not be expecting it, but Weijing wouldn't hear of it. "We can't even move," she said, "let alone escape." The next morning the guards agreed to let my mother summon the village barefoot doctor, and he set up an IV for Weijing; after this we were given no further medical attention. One of the local guards followed the doctor into our bedroom and was shocked at the sight of us. "Where's the humanity? This is an abomination!" he exclaimed. A few days later, we noticed that this guard was no longer working for the security team.

Our lives became even more circumscribed in the following months. Kesi had been accustomed to being allowed to play in the village; in late February, the guards stopped letting her go out at all. For some time, my mother's every move had been carefully tracked; beginning in March, the guards insisted on inspecting her bags, her shoes, her pockets—even the food she brought back—each time she exited and entered our yard. But these measures only strengthened Weijing's resolve to find a way to break the siege. "I support you," she told me soon after the vicious beating in February. I made ready to escape at any opportunity.

The guards redoubled their efforts to turn our home into a prison. On March 3, they nailed sheets of corrugated iron over the windows that opened toward the road; on March 6, they turned off the electricity; the next night they broke into our house to destroy our television antenna. On March 8 power was restored, but that morning Zhang Jian again led dozens of people into our home to take or break all our remaining electrical equipment, including remote controls, a DVD player, even old plugs. Weijing tried to block them from entering; confronting Zhang Jian, she demanded that he explain how he had the right to enter our house at any time and take whatever he wanted. Zhang Jian responded by punching her in the head. Two female guards standing nearby berated her, saying that if she had only kept quiet she wouldn't have been punched.

Ten days later, Zhang Jian and his goons came back. They were extremely angry—it seemed that word of our beating was getting out—and they brought with them a number of oversized nylon bags, into which they started stuffing all our books, including my Braille books, as well as our calendar, my cane, the children's toys, acupuncture needles, and everything on the walls. They were looking for anything that could have allowed us to send out a video or other message, and in the process they grabbed everything that caught their eye. They pried some of our wedding photos from their frames and stole a number of documents, including our marriage certificate, our children's birth certificates, the certificate of my release, and other materials I'd brought back from prison. Fortunately, they did not find either the voice recorder I had hidden or the cell phone, which Weijing had wrapped in layer upon layer of plastic and sunk in the waste pit of our outhouse. The phone's battery was almost dead and our phone chargers were gone, but we were desperate to hold on to the phone, our only lifeline to the outside.

A few days later, they returned to install more security cameras, this time on the southwest and southeast corners of our compound; now they could see everything in the yard. Afterward, Weijing said she didn't want to dry our clothes outside anymore; she didn't want them to see every article of personal clothing we owned.

Now more than ever, escape seemed to be the only viable option for survival. We began observing our captors carefully. The guards—a mixture of peasant boys hired for the occasion, township and county cadres, public security officials, and female directors from the family planning office—were for the most part in ordinary clothes. They were organized into three principal teams, with twenty-two people—later twenty-eight—on each team. Half worked the daytime shift, and the other half handled the night, though anyone could be called up at a moment's notice. Their shift hours varied, from six or eight hours at a time to twelve- or even twenty-four-hour shifts.

Every day, mountains of food were brought in from the township kitchen at government expense to feed the guards, and we often heard the guards discussing the price tag associated with their upkeep. As far as they were concerned, this was the perfect job: steady pay, regular meals, and decent equipment. Initially the operation relied on the electricity that came to the village, but our captors grew worried about power outages, so they had the electric company install a special line to handle all the cameras, floodlights, and space heaters. The blockade seemed completely impenetrable, though I knew there had to be cracks; our task would be to find them. And I was sure we could count on neglect.

Weijing and I felt virtually certain that no one would come to our rescue, but the release of our video was prompting more and more netizens and well-wishers to try to visit us in Dongshigu, to at least test the siege. Word of the beatings we had endured also began to get out, which made me determined to find a way to send another direct message to our supporters. Our best hope was to film a video on our remaining cell phone, but how on earth could we charge the phone's dead battery with no charger?

One day, rooting around in a pile of rotten firewood, I came across an ancient AA battery charger. Like many people in the countryside, we never threw anything anyway; you never knew what you might need someday. From what I had once taught myself about electricity, I knew that if I had good conducting materials, I could connect the cell phone's battery to the positive and negative ends of my AA charger. Soon I found two little twists of wire, and then by chance my mother turned up some long, thin aluminum sheets, about the thickness of a Coke can, that had been left behind by some men doing construction work. From these aluminum sheets I cut two little ovals, then bored small holes in them to run the wire through. The wire twists were meant to connect directly with the negative and positive poles on the cell phone battery—two little indentations at the top—but ultimately I found it better to use two key chain rings left over from a former neighbor's wedding twenty years earlier. I then wedged an old AA battery wrapped in clear tape against the little aluminum pieces to hold the wires against the charging plates, hooked up the wires to the cell phone battery, and plugged in the charger. The battery didn't charge quickly, but my contraption actually worked.

Later that spring, we used the phone to make a very short video about the beatings we had suffered. But how to send it out? Lightning storms in the countryside sometimes caused power outages, momentarily knocking out the mobile phone jammers our captors had positioned on our neighbor's roof. Afterward, the guards would have to climb up to the roof to start the generator, giving us a tiny window during which we could make the briefest of calls. One such stormy night in May we were lying in our bed, buried in quilts so the guards couldn't hear us. We were trying desperately to send the video message out with the phone, but it didn't go through, and the best we could do was to send a text message about our situation to a netizen who had helped us in the past, one of the few people we knew whose phone was not likely to be bugged.

We didn't have another opportunity to get in touch with the outside world until July 25, when another big storm caused an electrical outage. I called this same friendly netizen and asked whether the message we had sent him in May had been made public. Yes, he said, it had recently appeared. After months of silence, word of what was happening to us had once again leaked out. And once again we would pay for it.

On July 28, some seventy security people barged into our house and threw Weijing and me out the door, yelling, "Where's the cell phone!" They kept insisting that we hand over the phone; finally I retorted that they themselves had already taken our phones along with everything else they had stolen. In response, they struck me in the mouth with a bamboo branch and then beat Weijing, kicking her remorselessly, demanding that she procure the phone. They even asked Kesi where the phone was, but she bravely said that she didn't know. She cried wildly when she saw the thugs beating us again.

The security officers ripped open the sofa, our mattresses and pillows, and any boxes or containers that had somehow remained untouched in previous raids. No stone was left unturned in our yard, and every rat and mouse hole was dug open. Eventually they found the phone, but they couldn't locate the battery or the phone card we had used to make the calls. That afternoon they began snapping off all the branches of the trees in our yard and flattening the stalks in our bamboo grove, as these were blocking the unremitting gaze of the surveillance cameras. In March they had broken our TV antenna, but I had managed to improvise a new one, allowing us to watch some international news. This time, they took my homemade antenna and destroyed the little hole where it fit into the TV, jabbing it with a pair of pliers.

The next morning Zhang Jian arrived, demanding that I hand over the battery and phone card. I asked him how his actions were legally justifiable. "We don't care about the law—we can do whatever we want," he told me. "What are you going to do about it?"

Weijing was lying in bed, still recovering from the beating the day before. One of the security officers, Yang Xigang, went into our bedroom and demanded that Weijing give up the battery, saying they had orders from higher up to remove the entire contents of our house if they couldn't find it. Fearing another round of beatings, she handed it over, figuring they would locate it sooner or later.

I had hidden the phone card, but I refused to tell them where it was. Trying to protect me, Weijing said that she had let my mother burn it. In fact, she had earlier given Kesi a piece of a medicine box about the size of a phone card for my mother to burn in the cooking fire; this way, both Kesi and my mother—who is illiterate—could plausibly corroborate her story and take the guards off the scent. But the guards needed evidence to take back to their superiors, and we later found them burning a phone card to create their own evidence.

At one point, after brushing up against someone and realizing that he was wearing everyday clothes, I said, "You don't wear uniforms, and you don't have any legal documentation. That makes you seem more like bandits than police."

Yang Xigang replied, "At the moment, we aren't acting as police. We're here on party orders."

"You're just like the SS, then," I replied.

The next day our power went out again, and this time it didn't come back on for five months. The security forces set up more security cameras and floodlights than ever before, and our neighbors were warned against initiating even the slightest contact with us. My mother was restricted from going anywhere except the garden just outside the village, and starvation became a real prospect. We began planning for a small garden plot in our yard in the event that none of us could go out all.

The raid in late July marked a turning point in another way as well. Two months earlier, having watched constantly for an opportunity to escape but seeing none, we had decided to take a more drastic step: together, we drew up a plan for a tunnel, working out where it would pass under the road, where it would come up, and how to dispose of all the soil. Soon Weijing began the laborious, superhuman work of digging it out. She dug in the northeast corner of the courtyard, the one place the gaze of the security cameras couldn't reach, a spot just barely concealed from a guard on the other side of the wall. She took great care

People from all over the country tried to visit me to express their support. After they were beaten back, many took photos like this one—the characters read "Free Guangcheng: there is Light and Sincerity"—and put the images online.

自由光诚! FREE HIM!

One netizen devised a way for people to add sunglasses to their online photos to express solidarity for our cause. Another supporter who went by the name Crab Farm used the photos to create this composite image of me.

In December 2011 actor Christian Bale came to Dongshigu to see me, but he was roughed up by guards outside the village and turned away. I learned about the incident from Kesi, who told me that "Batman" had tried to visit me.

As one form of protest, we pasted this message over my sunglasses in the style of a poetic couplet: "Illegal house arrest of the old and young, the sick and disabled. / Breaking and entering, beating and stealing; brutal and inhumane."

Over time the guards stripped our home of nearly all our possessions; one of the few items they allowed us to keep was this calendar. Weijing consulted it for auspicious days as we planned my escape.

On the morning of April 20, 2012, I began my escape by climbing over the wall surrounding our yard and dropping into our neighbor's lot. I lay for some time on the flat-roofed building at the center of this photo, trying to stay out of sight.

Hu Jia

In this recent photo, Elder Brother stands beside the wall between our first and second neighbors' yards. I knew that a tree grew close to the eastern side of the wall; I tried to climb down it during my escape, but instead I fell.

My neighbors' mentally ill son, Chen Guangfeng, lives in a prisonlike room in my neighbor's yard. I did my best to stay out of his view and avoid their dog before climbing into a pen with several goats.

Many years ago this overgrown yard had been the site of my family's home. When I dropped over the wall surrounding the yard, I fell onto a pile of rocks and broke my right foot.

The night of my escape, I managed to partially dismantle the stone wall pictured in this photo (it was later repaired). The road opposite the wall was lit with spotlights; I was completely exposed as I crossed.

The terrain along the Meng River on the way to the nearby village of Xishigu is steep and dangerous. I periodically threw pebbles over the bank to help me gauge my distance from the river. I was extremely lucky that there were no guards posted on the bridge to Xishigu when I arrived there.

Friends and family brought me from Xishigu to a safe house in Beijing that had been secured by Guo Yushan (left). On April 25, Hu Jia (right) and his family visited me.

Zeng Jinyan

Ambassador Gary Locke (right) was attentive and generous in the days after I arrived at the U.S. embassy in Beijing, and he seemed fully committed to helping me achieve justice.

U.S. negotiators Harold Koh (left), Kurt Campbell (center), and Ambassador Locke (right) look on as I sign my name to a letter I dictated describing my persecution. I was promised that U.S. Secretary of State Hillary Clinton would personally hand the letter to Chinese premier Wen Jiabao.

Handout / Getty Images News / Getty Images

I tried to make a brave face upon leaving the U.S. embassy on May 2. Kurt Campbell holds my left hand, while Ambassador Locke holds my arm. Harold Koh follows to my right.

AP Images

I arrived at Chao-Yang Hospital in Beijing on the morning of May 2 and remained there for more than two weeks. Soon after entering the hospital, I was taken to an exam room on the ninth floor, where I was at last reunited with my wife and children.

ChinaAid photo

On May 4, I received a telephone call from Washington, where the Congressional-Executive Commission on China was holding an emergency hearing on my situation. From my hospital bed, I spoke directly to Representatives Chris Smith (center) and Frank Wolf (left), as well as other members of Congress. The call was placed by Bob Fu of ChinaAid (right).

Andy Jacobsohn / Getty Images News / Getty Images

My family and I flew to Newark airport on May 19, 2012; we were met there by my old friend Jerry Cohen, who drove with us to New York University, where I would soon become a student. Many friends and supporters—as well as a large media contingent—greeted us upon our arrival at NYU. To all who gathered there I said a few words, extending my deepest thanks to everyone who had supported me over the years.

Eduardo Munoz / Corbis

Two months after I came to the United States, I was welcomed by members of both political parties at an event in Washington, D.C. Left to right: Republican congressional representatives Ileana Ros-Lehtinen, Chris Smith, and Speaker John Boehner; Democratic congressional representatives Joseph Crowley, Minority Leader Nancy Pelosi, and Rick Larsen.

Fang Fang — VOA

I finally had the chance to thank Hillary Clinton in person at a Lantos Foundation awards ceremony in 2013. We shared a few words, this time with the help of my friend and translator Danica Mills.

Weijing and I have now made our home in America, and our children have embraced their new life here with unfettered joy. But I can never forget those I left behind, and my every effort is still bent toward achieving my dream of justice and freedom for all Chinese citizens.

to be completely silent. Breaking through the rocky soil with a short iron rod and then scooping the dirt out with a spoon, she scratched away during the day, when any noise she made would be covered by the sounds of the village. At night, she covered the hole with a cement slab.

After a week Weijing had carved out a hole about four feet deep, but then my mother found it and protested vociferously. Weijing took a break, and we considered our circumstances. We suspected that our chance of success was small, but in the end we decided that we had no other option. Soon Weijing went back to work, but her hands grew blistered and worn, and her body was red and swollen from the swarms of mosquitoes that fed on her. Her progress slowed, but she persevered and eventually dug down several more feet.

When the cadres raided our home that July, they discovered the tunnel. Furious, they immediately filled it in, and from that day forward they installed themselves inside our yard and house twenty-four hours a day, determined to keep watch over our every move. Guards would curse us and threaten us, even when we were using the outhouse, calling us traitors and turncoats and all sorts of unspeakable names. We weren't allowed to close any door in our house, even if we were sleeping or eating. "If we can't see you, we don't know what you're doing," they said.

By August it seemed the authorities had devised a campaign to drive us insane. Imagine this scene: we're inside our little house, with its modest living area—containing a table, a sofa, and a few miscellaneous chairs—and a small bedroom off on one end. The walls are bare, having been stripped clean except for a clock the cadres had broken earlier in the year. The windows are boarded up with iron sheeting, the electricity has been cut, no fans are working. It's the height of summer, sweltering heat both night and day. A dozen sweaty guards, each with his own chipped tea mug, sit on low stools on the floor, slump over chairs, and lie sprawled and snoring on the couch. Shirts come off; it's just too hot. Our couch is now soaked through with sweat. To walk across the room is a challenge—legs and arms and hands crisscross, akimbo. There's no air, no books, no phones, and nothing to do—they have taken everything from us. Weijing goes to our tiny bedroom to rest, or at least to feign sleep to escape their unbearable presence, only to find three of them sitting nonchalantly beside the bed, ogling her lewdly.

Into this stew of humanity and stink of bodies floods a tidal wave of verbal harassment, from eight in the morning until noon; after a break for lunch, it resumes again for another three hours, until dinner. They curse and yell and call us names; we are running dogs, spies for the Americans, in cahoots with the Americans, traitors. "You're barely human," they say. "Where did you get that wife, and why don't you get a better one? She's a snake." Meanwhile, twice a day another half dozen people are rifling through our things, turning the room upside down while searching for anything they believe we could use or anything they might want for themselves. As one of them told us, "This is not about breaking laws or harassing you or invading your rights. I'm telling you: what we're doing is pushing you against a wall. We want you and your whole family to be miserable, to have no way to go forward, no way to live, no way to go on. That's what we're doing." We did our best to ignore them, but our fury was almost impossible to suppress.

In time, the guards began to squirm with misery and boredom as well. After a week of taking turns yelling full-on, they began to falter. One group would take over for the next, but there were only so many things they could think of to say, and the pressure to come up with new insults began to take its toll. They recorded themselves for their superiors, competing for the harshest harangue, but eventually it was too much for them. They began to wilt, and after a few days I decided to debate with them, knowing that their arguments were completely illogical, and also that their leaders would hear the recordings later on. By the end of August they had largely given up on this kind of Cultural Revolution–style harassment.

As much a prisoner as the rest of us, Kesi could do nothing but play by herself or with us in the sand of the courtyard. Sometimes she cleverly got hold of newspaper pages that had been read by the guards; she folded them up as if they were her playthings and innocently walked them right by our captors. Weijing would unfold them, and I would eagerly listen as she read the latest news in a low voice. Of course we were nowhere in those pages.

Our daughter was now six years old, and Weijing forcefully told our captors that they could no longer delay her education, that they had to let her attend school in the fall. In response they said, "Our socialist nation won't permit your counterrevolutionary kid to go to school." We kept up her schooling at home as best we could, though we had almost no instructional materials or supplies. I taught her language and math, going over problems verbally; Weijing taught her characters, scratching out words in the dirt with a stick or a rock.

When word got out that Kesi was being denied the opportunity to attend school, scores of inflamed netizens made their displeasure known. The pressure must have worked: one day when Weijing and I were in the yard picking peanuts and my mother had just come back from the fields, Fourth Brother and Zhang Jian appeared. "You've been demanding that Kesi go to school," Zhang Jian said. "We've decided we're going to let her go, but there's one condition: she has to go to the county school, and she'll have to stay with Fourth Brother there. You won't be able to see her ever again." Of course we balked at such a ridiculous offer. Sulking, Zhang Jian stalked off, saying, "Fine, then you can just keep teaching her yourselves if you don't agree."

That September, after pressure from countless netizens had been applied, Kesi was allowed to start primary school in a nearby village. But she still faced unending surveillance: the guards drove her back and forth, and two or three remained beside her in school at all times. A little guardhouse was even built just inside the main gate of the school—as if our young daughter represented a counterrevolutionary threat. Every inch of her book bag was scrutinized at the beginning and end of each day, and the guards leafed through every page of her workbooks and textbooks, looking for communications we might be trying to send friends on the outside. Yet the party publicized the fact Kesi was attending school, and Kesi reported to us that on a few occasions someone came to take her picture while she was in class. In a similar Potemkin spirit, the party also renovated much of Dongshigu—not to improve it for the villagers but to put up a false front for a watching world.

That year, in our never-ending attempt to spread the news about our imprisonment, we had the idea to write messages for the surveillance cameras trained on our yard. At the very least, we wanted those who were watching us to be alerted to our plight, but we also nurtured the far-off hope that someday the footage could be used as legal evidence of the wrongdoing taking place. With a rock, Weijing scratched characters in the soft mud around our home, spelling out messages such as "Illegal detention taking place; brutalizing the old, the weak, the sick and disabled. Heaven will not tolerate such injustice!" Sometimes she used shards of drywall to write on the interior walls of our yard where the cameras were aimed. Of course we had no idea who saw our words or what reaction—if any—they inspired.

As if all their other abuses were not enough, in early 2011 the authorities had taken control of Second Brother's home in the village; he was living in the county capital at the time. First, they demolished the main building in his courtyard where we had gotten married and had lived for a short time. Next they began building a prison just for us, a single cage-like room with barred windows. On the outside, iron bars arched from the roof to the ground, just like in the detention center. My mother had had the habit of visiting Second Brother's home periodically, to look after it, but starting in May they wouldn't even allow her to walk in that direction. In late September, the guards ordered us to prepare ourselves to move there, the thought of which was terrifying for us. Would all our observation of the guards, all our knowledge of the nearby environment, now count for nothing?

On October 1, Zhang Jingbai came by to talk to us, saying he had just taken up his new post as Shuanghou party secretary and asking for my support. "Your living conditions here are pretty rough," he said, "but at the new place"—he was referring to our custom-made prison—"everything has been taken care of. Your moving there will help me out in my new job," he added. I was dumbfounded by this logic. Two weeks later, Zhang Jian and Wang Yunqing, both vice secretaries of the Shuanghou party committee, came to threaten us and insist that we move into the new prison, saying that I would be "transformed" faster there. When I objected, they replied, "It doesn't matter if you are willing or not—you're not the ones who will make that decision. You have to move."

We were still dreading the move when we heard a remarkable piece of news: on November 6, in the middle of the night, the authorities had brought in several bulldozers and demolished the prison, removing the iron bars and concrete slabs and dumping them at a site several miles away. We never found out why they suddenly changed their minds, though we did learn that the existence of the prison had been revealed by a Hong Kong news outlet. Once again, support and pressure from the outside world seemed to have saved us from a much harsher fate.

It was during this time—the darkest months of 2011—that a cause was born. We ourselves were only dimly aware of it, though we were right at the center of it, a new symbol of resistance. Dongshigu became an unlikely place of pilgrimage or adventure tourism, depending on whom you asked. A trickle of brave visitors, seeking us out in Dongshigu at great risk to themselves, gradually turned into a flood. Ordinary citizens, netizens active in online communities, journalists, lawyers, human rights defenders, even celebrities—all came to our village to show their support. They visited Dongshigu in September to mark the first anniversary of my release; they came for my fortieth birthday in November. Some came alone, for very personal reasons; others came in groups of thirty or more. Some let off large balloons carrying messages written on trailing strips of cloth that wished me happy birthday or good health; others crossed the river in the depths of winter to set off fireworks. At the time I didn't know the fireworks were for me, but I did wonder at them.

So many people were coming to Dongshigu that the cadres announced a 500 yuan reward for anyone catching a visitor. Obstructions were placed everywhere, including spike strips to deflate visitors' tires and a misleading sign at the entrance to the village: "Construction Ahead—Closed to Traffic." There was no way for the visitors to actually reach us; most were detained as soon as they arrived in Linyi, and many were assaulted or fined or had their possessions confiscated.

One early visitor was He Peirong, also known by her online English name, Pearl. A teacher in Nanjing, she was inspired by my story and enraged by my relentless persecution. She came to Shandong a number of times, even after her car was vandalized. In June 2011, she was held by the authorities after attempting to see us.

Upon hearing that Pearl had been detained, another supporter, Gao Xingbo, who had also made countless trips to our village, immediately flew up from Shenzhen to Linyi and checked into a hotel with the intention of searching for Pearl. That night the Linyi police paid him a visit, and soon afterward a man he didn't know appeared at his door on the pretext of delivering water. Once the door was open, a dozen other men burst into the room and started beating him viciously. They dragged him out of the hotel and took him to the city of Laiwu, about a hundred miles away, in the mountains. There they left him by the side of the road, completely naked except for a single sock on his left foot. He tried to hitch a ride, but no one dared to pick him up. He knocked on a few doors, but everyone was afraid that he was a criminal. Finally someone took pity on him, giving him an old pair of pants, a shirt, and shoes and letting him use the phone to call a friend, who came to pick him up. Gao's shakedown by the authorities was not unusual.

Many supporters, including Pearl and Gao, wrote about their attempts to visit us, and by doing so they made our situation come to life for people on the outside. Politicians such as Hillary Clinton began mentioning my case, as did many U.S. congressional leaders, European ministers, and British parliamentarians. Domestic and foreign journalists, representatives of major networks, and foreign diplomats began trying to contact us; all were threatened or beaten if they tried to come near. When reporters for CNN first tried to visit us, in February 2011, guards threw rocks at them. When CNN reporters returned ten months later, they were accompanied by the actor Christian Bale, who was in China working on a film. Bale said he simply wanted to shake hands with me, but the guards responded by pushing him and punching him. The video of this encounter was viewed around the globe, helping to spread the word about our situation. I didn't hear about this until much later, when someone happened to tell Kesi that Batman—that is, Christian Bale—had come to see me but had been forcibly turned away.

Though we never saw any of the many visitors ourselves and wouldn't learn their stories until much later, we began to get a sense from the guards that something was changing. On some days, instead of eating their lunch together as they usually did, the guards would all be out, off somewhere else in the village. Sometimes we could hear them talking among themselves about an upcoming event, and from time to time the number of security people guarding us would increase dramatically. From these clues we came to understand that people on the outside were taking notice of our situation, which lifted our spirits immeasurably.

The wave of activism surrounding my house arrest was unprecedented in modern China, and protesters used a variety of tools to engage with each other outside the system. One person made bumper stickers for cars, emblazoned with my face and the message "Free CGC." Another man, a netizen who went by the web name of Crab Farm, devised a way for people to add dark sunglasses—which by then had become the symbol of my resistance—to photos of themselves online. Thousands of users on Weibo, including the artist Ai Weiwei, created these self-portraits in solidarity with our cause. The power of such simple yet effective gestures, which the party had no way of suppressing, cannot be overestimated.

From the day I returned home from prison, I had never stopped thinking about escape. But after the guards discovered the tunnel and moved into our yard, escape began to seem all but impossible. The most we could do was try to eat and maintain our strength, no mean feat under the circumstances.

Yet I continued to hold out hope that we would find a way. Weijing and I discussed the idea of fleeing to a mountain cave and later managing to get Kesi and my mother out, too. We also considered having Weijing slip away on her own and returning for me once she got help. Finally, we came to the unlikely conclusion that although I was blind, the best approach was for me to make the attempt alone.

By the fall of 2011, we were constantly watching the guards and noting their routines. I listened to their conversations, trying to learn their individual habits and personalities; Weijing observed them surreptitiously while doing chores in the yard or up on the roof. When did the guards' shifts begin and end? When were our neighbors at home and when were they out? Where were the little obstacles the guards had set up to foil an escape? Sometimes we barely slept, eavesdropping on all the sounds and rhythms of the surrounding area. Weijing told me everything she learned, and I committed it to memory.

Among other things, we concluded that it would be a mistake to attempt an escape at night: there would be just as many as guards but a much greater chance of being heard because of the nighttime quiet. We also understood that dogs, commonly kept by rural households, would have to be avoided at all costs. Most especially, I knew that when my chance to escape finally came my ears would be my eyes.

Supporters continued their attempts to visit us, keeping up the pressure on the authorities. In late October, the vice chairman of the county Canlian, a man named Meng, came to see me, accompanied by Zhang Jian and two policemen. Pretending to show concern, Meng asked me how my life was. "At least I haven't starved to death yet," I replied; he didn't seem to get the irony. Then I explained to him the various illegal means by which my rights had been violated. "But you can't see anyway," said Meng. "As long as people give you enough to eat, what do you want with going out and doing things?"

Over the course of the meeting, he sat by my side and tried in various ways to get me to smile for the photographer they had brought along—I heard the shutter opening and closing throughout. After a while, he turned to the photographer and asked if he had gotten what he wanted. The photographer nodded and they all got up and left. Out of courtesy, Weijing and my mother put on a smile as they showed them out the door, unwittingly cheered to have a visitor—no matter the mission—who was not violent or aggressive. Within days, however, the government circulated photos of Weijing and my mother smiling, thus presenting "evidence" that our family wasn't being mistreated. On subsequent visits I taped written messages over my sunglasses for all to see, in the style of a poetic couplet: "Illegal house arrest of the old and young, the sick and disabled. / Breaking and entering, beating and stealing; brutal and unfeeling." From then on, it was impossible for the authorities to take sly photos for public consumption.

One morning in mid-December, three villagers came to our house holding a ballot box. The woman leading the group told me it was time to vote for our township and county representatives to the National People's Congress; as I knew well, this was the only chance we had to elect popular representatives in China. "Voting is a serious responsibility," I said, "but who are the candidates for these positions? Do you know them?"

"We don't," the woman answered.

"The candidates," I noted, "include Zhang Jian"—the very man who was in charge of my captivity—"but he's already the head of the township, so how can he also stand as a representative to the People's Congress? What are the campaign slogans of these candidates?" I asked. "If we know nothing about them, how can we vote?"

The woman replied that she didn't know but it wasn't important: all they did was get together and hold pointless meetings. I told her and the two other villagers that all these candidates had in fact been nominated by the party committee; I then instructed them to cross out all the candidates listed on the ballot and write in several names of villagers I thought would be fit for the job. As the villagers left, we saw the guards filming our ballots. They were playing their game well, trying to lead the outside world to believe that we were able to participate in a free and independent election.

During the final weeks of 2011, conditions improved slightly, undoubtedly because my captors were feeling pressure from the outside world. The electricity finally came back on; the surveillance cameras, lights, and other equipment in our yard were removed; and the guards withdrew back outside the gate. But our lives remained under lock and key, and my health continued to deteriorate—more blood in my stool, protracted periods of deep exhaustion. And although we did our best to prepare ourselves, materially and psychologically, for a siege that might last years, we thought constantly of escape.

One day in late December, Weijing was working in the yard when fourteen people suddenly appeared at our door. I was asleep at the time, and Weijing hurried over to wake me. I made sure to put on the sunglasses with the messages taped on them; several of the visitors were carrying video cameras. As they introduced themselves, I heard their Beijing accents and recognized two of their names—Yi Qing and Sima Ping-bang, both well-known apologists for the regime. These two were known as "big fifty cents," as opposed to the regular "small fifty cents," the people who were paid to write scathing remarks online about me or other party critics for, purportedly, fifty cents a line. I told them about the violations of my rights, the illegal detention, about being beaten and robbed. Somewhat to my surprise, they responded by encouraging me to find a way to persuade party leaders to sit down and talk. I said I would be happy to do so; for a long time I had made it clear that I was willing to meet with anyone who was interested in the truth, would talk reasonably, and act in accordance with the law.

"Our country is different now," they said.

"In what way?" I asked. "Truth is truth, and lies are lies."

They replied that facts are not always so clear.

I retorted, "What's not clear?"

At one point during the meeting, Yi Qing stepped over to Weijing. "I lived through the Cultural Revolution," he said to her, "and I know the Communist Party dares to do anything. This is China. One plus one doesn't always equal two."

"Then how much does it equal?" Weijing asked him. He didn't reply.

Weijing took the officials up to the roof of the kitchen building and pointed out the cell phone–jamming equipment stationed on the neighbors' houses and the surveillance cameras and lights dotting the village. They took photos. They filmed me while I spoke, too, and after they left I felt certain that if I hadn't worn my special sunglasses, they would have once again used images of me to deceive the outside world.

Some days later, the layers of guards reemerged, as if sprouting from the very earth, and the whole security setup in our yard—the flood-lights and the jamming equipment, everything except the cameras—was put right back in place. Our power was cut off again and the guards were ordered to reoccupy our yard. On December 31 they undertook another search, on the pretext of finding the messages I had taped over my sunglasses. But I knew what they were really worried about: they suspected that during the week when the guards had been kept beyond our yard, someone had passed us a cell phone or some other device that could make it possible for us to contact the outside world.

Early on the morning of January 25, 2012, I woke up from an angry dream, one of many such dreams I had been having since prison. A little while later, at about seven a.m., a guard told Weijing that Third

Brother was at the gate and needed to speak with our mother. This was strange indeed; it had been a long time since we'd been allowed to be in touch with anyone in my family.

Third Brother was carrying an upsetting message. "Second Brother is in the hospital," he said. "In fact, he has stomach cancer and is likely to die at any moment."

My mother immediately started wailing—this terrible news was such a bolt from the blue. Third Brother comforted her and told us we needed to think about what we would do. Should we bring him back here for burial, or have him cremated where he is? He also asked the guards if our mother and I could have a last chance to see Second Brother.

Weijing and I supported my mother as she walked out the gate, crying openly. A few of the guards were moved; they only made a show of trying to keep us from going out with her, and we were able to walk with her to the entrance of the village, followed by the guards. At that point Zhang Jian and several others hurried over and ordered us home. We refused to go back, and before long a crowd of villagers had surrounded us, lending their support. In the end my mother was allowed to go to the hospital, but Weijing and I were dragged back home.

An hour later, I was sitting in the yard when, in the distance, I heard the sound of my mother crying uncontrollably, and I knew Second Brother was gone. When my mother arrived at the gate, she was forcibly carried in by the guards, who ordered her to keep her tears inside the house. Through her sobs, she told us she had been too late. By the time she reached the hospital, her son's face was covered with a paper sheet; she had lifted it to see his face one last time.

I asked the guards to be permitted to touch Second Brother a final time, but this, too, was denied. The party then issued a strict order: Second Brother would be taken first to the funeral home for cremation, after which his ashes would be brought back to the village for burial. The cadres refused to allow the "bringing of the soup" to the grave, according to our local custom; after we objected, they finally let Kesi do it once, watched by two of our captors. While Kesi was taking part in the funeral rituals with our other relatives, my mother sat weeping in the yard, comforted by Weijing and surrounded by guards. I was extremely upset, and, not wanting the guards to see my grief, I had come inside. Suddenly, I heard the patter of little Kesi's footsteps approaching the door and stepping over the threshold. "I have something to tell you, Baba. It's very important," she said, leading me to the bedroom and closing the door. "Baba," she whispered earnestly as we stood there together, "Uncle told me to tell you that Batman tried to see you but the guards beat him off. He also said many other people keep trying to visit you, but the bad guys break their arms and don't let them come close." Elder Brother had quickly given Kesi the message when they were kneeling down together in the ceremony. I was grateful for this hopeful news in this terribly painful time.

The party had again behaved in barbaric fashion, denying us the right to bury and pay our respects to Second Brother properly. We couldn't even go to his grave—not me, not my mother, not Weijing. What kind of regime, what kind of system prevents a man from mourning his brother or a mother from mourning her son? My mother cried every day for weeks, and I still have yet to touch the spot where my brother's ashes lie buried.

On March 2, some of the guards passed us a message from Third Brother: it was our mother's seventy-seventh birthday, and he wanted to know what food should be bought to celebrate the occasion. My mother wanted to go speak to him, but the higher-ups didn't approve and the guards roughly blocked her way, pushing her back and causing her to hit her head on the stone door frame. She accosted them with bitter words: "What right have you young folks to hit an old woman? Don't you have a mother and father at home?" One of them had the gall to reply, "We young folks are just fine, it's you old folks who are no match for us."

This callous treatment of my mother caused me once again to feel consumed by rage. But in the days that followed, my anger congealed into a kind of desperate resolve: I would escape, or try to escape, and I would do it soon. I simply could not continue to live this way; our circumstances were intolerable. Besides, my health had grown steadily worse, making escape imperative. I would be fleeing not just for freedom but for my life.

Over the course of the past year and a half, I had come close to attempting escape dozens of times. We constantly watched the guards, waiting for that moment when their attention was elsewhere. Yet every time we spotted an opportunity and I made a move toward an escape route with Weijing, one of the guards would look in my direction, at which point I would immediately pretend to be doing something else. I became an experienced actor in this theater of the absurd, transforming my gait in an instant, turning a dash to the staircase into a visit to a faucet to wash my face or a chance to examine some new flowers. During these aborted attempts I never got caught.

With the arrival of spring, we had new advantages on our side: better weather and more foliage to cover sounds and obscure lines of sight. As well, my mother returned to the fields, making it easier for us to execute our plan without her noticing. Then, on April 13, our neighbor's dog disappeared; he was as vigilant as any guard, so this was a piece of good fortune, one we were determined to take advantage of.

I began spending even more time in bed than usual—in part because of my health but also because I wanted the guards to get used to seeing less and less of me. Weijing continued to scout the different routes and report everything she had seen. We repeatedly reviewed our possible plans together, going over every detail until I knew each step I would take by heart.

We had been living under house arrest for more than a year and a half, and now the moment for escape seemed ripe. We needed just the tiniest of openings, then a first move perfectly executed.

"It's now or never," I said to Weijing.

But to me that was no choice at all. *Now.*

CHAPTER ELEVEN

Breaking Free

The morning of my escape, I had crept up the stairs and crawled atop the wall around our yard at a little after eleven; now, eight hours later, I lay in agony only about one hundred feet to the east. After dropping into the abandoned courtyard of our old home and landing on a pile of rocks, I knew my right foot was likely broken in several places. I wanted nothing more than to lie there and focus all my attention on managing the pain, but I could not linger: with each passing moment, the likelihood of capture increased. I rolled over, got on all fours, and headed toward the back of the house of a childhood playmate and his wife. I thought I could get their attention by calling to them through the rear window, but I'd forgotten that the window was so high. Besides, I could hear their TV blaring just inside—they would probably never hear me.

Desperate to get their attention, I crawled alongside my friend's house until I came to the low stone wall that connected the corner of his house with the edge of our old yard. The wall was no more than two feet high, but now even this climb was daunting, given the shooting pain in my foot. I finally managed to get myself over the wall and then crawled around the corner of the house and over to a second, much higher wall that ringed his yard. I could never scale this in my condition, but I knew the configuration of sheds and paths in my friend's yard: if I called to him in a low voice, the sound would bounce off the building just ahead of me and ricochet into their front door, which I guessed was probably open.

I braced myself against his wall and called out—only to hear their dog begin barking furiously. Mao Ling, the wife of my childhood friend, seemed to be home alone. I heard her push open the screen door and step outside. She walked around the perimeter of their yard, her sandals squishing in the mud, searching for whatever had made the dog bark. Once again I called out, but the dog's barking drowned out my voice. Mao Ling soon went back inside.

To be so close but unable to get her attention was agonizing. For a while I stayed near my friend's house, unsure about what to do next. Sometime around nine p.m., I felt a few drops of rain on my face. I knew the rain would send the guards up to the roof of our neighbor's kitchen building to cover their mobile phone–jamming equipment, and from there they would have an unobstructed view of me, unless I moved. By now night had fallen, but high-powered spotlights glared into every nook and cranny of our neighborhood. I scurried as quickly as possible back behind the corner of my friend's house.

A couple of minutes later I heard the guards climb up to the roof, chatting as they pulled tarps over their equipment. The dog in the yard of our mentally ill neighbor began barking and didn't stop until the guards climbed back down the steps, ten minutes later. Lying there, waiting for the noise to subside, I considered my options. I desperately wanted to make contact with Mao Ling or her neighbor next door, but even if I could, how could they help me? Neither family had a car, and if I asked one of them to call a taxi for me, the arrival of a vehicle would immediately cause a stir, since neither had ever used a taxi service. I could see now that no one could help me. I would have to escape on my own.

As the village descended into the quiet of evening, I could hear its many sounds with absolute clarity. Guards settled in at their posts for the night in pairs, talking casually or playing games on their phones. I heard the patter of the light rain and a gentle breeze rustling the budding trees. I followed a person's path, by ear, as he or she walked through the village; I traced the succession of barking dogs, each of which I knew well. I could even hear the occasional car, traveling on a distant road beyond the village. Every sound stood out as separate, and I knew that any noise I made would easily be heard by the guards.

It was time to move. Turning away from my friend's house, I began to make my way east, half-crawling and half-stumbling through what seemed to be a thicket of newly planted saplings. I tried to use one to help me stand, but it nearly broke under my weight. At the far edge of the space, I discovered a new stone wall about five feet high, where previously there had been a rough wooden door. The wall seemed loosely put together, not at all suitable for climbing; instead, I decided to dismantle it, stone by stone, and make an opening to crawl through.

My foot was now so swollen it felt as if my shoe might burst, and when I stood up to reach the highest rocks on the wall, I nearly screamed with pain. But over the next hour or so, I carefully dislodged each stone and then gently placed it on the ground, knowing that the guards would hear even the slightest knock. At last, with the rain still falling, I was able to create a sufficient opening, and I stumbled through.

I felt my way up to the gate of a family compound to the left of the wall. Alongside it ran the concrete road that snaked through our village. Trying to understand these new surroundings, I strained my ears for the slightest sounds. I knew the road was lit with spot beams from poles that reached high above the roofs of the village houses. In crossing the road, I would be completely exposed; I could make no mistake.

A sudden wave of nervousness came over me, and some instinct drove me back through the wall I had partly dismantled. Just as I had found a good place to crouch on the other side, I heard footsteps approaching on the road; it was probably a foot patrol checking on the night guards stationed throughout the village, making sure that none were asleep. My heart jumped: another minute's hesitation and I would have been found out.

By then it was past midnight. The rain and wind suddenly ceased, leaving a heavy silence hanging over the village. I heard a guard drag his bench along the road on the other side of the wall. I feared I had missed a crucial opportunity: now he would be able to hear my movements all too clearly. Having no choice but to wait, I sat in the darkness, using a stone as a seat to keep myself out of the mud.

After an interminable stretch of silence, a rooster crowed into the darkness, shattering the stillness. I could recognize all the roosters in the village by their cries, and this one was from my house, its first call coming regularly around one-thirty in the morning. I thought of my family at home: were they asleep or lying awake and wondering where I was? They had no way of knowing that I was crouching in the darkness just a few houses away, and that I had heard the rooster, too.

A few minutes later, I felt a few drops of rain on my face. Then more rain fell and the new spring leaves began to rustle in a light breeze. For a second time, I heard the guard around the corner scooting his bench along the ground. Suddenly it made sense: he was moving himself back out of the rain, abandoning his regular post and taking cover under the eaves of a nearby house. Now was my chance: I had to get across the road as soon as possible, before dawn began to break.

Once more I strained my ears for any signs of movement. Hearing none, I struggled through the opening in the wall once again, but this time, instead of bearing north, toward the gate, I headed straight for the edge of the road. I briefly weighed walking versus crawling, then decided that crawling would be quietest. I also drew on an old skill I had developed when I was just three or four years old, a kind of batlike echolocation. By making just the slightest *shhhh* sound, no louder than a light wind in a pine tree, I could determine from the returning sound waves what was in front of me, whether large object or wall, forest or field. I hissed under my breath and listened carefully to the patter of the raindrops for clues about what surfaces were ahead of and around me. I also walked my hands on the road a few times, pleased that even I could not hear the sound they made.

Once I was confident that nothing large blocked my way, I made a break for it. A sighted person could have easily seen me, lit up like the day under the spotlights: a body hunched over on all fours, head low, scuttling like an insect across the road. My heart raced and for a moment I was sure I'd be caught, but when I reached the other side all remained quiet.

In the distance I again heard the crowing of our family's rooster. It was now about two a.m. I had traveled less than a hundred yards and scaled seven different walls. My glasses and watch were shattered, my foot was throbbing in pain. In just a few hours it would be dawn, and my escape would be doomed unless I could reach the neighboring village of Xishigu by then. Beyond the protection of family yards and walls, I would have nowhere to hide. Though I knew there were no spotlights in the fields beyond the village, the guards carried strong flashlights and would flick them on at the slightest sound.

Still, having crossed the road, I had survived the most treacherous stretch. I had made it past the innermost circle of my captors, the ceaseless patrols guarding my home and the homes of my neighbors on every side. I hadn't eaten or had any water in more than fifteen hours, and I was still a long way from freedom. But if I could keep moving, I might make it to Xishigu. And then I would need water, shelter, and a car that could take me far, far away.

I crawled a few feet beyond the road and soon was picking my way through a landscape I barely recognized. The communal vegetable garden I remembered on this side of the road had been partly paved over with a cement path about three feet wide. Gripping the roots and branches of trees, half-crawling and half-walking, I followed the path until it ended abruptly at an old greenhouse. I tried to cut through it, but the exit was blocked and I had to double back. Once outside again, I encountered a number of raised beds, several of them planted with garlic. I pushed past a number of shrubs and small trees that blocked my way; following my ears, I found the wall that surrounded the garden. Remembering that a sloping floodwall abutted the garden wall, I hauled myself up, carefully positioned my body, and then slid down the floodwall to the rough dirt road just below.

I scrambled across the dirt road, crawled into a shallow gulch through which rainwater drained into the Meng River, and climbed up the opposite side to a copse of trees. Weak with hunger and fatigue, I ran my hands over the ground, looking for a walking stick with which to support myself. Unable to find one, I kept on crawling, picking my way along an uneven path that was muddy and slippery from the rain. Occasionally I tried to stand, putting my weight on the heel of my injured foot, but the pain was so searing that I immediately fell to the ground. Gritting my teeth, I moved forward on all fours until my elbows and my knees were rubbed raw and blood soaked my clothing. At one point I was overwhelmed with the urge to lie down right then and there, to sink straight into the wet black earth. But I knew that somehow I had to keep going—stopping now would mean certain disaster.

Slowly, awkwardly, I kept thrusting myself forward, and finally I came to another path, one I remembered from many years before. It was now overgrown with small trees and bristling with thornbushes. I recalled that jagged stones lay scattered to the east of the path; to the west, the ground dropped off into a sandy pit, which sometimes pooled with as much as thirty feet of water. I hobbled along, occasionally picking mud from my shoes, the little cloth slippers that had allowed my soundless escape. I still moved as quietly as I could. There were guards here, too; my mother had told me where they were stationed, and I tried to stay far away from where I thought they might be.

I made slow progress, but after pushing ahead for nearly two more hours I reached a jagged, rocky drop-off at the edge of the Meng River. Frogs croaking from the riverbed allowed me to determine both the path of the river and my distance from the water. The terrain here was particularly steep and dangerous, and the going extremely rough. I wanted to follow the water, sticking close—but not too close—to the steep edge of the cliffs, so I periodically threw pebbles or sand over the bank to help me gauge my distance from the river.

At last I reached another landmark, an old water-pumping station where, during my childhood, my father had taken me to play. One side of the station edged against the river's rocky bank; the other abutted a large stone aqueduct that used to carry water out to the fields. Remembering a small opening at the base of the aqueduct and the pumping station, I squeezed through it and continued on my way.

Crawling and hobbling west, I followed the forested shore of the river, listening to the frogs. By now a few early morning sounds were beginning to join in: sparrows calling overhead and the far-off purr of auto-rickshaw drivers starting up their motors in the village. I knew dawn must be breaking, and my spirits lifted a little. Though I still hadn't crossed the river, I was technically in Xishigu.

Soon I came upon a gully, where a small creek, twisting its way down from a mountain in the south, flowed into the Meng. By this time I was soaking wet from the rain. I searched at length for a stepping-stone bridge I remembered from long ago but was unable to find it. After crossing the stream on my hands and knees, I moved slowly along a narrow footpath, looking for the old, uncovered well I remembered from twenty years back that jutted into the path. Once I found the well and crawled safely around it, I came to a field of peanuts. The new plants were covered by sheets of plastic, in which rainwater had collected overnight. I bent down to sip the water but wasn't able to get more than a few drops.

I paused for a moment, listening carefully to the sounds ahead. Not far off, I could make out the rippling of water passing under the Xishigu Bridge. Stumbling forward, I came to Xishigu's communal vegetable garden—reaching out, I ran my hands over chives, onions, garlic, lettuce, and rapeseed. Both knees and my injured foot were burning with pain, but I was now at the bridge, the very edge of the village.

Some months earlier, my escape might have ended here. When security was at its most extreme, eight guards had been stationed on this bridge, but lately my captors had eased off. After considering how dirty I must look, I wondered whether anyone would dare to help me. Should I take a few minutes, I wondered, to bathe in the river? Knowing that the day was growing brighter with every passing moment, I decided to push on into Xishigu, where the path would be more level and the going easier.

Using a tree branch as a crutch, I limped my way over the bridge and stumbled into the village, still mostly quiet at this hour. I hoped that people here would know who I was, that they would be sympathetic to my struggle and help if they could, but I couldn't rule out the possibility that someone might turn me in. I heard snores from within one of the yards, and from the smell I could tell the family raised chickens there. I slipped inside that yard, knocked on the door of the house, and heard grunts. I asked for water; no response. I kept heading west, along the north shore of the river, dogs barking like mad in each compound I approached. A few of their owners emerged to see what the fuss was about; one saw my mud-covered figure, turned on his heel, and quickly shut her gate. My heart was pumping with fear: Would I find help here? How much longer could I go on?

I had little sense of Xishigu's geography, so I let my ears guide me. From the gutters of someone's flat-roofed outbuilding abutting the road, I heard water pouring down from the recent rain, and I was able to use it to wash my hands and clean some of the mud off my body. I kept moving forward, then found a door. Hearing a noise inside, I knocked and asked, "Can you give me some water to drink?" In reply, someone told me to wait where I was. Soon a woman whose voice suggested that she was about fifty years old came out with a dipper of water; I took a step inside the gate, drank deeply, and thanked her.

"Where are you from?" she asked.

"From the east." It was the first time I'd spoken to anyone in many hours.

"Where in the east?" It was obvious she didn't recognize me.

"I'm Chen Guangcheng, from Dongshigu."

She was stupefied. "How did you escape?"

"It's a long story. Can you help me?" I asked.

"What kind of help?"

"Help me find a taxi."

"We have no cars here in the village," she said. "You would have to go pretty far before finding any cars." This came as no surprise: few people in the Chinese countryside have private vehicles.

I asked the woman if she knew a villager named Liu Yuancheng; how far was it to his house? I'll go right away to get Yuancheng, the woman replied, saying it would take about fifteen minutes. At first I made to follow her, but then I realized I couldn't move at all; my hunger and pain had finally overpowered me. Exhausted, I leaned against the wall and waited for the woman to return.

I first met Liu Yuancheng in 2005, shortly after he had been beaten and left unconscious by the side of the road during the family planning campaign. While working closely together on his resulting lawsuit, we had become friends; now I hoped he would help me.

Soon the woman returned with Liu Yuancheng's wife. "Who are you?" she asked, no doubt startled by the filthy and bedraggled figure who stood before her.

"I'm Guangcheng!" I almost shouted at her, desperate to convince her that it was me.

Shocked, she asked me about my escape and my wounds, but I insisted that we had to keep moving. We made our way on to Yuancheng's house, where his wife ushered me into a little outbuilding. "They almost certainly won't find you here," she said. "We usually keep grass for the cattle in this shed, and no one ever comes in."

Now, for the first time since my escape, I felt a small measure of comfort. Before long, Yuancheng himself appeared and promised to help in whatever way he could. His wife brought me three bowls of water, which I gulped down in quick succession. I took off my soaked and mud-spattered clothes and put on fresh ones belonging to Yuancheng's son. Every inch of my body seemed to have its own aches and pains.

"Sister-in-law," I said to Yuancheng's wife, using the familiar village term, "find me a taxi to get me out of Shandong. I can pay the driver, and then friends will come meet me." I had a small amount of money in my pocket that I'd taken from home; Weijing and I had been saving it for my escape. Yuancheng's wife agreed and set off. Yuancheng urged me to rest, and as soon as I lay down in the straw in the shed, I thought I would never get up again. My body was terribly sore, but my mind was alive with the worry that Yuancheng's wife wouldn't be able to find a taxi.

She returned about an hour later. "Did you find me a car?" I asked.

"No," she said quietly. "I went to the edge of the village and then rode my bicycle over to your village. I saw guards at every intersection, and though it seems that no one has yet discovered your escape, it's far too dangerous for you to continue on your own. Then I went to your elder brother's house," Yuancheng's wife continued. "He's in Linyi, but I found your sister-in-law there, and she said she'd find a secure way to reach him."

Grateful though I was to this brave woman, I felt obliged to warn her that she had taken a serious risk. Cameras were everywhere in Dongshigu, and they had surely recorded her visit. "It's okay," she replied. "You already made it out."

She cooked up a bowl of noodles, and I did my best to get it down. I was starving, yet I found it strangely hard to eat. "All of us on the outside have been so worried about you," she said, "but there was nothing we could do—they punished or beat anyone who got close. Your sister-in-law said she'd come by around noon," she continued, "so you'd better lie and rest until then."

I slept until late afternoon and awoke to find that nothing had happened—no one had any news, no one knew what to do, and my sister-in-law had not yet arrived. My body ached so much I could hardly move. Liu Yuancheng and his wife were nervous; they had walked back and forth to the Xishigu village entrance several times.

"Help me find a car," I told Yuancheng. "I'll take care of everything else." He firmly objected. "Right now it won't work," he said. "If they see you, they'll kill you. There are party men at the bus stations and train stations; they are everywhere. Your sister-in-law will think of something," he assured me.

By nine that evening, she still hadn't come. I was determined to set off on my own, but Yuancheng gently insisted that it would be too risky. I told him that my nephew Chen Hua might be willing to help, and Yuancheng's wife agreed to seek him out first thing the following morning. Full of agitation, I waited for dawn to come.

The next morning Liu Yuancheng's wife walked into the hills where Chen Hua lived, carrying a basket on the pretext that she would be gathering wild herbs. She found my nephew at home and quickly briefed him about what had happened. Chen Hua promised to come down later, by himself, so as not to arouse suspicion.

At around eight that morning my sister-in-law finally arrived. She hadn't come the day before, she said, because she'd had to walk to a neighboring village to find a secure way to call my older brother Guangfu, who was working in Linyi. When she eventually got through to him my brother promised to do whatever was necessary to help me.

I needed somewhere to go, but I wasn't sure where. Yuancheng advised me to head deep into the mountains and live there for a few years; he felt that my situation was much too dangerous now. My sister-in-law agreed, adding that she had heard my brother talking about a recent incident involving a man who had sought refuge at an American consulate—the police had surrounded the place until he walked out.

"Who was that?" I asked, wondering if he was someone from the human rights community. "He was an official, and was taken away by the party," she replied. I had been closed off from the news for over a year and so had no way of judging the significance of the story.

I then asked my sister-in-law if she could do something for me: I needed her to go back to Dongshigu and find a way to deliver six apples to Weijing—or, if not apples, six of something, anything. She said she would try.

As soon as Chen Hua appeared, I asked him about the chances of finding a car, and he went off to see what he could do. About an hour later he came back with a taxi, saying that the driver was waiting outside. At first he had sought out a friend, but the friend was too scared to get mixed up in my case; the money my nephew offered made no difference to him. Next Chen Hua had gone to the bus station and told a taxi driver that his older brother was sick and needed a ride to the hospital.

The lane outside Yuancheng's house was extremely narrow, and it was some time before Chen Hua and the driver could figure out a way to position the taxi right next to Yuancheng's main gate. Hearing the car, villagers came out to see what a vehicle was doing there. When they asked where we were going, Yuancheng replied that we were driving to Jiehu, a town in the opposite direction of where we were really heading. Yuancheng then took some bundles of corn stalks he had piled nearby and stood them up between the car and the wall of their yard to block the onlookers' view. Chen Hua wanted to make sure that even the driver couldn't see me—we had no idea where his loyalties lay. Yuancheng invited the driver inside for tea while Chen Hua gathered up the few things we needed. I had Chen Hua cover my head with my coat. "If someone asks," I told him, "tell them I'm sick and afraid of the breeze."

Chen Hua quickly led me out of the shed and into the taxi. I lay flat on my stomach in the backseat, while Chen Hua took the passenger seat in front. Yuancheng brought the driver out of the house, and at last we got under way. Only then did something like calm begin to come over me. A little over an hour later we reached Xintai, a town on the road to Beijing where Chen Hua's aunt happened to live. My nephew helped me out of the car and paid the driver, who drove off.

It was now Day 3 of my escape, around one in the afternoon. We sat down to rest in a public park, and I asked Chen Hua to go buy water, dumplings, and the cheapest shortwave radio and secondhand cell phone he could find. The phone he brought back still had some battery power left, so I immediately called two contacts—Liu Guohui, who had visited us over Chinese New Year in 2011, and another supporter we knew of. I got through but had to wait for them to call back.

Hearing the large crowds milling all around us in the park, I was beginning to get anxious, so I asked Chen Hua to take me somewhere more secluded and secure. After limping around with his help for nearly three hours, we eventually settled in the one place that appeared safe, a set of little stone stairs down by a river. We ate a bit of food and talked of what had happened, and then I sent him to his aunt's house to charge the cell phone and try to find more help.

I waited there by the river until well after dark, listening to the radio. That evening I heard about the case of the politician Bo Xilai, whose dramatic fall from power was just then playing out. I learned that Wang Lijun, Bo's former deputy, had fled into a U.S. consulate—and then swiftly been turned out. This was the incident my sister-in-law mentioned earlier. The news gave me much to consider as I thought about my own options.

Just as I began worrying about where Chen Hua could be, I heard his voice calling, "Fifth Uncle, Fifth Uncle." I answered, "Come on, I'm here." Chen Hua ran over to me and said, "I've brought people who will help you."

"Who?" I asked.

In reply I heard Elder Brother's voice. "Guo Yushan and Pearl have come for you," he said. "Quick, you need to change your clothes, and then we can go."

"Where are we going?"

"To Beijing."

A moment later I heard Guo Yushan running toward me. I immediately called out, "Yushan, brother!"

"Brother!" Yushan cried joyfully in reply, hugging me. I hadn't seen my old friend since our work together in 2005, since the difficult times we had experienced while investigating the family planning campaigns. Now, under these strangest of circumstances, we were reunited again.

Yushan gave me fresh clothes, made me put on a hat, and said we had to leave immediately.

"Where are we going?" I asked again.

"Beijing," replied Yushan.

"Is it safe in Beijing?"

"I've taken care of everything," he said. "There's no way they'll find you."

Yushan held my arm as I got into the car, a Volkswagen Passat. The driver of the car, a university professor and a trusted friend of Yushan's, was flabbergasted to see me. "So you really are Chen Guangcheng! Take your glasses off so I can take a good look at you," he exclaimed. And of course I did so.

I said good-bye to Chen Hua and urged him to hurry back to his aunt's home. Then I wedged myself into the back of the Passat, between my brother and Chen Hua's father, who had brought Yushan to meet us. Yushan himself sat up front. Behind us, in another car, were Pearl and a friend of Yushan's named Ding Ding, ready to create a diversion or screen us in case we were tailed or pursued. We also wanted to avoid the possibility that we would be caught and all taken in at once.

We had been on the road for only a few minutes when the Passat sputtered to a halt and would go no farther. Blood was thumping in my temples: what was it? A flat tire—at a time like this! Nervous, Yushan's friend had momentarily lost his way and gone careening over a speed bump. As our driver changed the tire, we waited anxiously, fearing detection right there on the side of the road. It was ten p.m., and with few cars around there was nothing to stop a police patrol from pulling over, demanding identification, and unraveling everything in an instant. But soon we set off again, and I began breathing easier.

I stayed low in the back, talking with Yushan about how best to proceed. Before long we made the decision to have Pearl and Ding

Ding take Elder Brother and Chen Hua's father back to Dongshigu. After pulling over again, trailed by the second car, Yushan got out of the Passat and told Pearl to come say hello to me. Pearl and I shook hands and then hugged—this was the first time we'd met, though I had known a bit about her visits to Dongshigu on my behalf. She was almost bashful, but we were both deeply moved, and I was grateful for what she had done for me. After Yushan explained what she and Ding Ding should do, we agreed that we'd all rendezvous again in Beijing.

Ding Ding drove off with Pearl, my brother, and Chen Hua's father, and then we settled in for a long night on the road. Once we turned onto the expressway at Tai'an, three hundred miles south of Beijing, I began to relax, knowing that the police were less likely to stop us now. A few minutes later we began skirting holy Mount Tai, a pilgrimage site for over three thousand years and a famous symbol of birth and renewal. I hoped a rebirth awaited me in the days ahead, though as I ran for my life I had no idea how such a thing could happen.

The days after Guangcheng's escape were unbearable, and we could hardly eat or sleep. Though the guards hadn't seemed to notice anything amiss, I was terrified that they had already found him, that maybe my husband had been captured or even killed. I had to feign complete calm and go about my day as I normally would, even as my heart beat wildly and my mind raced.

On the afternoon of April 22, two days after he left, my mother-in-law was heading out to see if she could get wind of Guangcheng's whereabouts when she was stopped at our main gate by the guards. Handing her a small package, one of them said, "Your eldest daughter-in-law left some things for you."

She carried the package inside, and I hurriedly opened it up: dried noodles, six packets of dried noodles. I was overcome with joy. Though I wanted to sing out with relief—Guangcheng was safe!—I ran to Mama, bent down to her ear, and quickly whispered that I was sure he was okay. Of course she had no idea what I was talking about, since we hadn't told her about the escape plan or the significance of the number six.

We continued to perform our daily chores as though nothing had changed. Kesi maintained her habit of calling for Baba every day when she came back from school; I cooked, cleaned, took out the chamber pot, and went through the motions of washing Guangcheng's feet each night, preparing the basin of warm water and later emptying it outside.

Two days later, on April 24, my confidence was shaken. As we prepared for bed that evening, a driving spring rain beat down on the windows. I lay awake in the dark, watching the beam from a guard's torch illuminate our stark surroundings as he made his periodic rounds. Around nine p.m., a stiff wind kicked up; suddenly the beams multiplied, and I heard footsteps and anxious voices in the yard. I crouched by a crack in the door, watching with one eye, occasionally poking my head up to look out the window. A guard trudged through the mud with a flashlight and an umbrella and sat down right outside our front door, blocking the exit.

I was terrified that Guangcheng's disappearance had finally been discovered. The guards seemed to be looking for something, turning everything over, shuffling through some wood and planks near the steps where Guangcheng had left our yard. Then I heard one of them say, "It's nothing, just a branch that got blown down in the wind." I breathed a sigh of relief—the guards were simply responding to the unexpected sound of the falling branch and had no idea Guangcheng wasn't here beside me. One by one they headed back to their posts.

We did everything we could to give Guangcheng the cover he needed to get as far away as possible. One day Kesi noticed that the bamboo in our yard had grown quite a lot. At my suggestion, and under the watchful eyes of the guards sitting nearby, little Kesi ran eagerly inside the house, shouting, "Baba, Baba! The bamboo has grown so fast! Now it's even taller than I am!" I was continually amazed by her courage.

Seven years had passed since I'd last been on this expressway. In September 2005, after being kidnapped in front of Jiang Tianyong's apartment building in Beijing, I had been traveling in the opposite direction, back to Shandong, and I had been held captive ever since. Now, thanks to the brave efforts of friends and comrades, I was once again a free man.

As we barreled toward the capital under cover of night, Yushan and I talked. We marveled at and mourned all that had happened in just seven years—in our own lives, in the lives of our fellow activists, in China, and around the world. Yushan told me about everything that had been happening outside Dongshigu, about the netizens who had tried to visit me, and about some of his own travails in recent years. We talked about the struggles of such comrades-in-arms as the artist Ai Weiwei, whose ever sharper critiques had ended in detention and house arrest, and Liu Xiaobo, who was still imprisoned and unheard from, despite the Nobel Peace Prize that had brought him international fame.

Yushan also described some deeply disturbing events I'd had no way of hearing about while in prison and under house arrest. During the Arab Spring, China's leaders had grown extremely anxious about a copycat uprising in China, and they had begun a severe crackdown. Some two hundred people had been jailed or disappeared; among them were a number of high-profile activists and lawyers, many of whom had been subject to unspeakable cruelties. Some of those who were imprisoned—such as Teng Biao, Jiang Tianyong, Tang Jitian, Zhang Yongpan, and Xu Zhiyong—had come out of detention weeks and months later, utterly traumatized and unable to talk normally. Jiang Tianyong, for one, described being stripped naked and beaten. Hearing about what my friends and colleagues had suffered at the hands of the government, I shuddered, thinking back to my own experiences in black jails and detention.

By now I was tired and very hungry, yet somehow I couldn't bring myself to sleep or eat. The hours of intense conversation lifted my spirits, and with every mile we put between ourselves and Dongshigu, I felt my anxious mind become a little quieter and the screaming pain in my foot a little less insistent. As Yushan and I talked about what we would do once we reached Beijing, I became convinced that I had to draw attention to my case from the highest levels. If I couldn't achieve freedom and justice for myself and my family, nothing else would be possible; as well, I had to attend to my health right away. In the capital, the presence of journalists and diplomats would make it more difficult for the party to act with impunity. And there was one place in the city, perhaps the only such place in all of China, that we considered absolutely safe: the U.S. embassy.

Shortly after five a.m., with dawn approaching, we entered the orbit of Beijing on one of its concentric ring roads. Our driver, steady at the wheel for almost eight hours, refused to let Yushan take over. Near a university campus, we came to a small apartment, the temporary safe house that Yushan had arranged for me. Staying with me would be He Zhengjun, a reliable activist at Yushan's NGO. After the driver hurried off to a class he was teaching, Yushan got me settled in and asked what I needed. "A shortwave radio, a talking watch for the blind, and a pair of sunglasses," I answered. No matter what, we agreed, I would let no one into the apartment. Zhengjun and Yushan would have keys, but since my whereabouts were unknown to everyone else, no one ought to be coming to the door. Now I would rest, and tomorrow we would plan.

Yushan and Zhengjun left, promising to return that evening. It was Day 4 of my escape, and after everything I'd gone through, this ordinary, middle-class Beijing apartment seemed a small miracle of everyday life. I had slept barely a dozen hours since fleeing my home; now, under clean sheets, in an atmosphere of unaccustomed privacy and safety, I dropped off almost instantly.

But I didn't sleep long: around eleven that morning, I woke to troubled thoughts. What was happening to my family and friends back home? Who in Beijing could help me find a way to keep my hard-won freedom? And how could I get to a doctor? I was still in very bad shape. My right foot was terribly painful and increasingly swollen, and once again I was besieged by diarrhea.

I boiled some water for tea and listened intently to the noise beyond my window. For my own safety, I needed to learn the normal soundscape here so I could discern any deviations. I also wanted to take in the ordinary sounds I hadn't heard in years: the scattered footfalls of children going to and from school, the rhythms of a distant basketball game, all the floating music of city life.

At three p.m., someone rang the doorbell. They rang twice, but I didn't open the door. Ten minutes later, someone rang again; I still wouldn't open up. I was on high alert, listening carefully to every sound, fearful that the police had at last tracked me down. After a few minutes, I heard a key turn in the lock and He Zhengjun walked in. I asked him if he knew who had come to the door, and he explained that two men had tried to deliver a bed to the apartment. Now I understood: the small apartment had only one bed, the one I had been using, and Zhengjun also needed a place to sleep.

That night Yushan and his wife, Ah Pan, came to the apartment. We made plans to record a video statement that would be released online—and since I might be caught at any time, there wasn't a minute to lose. Zhengjun, who had some experience with film, would shoot the footage, edit it as needed, and get it out to the world; my job was to craft what I wanted to say. To speak out publicly, fluently, and convincingly was no simple matter in my condition. A more serious concern, however, was our safety. We chose to film my statement in the most generic spot in that very generic apartment. While testing the equipment, Zhengjun noticed that my sunglasses gave off a slight reflection of him behind the camera, so we melted chocolate and smeared it over my glasses.

We filmed three long takes over the next two days, and the fifteen minutes we ultimately released consisted of me speaking directly to the camera. "Dear Premier Wen," I began, "I finally escaped." I made three straightforward demands: I wanted a full investigation, I wanted my safety and the safety of my family guaranteed, and I wanted to see the officials responsible for my illegal treatment punished. In the unreleased footage I described my escape, but I also recorded a short message to Christian Bale: "Hi, Mr. Bale, I'm Chen Guangcheng. You're not just a knight when you're acting. You are in real life, too."

Two days into my stay at the safe house, we took our chances and arranged a small reunion of all those who had driven down to Shandong and tried to save me. Emotions ran high that evening. When Pearl—the "female knight" who had worked with devotion on my behalf for over a year—arrived, she ran to me and wept with her head on my chest. I felt no real sense of triumph that night, nor did anyone else. Instead, an inexplicable sadness prevailed, a bittersweet sense of both endurance and uncertainty. Would I stay in China? my friends asked. I admitted that I hadn't really thought about it but that it was certainly my aim to remain in my native land and work for justice here. We took some group photos to memorialize our evening together; even now, with my own kind of mental camera, I can access the image.

The only other visitors I had in that safe house were the activist Hu Jia and his wife, Zeng Jinyan, who came to see me on April 25. They were bold fighters both. Though they had helped me and Weijing when I was in jail, I had known them only from a distance.

"Hu Jia, my brother," I said to him, "at last we meet."

"Guangcheng, my brother," he replied. "Indeed now we are together."

Few people could understand as well as Hu Jia and Zeng Jinyan the path I had chosen and the price I had paid. Jail time for an invented crime, the resulting strain on a marriage, the victimization of one's family members—all these things we shared, and I found myself frankly and openly weeping beside them, reaching depths of feeling that I'd been forced to ignore during my seven-year fight for survival.

As Hu Jia and Zeng Jinyan were leaving, Jinyan told Yushan that I should think seriously about contacting the American embassy. When Yushan asked my opinion of the idea, I said I had considered it but was hesitant because of the news that Wang Lijun—the official implicated in Bo Xilai's case—had been sent away from the American consulate just two months earlier. "You can still try," replied Yushan, and I agreed with him. I was hopeful that popular pressure, spurred on by the release of our video, might finally force the higher-ups to investigate my case, but I acknowledged that getting in touch with the U.S. embassy was the only other option.

That evening, Yushan, Zhengjun, and I finished filming the video, and then Yushan sent an e-mail to contacts of his at the embassy. An hour or so later we heard back; embassy officials wanted to arrange a brief meeting so they could talk with me in person. Perhaps they were skeptical that a blind man had escaped on his own, or perhaps it was their penchant, typical of foreigners, for wanting to be "99 percent sure" of something before moving forward. In any case, Yushan hatched a plan for us to rendezvous the next morning at six a.m. in Wudaokou, a student neighborhood close to the Tsinghua University campus.

The whole world seemed to be asleep when Ding Ding picked us up on the morning of April 26, this time in a car with tinted windows. We hastily packed the few things I would need; even if the embassy refused to provide me with emergency shelter, it was clear that I couldn't stay in the safe house. We arrived at our rendezvous point a few minutes early and pulled over, the car idling in the predawn street. Soon enough a car from the embassy appeared, and a moment later two staffers popped open the doors and slipped into the seats on either side of me. As soon as they saw me, they expressed both amazement and concern. I allowed them to take a quick photo to prove that they had really met with me, and then I told them I wanted to go to the American embassy to escape danger. They promised an answer as soon as possible—with luck, they said, they would have it within the next five hours, although it could take longer because the decision would have to be approved by Washington. With that, they climbed out and drove away.

Now all I could do was wait. Ding Ding and I spent the next couple of hours driving around Beijing; occasionally we would park somewhere for a few minutes, but it was far too dangerous to step out of the car. Eventually it occurred to us to head for the Bird's Nest, whose design Ai Weiwei had collaborated on; also known as the National Stadium, it had been built for the Olympics but was now barely used. As Ding Ding pointed out, there was ample public parking but few people around, so it was a good place to rest for a while.

As we waited, I tried to imagine what we would do if the embassy refused to take me. As we sat there in the car, time seemed to come to a halt. Ding Ding told me his life story, describing his father, his childhood, his political ideas. We had a case of bottled water in the back, and by eleven a.m. I had already drunk three bottles. Running to a bathroom was out of the question, so with Ding Ding's permission, I discreetly filled up the bottles I had just emptied.

Just after eight a.m. on April 26, three guards came into our living room. "Where is Guangcheng?" they asked abruptly.

"He's asleep," I replied.

Knowing that he spent most of his time in bed, they seemed satisfied and walked out. I was nervous, though, so I quickly rolled up a quilt, shoved it beneath the covers, and shaped it into an approximation of a human form. I also set out Guangcheng's shoes beneath the bed, just the way he always did.

Minutes later, the three guards were back. "Our boss asked us whether we actually saw Guangcheng. Let's see him."

"Okay," I said, "but you know that after he has breakfast he goes to bed." I opened the bedroom door for them, and when they saw the shape in the bed and the shoes beneath, they were reassured.

But the higher-ups must have known something was amiss: they sent the three fools back yet again, and this time they entered the bedroom and poked among the bedclothes and saw that they'd been duped. They ran from the house as fast as their legs could carry them, and soon dozens of cadres were back in the house, searching up and down, interrogating me, poking their noses everywhere. Before long, I was taken away by a crowd of burly security police officers and forced into their car. Just as the guards slammed the door shut, I yelled out, "Mama, I'm being taken away!"

I was driven to a nearby hotel and interrogated. "When did Guangcheng escape?" the officials asked. "How did he escape?"

I said I didn't know, then turned their questions back at them. "Why is he not allowed to leave his own house? Do you tell the whole world every time you leave home?"

Furious that I'd spoken to them in this way, they shouted at me to tell them where he was.

"You've got layer upon layer of guards out there watching us," I said, laughing. "And now you don't know where he is. I've only got one pair of eyes. With that many pairs of eyes working for you, don't you think you should know where he is?"

My interrogators were livid and embarrassed. At one point one of their leaders came in and announced that Guangcheng was in Beijing, but I wasn't sure if they were just trying to trick me. Later that day I was taken to the Yinan County Public Security Bureau, where two female police officers did a full body search and then bound me to a chair. They kept switching in new people to question me, but I told them nothing.

By that evening my feet were swollen and my whole body was numb from being tied up for so long. I repeatedly asked to go to the bathroom; eventually they allowed me to use a small pan in the corner of the interrogation room. Just moving was very painful, and I was overcome with worry about the rest of my family.

* * *

Yushan called us around noon with some news: the Americans had agreed to give me shelter, and we were due to meet some people from the embassy at one o'clock. After pulling out of the Olympic stadium's parking lot, Ding Ding started driving toward the rendezvous point, but a few minutes later Yushan called to say that the meeting had been changed to one-thirty. I wondered if I would be safe once I reached the embassy's car; would the car itself be considered American territory? Soon Yushan called again to say that four suspicious cars were now tailing him.

At precisely one-thirty, all seven cars—our own, the embassy's, Yushan's, and the four that belonged to our pursuers—converged at the rendezvous point, which was near a McDonald's on a main street. Ding Ding parked just down the street from the McDonald's and picked up Yushan and Zhengjun; as soon as they hopped into our car, Ding Ding stepped on the gas. Two pursuing cars immediately fell in directly behind us, while the other two followed the embassy car.

As Ding Ding pulled away, Yushan gave me a cell phone and some cash. Then we settled in for what became a car chase. For more than twenty minutes, a tight cluster of six cars raced through the streets of Beijing. Cool and confident, Ding Ding made short work of the jam-packed boulevards, but so did our pursuers. At first, Yushan and Zhengjun reported that the embassy's driver was doing a good job of keeping up, but after a few minutes two of the pursuing cars separated us from the embassy car.

Still unable to shake our pursuers, Ding Ding steered us toward the west gate of Beijing Forestry University, thinking that the enclosed layout might give us more chances to dodge them. We raced east through the campus and then took a quick right toward the south gate, only to discover that it was closed. Braking hard, Ding Ding made a fast three-point turn, cutting off our nearest pursuer, who had tried to follow suit. The embassy car now seized the moment, overtaking the car immediately ahead of it and stopping just three or four feet from us. Moments later all six cars had come to a halt, all facing in different directions. Our pursuers almost encircled us, but Yushan judged that we were just close enough to the embassy car to make the switch.

"Quick, get out!" he urged. This was our chance. Yushan and Zhengjun jumped out of the car and hailed the Americans. Then they grabbed my arms and hurried me over to the open door of the embassy car—together we crossed that tiniest, most crucial bit of distance.

"Get in, get in quick!" came the voice of Yang Junyi, one of the staffers I had met earlier, and I felt my arms being pulled just before he slammed the door shut. Outside, Zhengjun made a run for it on foot, while Ding Ding and Yushan sped off, two cars following their car. The other two cars stayed with us, a snarling little escort containing invisible enemies.

"Thank you, thank you" was all I could say to these unknown rescuers from a distant land. Yang Junyi then introduced me to Robert Wang, the U.S. deputy chief of mission. Taking my hand firmly, Wang told me that my troubles were over.

Wang turned to the driver. "Step on it," he said. "Back to the embassy."

At last I was on my way to the one safe place in all of China.

CHAPTER TWELVE

Eye of the Storm

Trying to elude our pursuers, our driver wove in and out of traffic, accelerating and then braking suddenly, jerking us back and forth in our seats. Deputy Chief Wang finally told the driver to take it easy, fearing that an accident or some other mishap would draw the unwanted attention of the police. To me, he said simply, "Don't worry, you're safe now. You can breathe easy." He held my hand tightly, which felt wonderfully reassuring and caring after everything I'd been through.

Slowly my heart was returning to something like a normal rate, but I would feel real relief only when we were inside the embassy itself. Even there, I knew, I would be marooned on an island of freedom set in a sea of party rule; for now, though, I was overwhelmed by spontaneous gratitude, a drowning man pulled out of a river who at last gasps the open air. When the danger is real, I thought, America lives up to its most basic values. Deputy Chief Wang, Yang Junyi, and a man in the front seat were continually taking phone calls as we drove, including at least one from Washington. Their phone conversations were all in English, but there was one phrase I thought I understood: "in the car." Wang told me that Secretary of State Hillary Clinton had sent me a clear message of support.

When we reached the embassy gate, Yang instructed me to put my head down: the guards outside were Chinese citizens, and I needed to stay out of their view. The other two cars followed us right up to the gate and stopped—I was safe. I thanked our driver, who surely didn't find himself in such car chases every day but had proven himself to be remarkably skilled.

Wang stepped out of the car and led me inside, still holding my hand. He was concerned about my foot, repeatedly asking if it hurt. In fact, I was no longer bothered by the pain; I'd been too overwhelmed by recent events to pay it much heed. Several embassy staffers followed us up to the third floor of one wing of the compound, where the marines charged with defending the embassy in an emergency live. My presence in the embassy was kept quiet, known only to a handful of diplomats in the political affairs department.

Wang led me to my room, which had a bed, a table, and a large wardrobe. While I rested in an upholstered chair, the embassy staff set to making the bed with fresh sheets and blankets. Everything felt new and plush—the carpets, the towels, the pillows. The bed was high, and difficult to get onto with my injured foot.

In the chaos of the car chase, I'd left my few possessions in Ding Ding's car, but Wang and his staff saw to everything, graciously and efficiently. Much of what they gave me had been brought from their own homes, including new dress shirts taken directly from one of the diplomats' own closets. I soon had a shortwave radio, a little voice recorder, a cup, a toothbrush, and toothpaste. I asked for a computer and was told that the embassy would find something for me as soon as possible. Staffers also brought me food and a crutch from the infirmary; I had to use it just to get across the room. "Whatever you need," said Wang, "just tell me. Washington has made it very clear that we should do everything possible to help you." These words filled my heart with warmth and gratitude.

Throughout the day, Deputy Chief Wang stopped in numerous times to see how I was doing. There was a sincerity and a genuineness of spirit in him and the other officials that moved me greatly, and I felt full of hope that America would live up to its role as a leader in human rights, that justice could finally be achieved. Secretary of State Clinton was truly a person of vision, I thought. The significance of the gestures made by the United States government on my behalf went well beyond me; indeed, they validated for all humanity the importance of the universal values of human rights and dignity, so often diluted by commercial interests.

That evening, I told Wang about the videos I had made with Zhengjun and Yushan. I still had no information about the friends who had helped me escape, and I feared for their safety. Wang told me that Pearl had already contacted the media; indeed, later that night, nearly one week since I had slipped away from home, the earliest Chinese-language reports about my escape came out and the video made in our Beijing safe house was released. As word spread on the Chinese Internet, my name was banned as a search term; so was "blind man," and then even the word "embassy." Netizens managed to stay one step ahead of the censors by making coded references to the movie *Shawshank Redemption*, with its famous prison break, and by using the phrase "going into the light," playing on the meaning of my name in Chinese.

The following day, April 27, Ambassador Gary Locke returned to the embassy, having cut short his vacation because of my arrival. That morning, he and Deputy Chief Wang came to see me, expressing great concern about my injuries. I thanked them and told them I was extremely worried about my family and friends. They informed me that a team of high-level American diplomats would soon be arriving in Beijing, led by Secretary of State Clinton and Treasury Secretary Timothy Geithner. Beginning on May 3, the American team would be holding a two-day "Strategic and Economic Dialogue" with top Chinese officials. I wondered how my situation would sit with their agenda.

Yang came by later and let me use his phone to call Yushan. He and Pearl were safe, he said, but he had heard news that my nephew Kegui had been injured in a confrontation with Zhang Jian, a ringleader in our house arrest. The details were as yet unknown.

Those first two days in the embassy were productive and restorative. Aside from being attentive and generous, Ambassador Locke and Deputy Chief Wang seemed fully committed to helping me achieve justice and pursue my work. Diplomats from the political affairs department brought every meal directly to my room; many of them said they felt that the United States was doing something profound and important in helping me. I was filled with gratitude and affection. They asked repeatedly whether I wanted to go to America; I told them that for now I hoped to stay in China so that I could continue pushing for the rule of law and promoting human rights.

A nurse had seen me soon after my arrival at the embassy on April 26, and she'd given me medicine for my ulcerative colitis that helped immensely. The next day, a doctor came by as well. Carefully examining my injured foot with his hands, he discerned that I had broken at least two bones, possibly three. I was touched by his gentle manner, so professional and yet so compassionate, in stark contrast to the treatment I had grown used to over the past seven years. Everyone agreed on the need for an X-ray; the only question was how I could get one, given the obvious dangers of leaving the embassy to visit a hospital. Yang was only half joking when he asked whether we could use the X-ray scanner at the embassy security check, though of course the doctor didn't think that was such a good idea. "Well then," said Yang, "we should look into purchasing an X-ray machine for the embassy, with support as strong as it is in Congress for your case." I was struck by the dedication and enthusiasm of my hosts, who seemed willing to go to any length to help me.

Later that afternoon, Yang brought me an iPad and read me the news. I had never held such a device, having only heard about it on the radio while listening under my quilts in prison. He read some of the messages Chinese netizens were leaving on the embassy's website, thanking the Americans for taking care of "our light." He also helped me look up information about my nephew, and we found a recording of a conversation between Kegui and an American netizen, during which Kegui described what had happened. I wept as I listened, and Yang comforted me.

From this and other sources, I would eventually learn the details of how on April 26, Zhang Jian had led a horde of thugs to Elder Brother's house. They broke in, scaling the walls of the family's yard and storming inside; they hooded Elder Brother and took him off to the police station, where he would endure three days of torture and interrogation.

Other cadres attacked my sister-in-law, while another group surrounded Kegui and beat him with clubs until he was covered in blood. Fearing for his life, Kegui grabbed a knife to defend himself; Zhang Jian and two of his cohorts sustained minor injuries in the melee. Kegui would later be arrested, detained for "intentional homicide," and sentenced to over three years in prison, in obvious retaliation against me.

After listening to Kegui's account, Yang helped me find Radio France's online news program. He then stepped out for a meeting, leaving me to revel in the clarity of the program, which I was hearing for the first time without signal interference.

Alone in my room, I listened to the news until the iPad suddenly shut down, at around six p.m. I was unable to turn the device back on, so I put it on the table and waited. I expected that Yang would be back around six-thirty, but in fact he didn't return until around nine that night. Aside from the person who brought my food, no one else came to see me, in stark contrast to the regular appearances they had been making so far, both day and night. When Yang finally returned, I could tell he was both saddened and deeply disturbed. I asked him to help me go back online, but he said it was late and that he had to head home to his wife. I don't like pestering people, so I didn't press him.

After he left, I sat in a chair beside the window with my foot propped up on a stool, my crutch on one side, the table with the iPad on the other. From my brief conversation with Yang and from the shift in the other staffers' attentions, I understood that something had changed dramatically. Apparently, at a meeting on April 27 of the National Security Council with President Obama in the White House, the "policy had changed." The new directive was that from then on, no one was to help me go online, which, given my disability, made it impossible for me to know what was happening beyond the confines of the embassy. Moreover, it was agreed that my case shouldn't damage the relationship between the United States and China, and thus my situation should be resolved immediately—language I took to indicate that the White House no longer supported me and that I was to leave the embassy in short order. Most disturbingly, I learned, some officials at the meeting had suggested that democracy and human rights in China were not in America's best interest. Apparently, not a single person at the NSC meeting had spoken up to argue that America should protect human rights or to insist that the U.S. government should stand up for its founding doctrines and essential values.

When I heard this, I was dumbfounded, stung. So this was the America we all put on a pedestal, the concrete manifestation of what is good and just in humanity? Out of all the nations in the world, and all the embassies that could have provided a safe haven, I had sought the succor of the United States, believing with every cell in my body that this country, above all others, had both the commitment and the strength to protect the rights of the individual over the interests of a dictatorship. The moral authority lay unquestionably in the hands of the Americans; why, then, would the country we all revered for its values choose to turn away from human rights?

The following morning, April 28, Deputy Chief Wang appeared in my room. He told me that normal embassy rules dictated that everyone who came into the compound had to go through security. Of course, my situation was different, he added, and nothing had been checked when I arrived, but now Washington was asking that I hand over all my electronic devices for a routine security check. I could tell he was under pressure. I sympathized with him and handed over my talking watch, cell phone, and chargers.

In the afternoon, my watch was returned to me but not my phone—Wang said they would give it back when I left the embassy. He also told me that Washington had wanted the embassy to check the radio, but he hadn't bothered to take it. The iPad was left in my room, but I had no way of using it on my own. From this point on, I was effectively cut off from the outside world.

It was fast becoming clear that some Americans hoped my stay here would be short. Embassy staffers were still friendly and enthusiastic when providing food or arranging medical care; these small acts of kindness now seemed to be the only way they could express their concern. Otherwise, most of them seemed worried about something they weren't able to talk about. I felt like an invisible wall had risen between me and the staff, one I was reminded of each time I got up from the bed and inadvertently ran my hand over the unusable iPad on the table.

Of course I knew that the diplomats here in Beijing, however generous and willing to help on a personal level, ultimately had to answer to Washington. Secretary of State Clinton might have voiced her support, but the order to prevent me from communicating with the outside seemed to have come straight from the White House. "Don't be disappointed," Wang said, "this is how it goes with politics." In my own view, as so often in human relations, greed was likely coming before justice, and economic considerations were being given more weight than people's fundamental rights. The specter of profit constantly haunts the world's dealings with China, and the United States was far from immune. Is there no country that truly represents and embodies the most basic values of humanity? I maintained my faith in the American people, knowing—hoping—that a democratic country would not just eject me from the embassy, could not just throw me to the wolves. For now I said nothing, but I was on guard. The high-stakes political maneuvers were just beginning.

At noon the following day, April 29, Ambassador Locke, Deputy Chief Wang, and I spoke in the garden while we waited for the arrival of the other diplomats who were forming a negotiating team to work out my situation. I told Ambassador Locke that I was extremely concerned about my family, especially after hearing the news about my nephew, and that before we discussed anything with the Chinese authorities, the persecution of my family had to stop. Ambassador Locke assured me that my family's safety was their number one concern as well.

Soon, Harold Koh, the legal adviser for the State Department, along with another key negotiator, Kurt Campbell, assistant secretary of state for East Asian and Pacific affairs, arrived at the embassy and joined us in the garden. We moved chairs around a circular table to make ourselves more comfortable; I felt the sun warming my face.

Koh and I had met briefly the day before; he had described how his father had come to the United States as a South Korean diplomat, later becoming a dissident in the 1960s. Campbell was introduced to me by

Locke, who announced that the assistant secretary's primary responsibility was to make sure human rights were not obliterated by the Strategic and Economic Dialogue about to take place. Both Americans impressed me as being capable, steady, and focused.

Campbell told me that he and his team had already met with their Chinese counterparts to talk about my case. "We have our principles, and we will protect your interests," he said, adding that the team was considering various proposals in an effort to come up with a workable solution. "However," he assured me, "our first priority is the humane treatment of you, your children, your wife, and your mother." When I mentioned my concern for my oldest brother's family, Campbell said the Chinese central government should undertake a careful investigation and that there needed to be a process that the central government would "accept and acknowledge."

I was encouraged by his words, then surprised when he passed on some unexpected news. New York University, with one of the best law facilities in the world, was opening a campus in Shanghai. "They want to offer you a three-year scholarship, including a stipend," he said, "so that you can complete your studies. This is a unique opportunity that has been put in place quickly to allow you to be able to start a new life." He went on to say that I would be able to leave Dongshigu and study with NYU law professors such as Jerry Cohen. He also said that his team had already written out this proposal and presented it to the Chinese government.

"Our time is extremely limited," Campbell said, "and we are in the process of working out the parameters of the proposal. First of all, they need to acknowledge that they won't take legal action against you simply because you came to the embassy. Secondly, they need to allow you to study and live in peace, and your civil rights need to be guaranteed." I thanked the Americans profusely for their efforts on my behalf, adding that I was also concerned about my right to leave and enter the country.

Campbell then told me that they had been informed that the Chinese government would agree to hear my story and that, in fact, the Chinese leadership had been concerned with my case for some time. "They acknowledge that your civil rights have been violated," he told me, "and there are at least a few negotiators on the Chinese side who respect and support you. The only way to achieve our goals, however, is if we act quickly."

I found it odd that he kept emphasizing that the situation needed to be wrapped up quickly. I had lived under persecution for over seven years, after all, and I told Campbell that I wanted to make sure that the proposals were watertight.

"I now want to ask something of you that might be premature," Campbell said. "I need you to believe in Ambassador Locke, Mr. Koh, in me, and in Deputy Chief Wang. We need you to trust us. We will work to protect your interests, and to help and support you and your family."

I said I trusted them implicitly and was grateful for all they had been doing.

Campbell told me that the Americans were hoping to work out an agreement with the Chinese within twenty-four to thirty-six hours. "Now, there are two choices: one, come to an agreement with the Chinese government, be reunited with your family, and have your rights guaranteed," he said. "This will be a formal written agreement between the two countries. Another option is that you would stay at the embassy indefinitely, but in that case we would have no idea whether or not the government would actually allow you to leave the embassy, or even China. I would also, in that case, be concerned for the safety of your family and of your friends and supporters." He again said, "You must believe in me," reiterating the narrow window of time.

Actually, I already believed in Campbell and the other diplomats, and I wasn't sure why he kept telling me that I should trust them. My greater concern was the time frame. Though it might be possible to reach an agreement with the Chinese government in the next day or two, a proper investigation of my case would take much longer. In my mind, there could be no resolution without a thorough, transparent inquiry that led to the prosecution of those responsible for the injustice done to me and my family.

As our conversation came to an end that afternoon, Campbell said, "I promise you that we will find a good school for your children, and that

I will help to find a good place for you to study, in your own country, to live peacefully." He then added that with the assistance of the embassy, I should call Weijing that evening and tell her to pack her things: staffers would pick her and our two children up in Shandong the following day. We had no phone in our house, but the diplomats said they would find a way to get through. If all went as planned, they said, I would be reunited with my family the following evening.

Before Campbell and the others left to continue their discussions with their Chinese counterparts, Harold Koh asked Wang to read me the letter from the president of New York University, offering me a three-year scholarship at NYU. The letter invited me to study at NYU's new Shanghai campus, as well as the university's main campus in New York City in the future. Wang handed the letter to me when he was finished. I told them I would happily accept the invitation and that I would tell Weijing about it when I spoke to her later that night; I thanked them again and again for their efforts and concern and again mentioned the safety of my family and friends, urging the Americans to raise the issue at the next meeting.

After Campbell, Koh, and Locke left to continue negotiations, Wang helped me back to my room, asking me what I thought. I said I was optimistic, and impressed with the dedication of the American team. "My ultimate goal is not to oppose the Communist Party per se," I told him, adding that I would be against any party that maintained a dictatorship and would also support any party that embraced democracy and the rule of law. Wang left soon after to join the next round of talks. For the time being I stayed in my room alone, playing through everything that had happened and wondering how the Chinese government would respond to the Americans' proposal.

That evening, Campbell, accompanied by Wang, came back with a report that I found deeply troubling. He prefaced it by saying that my case had gone to the highest levels of the Chinese government and that they had already come to a decision. There was some good news and some bad. "First," he said, "they agree to let you reunite with your family. Second, they will make sure the abuse stops. Third, they hope you will stay in Beijing for a while to enable them to take a record of your treatment." The Americans would need my support to help achieve these basic goals, he said.

Then came the bad news: although the Chinese authorities would agree to let me go to another city in Shandong Province, they would not allow me to go to NYU in Shanghai. "They aren't pleased with the idea of your going to a Western institution to resolve the situation," Campbell said. "It makes them feel like they are losing face." As long as I was away from the petty tyrants of Yinan County, they seemed to be saying, all would be well. The idea that going somewhere else in Shandong would end my persecution, though, was a farce. I had been told on numerous occasions that the orders pertaining to my treatment were not confined to local actors and, most likely, came from the highest echelons of the party and government leadership.

"I don't think I can accept that," I said. "If they are worried about losing face, then they shouldn't do things like this, especially in the age of the Internet. They still think that if they do something bad, they can just cover it up."

"Besides Shandong," Campbell asked, "where else would you consider living? Beijing?"

"If there were guarantees about my safety, then I would consider Beijing. I'm not so concerned about exactly where. It's more that their demands are incredibly conservative and controlling. A citizen has the right to movement and should be free to choose where to live. They have no right to limit my choices, to say they are giving me a choice. They shouldn't ask if I'm living here or there—I should be at liberty to make that choice myself. If they are going to interfere with this, then how will I know my civil rights will be honored in the future?"

We debated these issues a while longer, and before heading off to take a call from Washington, Campbell agreed to raise my concerns in the negotiations the following day. Again I was left in the room with Wang, who concurred with Campbell that the Chinese didn't want the Americans to get too involved in a situation involving a Chinese citizen. I found it strange that when it came to practical solutions, the facts of my treatment—namely, that I had undergone over seven years of abuse at the hands of the authorities with whom the Americans were now negotiating—seemed immaterial.

"It's like this," I said. "If it weren't a question of my safety, then why would I have come here? If there were anywhere else in China I could go where I felt safe, why would I have come to the American embassy? In 2005 I went through the officially sanctioned process and reported my case to the police, and as a result I was detained. And no one paid any attention. Why would I do that again? The officials in the central government never want to look at themselves for the root of the problem—as long as they hold on to power—but will do anything to avoid losing face." It was clear to me that the issue of "face" raised by the Chinese government was simply a distraction tactic—and one that was particularly effective with Western governments.

The embassy never arranged for me to talk with my family that night, and I never found out why. Reflecting on the day's discussions, I concluded that the Chinese side had indeed done a lot of work on the "face" front and that it might help matters if I wrote up a few things in response. The next morning—April 30—I dictated a memo delineating five points to Wang, which I wished him to give to Campbell, the head of the negotiating team. The points were as follows:

1. Freedom of movement. It is my right as a citizen, not the Chinese government's, to choose where I go and where I live. In carrying out their promises, the Chinese side should be acting in service of my rights, not controlling my rights.
2. Would I have come to the American embassy if my safety was protected on Chinese soil? I came to the embassy because of a real and present danger, a circumstance protected under Chinese law; as such, I should bear no legal consequences.
3. On the surface, my going into the embassy may seem like a foreign affairs matter, but in reality it is a question of human nature and basic humanitarianism: saving a life. Every country—not just the United States, a nation founded on the principles of democracy, freedom, and human rights—has a responsibility to save someone from imminent death or face strong criticism for inaction.
4. In Chinese law, a basic principle is clearly enunciated: a citizen may do anything, as long as it is not prohibited by law. That is to say,

according to Chinese law, there are no restrictions regarding whom I may associate with. Therefore, I may associate with whomever I choose. If you feel uncomfortable with my associating with Americans, for instance, that is due to the fact that you still harbor sentiments left over from the Cultural Revolution and have not fully implemented Deng Xiaoping's ideas related to "seeking truth from facts" and liberating one's thinking, both of which have already been integrated into the party's mission and the nation's constitution.

5. I demand a transparent, public investigation leading to the prosecution of the officials in Shandong who were involved in my case. If, in the process, other officials are implicated, they all need to be investigated thoroughly, no matter how many or from what rank; a schedule must be announced. If, after the Strategic and Economic Dialogue is over, you continue to procrastinate, this will not be acceptable.

Wang promised to pass these points on to Campbell, and I spent the rest of the day in my room, weighing the potential scenarios and possible outcomes and wondering what the Americans would bring back later that night. I've often observed that the Chinese government will strike an aggressive stance but will give in easily if an opposing side holds its own. I was certain that if the Americans drove a hard line in the negotiations, their Chinese counterparts would likely capitulate.

That night, Harold Koh and Kin Moy, the deputy assistant secretary of state in the Bureau of East Asian and Pacific Affairs, as well as other embassy staffers, came to my room with an update. Koh said they had spoken at length with representatives from the Chinese government, that they had a lot of information to give me, and that I should listen hard and be prepared to make a decision. "It was not easy," Koh told me. "They are quite angry with you, and also angry at the U.S."

"Are they angry with themselves?" I asked, amazed at their audacity.

Ignoring the chuckles from others in the room, Koh said, "They are angry at Shandong and don't understand why Shandong officials would treat you that way. We discussed a proposal with the Chinese side, and you can decide for yourself if you want to accept it or not. The

Chinese side won't make any other offers, and after this there are two other choices, neither of which is very optimal. One would be that you stay here at the U.S. embassy indefinitely, without your family. The other would be that at some point you might be able to go to America, but alone, not with your family, and no one could say for how long; moreover, we wouldn't know if the Chinese government would even allow this.

"If you choose to accept this proposal—that is, if you leave the embassy tomorrow and go to Beijing Chao-Yang Hospital—you will be able to be seen by Chinese doctors for a few days, maybe one or two weeks, while they do an evaluation. Embassy doctors and officials will continue to visit you at the hospital, as the hospital is not far from the embassy."

When I heard this, I was confused: Chao-Yang Hospital, though well known and respected, was under the control of the Chinese government. Embassy officials had previously said I should go to an international hospital, ostensibly under the auspices of the United States and other democratic nations, as they believed my medical and personal safety were of utmost importance. It sounded as if the Americans had allowed their negotiating position to be significantly eroded.

Koh continued: "During these one or two weeks, you will not be allowed to have contact with the media throughout the period of the strategic talks. But there are two good things: you will be reunited with your family and an official will come to the hospital to document the abuse you and your family suffered, and will later carry out an investigation.

"At a later point," Koh said, "Secretary of State Clinton and President Obama will raise your case with Hu Jintao, Wen Jiabao, Xi Jinping, and others"—that is, the Chinese president and premier and the general secretary of the Communist Party—"and will let them know that they are concerned about you and your family and express that they believe you should be treated humanely. They will also bring up the situation with regard to the people who helped you escape from Shandong. High-level U.S. officials will continue to pay attention to your case and will continue to hold the Chinese side accountable to its promises. President Obama and Secretary of State Clinton will raise your case with the Chinese leadership—i.e., Hu Jintao and Wen Jiabao—during the period of the strategic talks and beyond. This will help ensure the safety of you and your family. In two weeks, the Chinese government will allow you to leave to go to university and will give you a housing and living stipend. They have already found seven schools where you can study, though they won't allow you to go directly to the NYU Shanghai campus."

I asked why I couldn't go to NYU's Shanghai branch when I already had the university's letter inviting me to study there for three years.

"We don't know. Probably because it's an American institution."

"Isn't Bo Guagua"—Bo Xilai's son—"studying at an American university?" I said. "Why are they letting him go? And isn't Xi Jinping's daughter at Harvard? Or is that not an American institution?"

"I believe they're afraid you'll have contact with Western media," Koh said.

"It's my freedom of speech," I protested, exasperated at having to defend the idea of basic freedoms to American officials. "This is a civil right protected under Chinese law, and it's also one of the things I need them to agree to protect. If they are going to continue to limit my freedom of speech, then it's a farce for them to say—like they did earlier—that they are going to protect my civil liberties. Civil rights are not just about living accommodations and having enough to eat, as they would like to have it."

I gathered that the American side thought I would accept the conditions presented by the Chinese, and indeed they began pressuring me to come up with a decision. Oddly, the admissions of guilt and wrongdoing on the part of the Chinese government had evaporated, and the Americans didn't seem to think it necessary to keep this on the table.

Time in the hospital was certainly a necessity, as there was only so much care the embassy could provide on-site—but surely the American negotiators understood the potential dangers for me at a Chinese-controlled hospital? It was also true that I wanted to study the law more formally than I had before, but otherwise this "deal" was absurdly inadequate, deftly avoiding all my important demands and indeed even further infringing on my basic rights. I would not accept two weeks without contacting the media, but I also found it extraordinary that the Americans seemed to think it would stop at this. And why, I wondered, should I renounce my right to freedom of speech at a time when the media's oversight role could be pivotal? Why should I wait two years before going to NYU, where I'd been invited—and why this list of seven universities chosen by Chinese officials? When Koh read me the list of schools, I discovered that it included my alma mater Nanjing University of Chinese Medicine. And what did I care about the authorities paying my tuition, providing a kind of measly minimum wage, when they were clearly spending millions on my detention and wouldn't meet my basic demand that they investigate my case?

"If you agree to our proposal," Koh said, "you can choose one of these schools, either today or, at latest, tomorrow. I urge you to accept this proposal."

"I don't trust them," I said, dumbstruck. "You can see how anxious the Chinese government is to have me leave the embassy, but after I leave they are clearly planning to continue to restrict my freedoms. I can't accept this. The thing I proposed was that they immediately cease the persecution of me and my family and protect my civil rights. They even mentioned on the first day that they were in the wrong in some areas and admitted that I had indeed been abused. They should immediately cease the abuse and guarantee my freedoms, not because of anything outlandish but because these are the most basic human rights. I don't think they should be adding any more restrictions."

I felt that I had to explain further: "In 2005 I was illegally detained; then they put me in jail for over four years, having fabricated a crime. When I got out of jail, they put me under illegal house arrest. Altogether that's seven years. Do they think that's not enough? They still want me to waste another two years?" I asked incredulously. "They aren't interested in solving anything. The only reason they are doing this is to make me leave the embassy, because if I do, they can continue to exercise control over me. Moreover, at the same time that they are in dialogue with you, they are persecuting those who helped me escape Shandong, and from April twenty-sixth on, they have arrested my family and friends. While they are talking with us, they are just continuing their old ways. If they want me to trust them, they need to immediately stop all illegal persecution, they need to respect my right to make choices, and they need to guarantee all of my rights as a citizen."

"Because you chose to come to the embassy," Koh responded, "you have begun a relationship with the United States, and we need to strengthen this relationship. The first time we met, I told you that time was of the essence. I don't think you should refuse an offer that's already in hand. This is a good proposal. You will be reunited with your family, and you have the invitation from NYU." The three-year invitation, the Americans indicated, was effective indefinitely and had no requirements as to a start time; they seemed to be suggesting that after an indeterminate period of political sensitivity had passed, I would be allowed to attend NYU.

"Mr. Koh has repeated the positive points of the proposal over and over," I said, "but I maintain my concerns that my rights are not being guaranteed. For example, if they really want to go ahead with this, there is no reason that it all needs to begin tomorrow, with me leaving the embassy. I need to see what they will actually do first. If they are unable to make any steps to repair any of their mistakes and tomorrow I go to the hospital, then there's no way to predict who, if anyone, outside of the embassy staff, will be able to see me, and for how long. After two weeks, if there is always someone there monitoring me, and there are cars and people following and surveilling me wherever I go, I just can't accept it. I don't believe that they will protect my rights as a citizen. This is all about coercion. They are forcing me to leave, to not have contact with the media for two weeks, but even after that time, what can anyone do if suddenly they decide that they don't want me to have any contact at all with the media from then on?"

I made clear to the negotiators that we should reject the proffered Chinese "deal" wholesale and stick to our demands. Yet the Americans now seemed suddenly in league with their Chinese counterparts, as if a secret agreement had already been made between the leaders of the two sides. Throughout the day, I met with Campbell, Koh, and Locke, with Wang always translating, but I no longer felt that they were on my side. They kept encouraging me, as if I were a child, to see just how beneficial the Chinese terms were. I should trust that my safety really would be guaranteed, said Campbell, because with America I now had a "big brother" on my side. If you accept, they kept emphasizing—quickly adding that it was up to me, of course—you can stay in China, be with your family, be a hero to the Chinese people, and continue your work, which would surely be well funded. "We'll create a support network to sustain you," Campbell told me, saying that it would include both international donors and governments. What's more, he said, a high-level Chinese official from the central government would make a record of my case. "I'm confident that this is the very best the United States can do," he added, then swapped the carrot for the stick: "If this goes on any longer, they will accuse you of treason."

"As for Chinese officials coming to hear and record my treatment," I said, "you're not going to get any real promises on this count. I'm guessing that they might come and listen, but following that, there will be no way to hold anyone responsible or to deal with those who are responsible. It's just like all the petitioners. The central government sends the cases back to the local authorities, where the problem began originally. Once the Strategic and Economic Dialogue is finished and you all go home, they won't pay much attention if embassy staffers seek them out. Over the past year, many people from the American government have raised my case, and Chinese officials haven't responded at all. Last year on January fourteenth, Secretary of State Clinton raised my case in front of the Chinese ambassador in the U.S., but China had no motivation to respond. That's why I think we have to be stronger and insist on them stopping the persecution and guaranteeing my and my family's rights, now. They have already admitted that they made mistakes and that I was abused. If we begin with this as a basis, I don't think they can refuse.

"If I have no assurances," I continued, "then I'm just switching locations, from being under illegal house arrest in Shandong to another place of my so-called choosing but still under house arrest. This is not a way to resolve this situation."

Koh said, "But they have already promised that you can be with your family . . ."

I laughed bitterly. "If I hadn't escaped, I would still be with my family, right? I really don't think I should accept simply being with my family as a condition."

I could tell that Koh was disappointed and that he believed that I wasn't enthusiastic enough. They seemed to think I was incapable of making a rational decision. They had avoided responding to my demands, and at the same time they were passing on the demands from the central government. Koh wanted me to clearly understand that by the next day I would have to accept the proposal, and he kept saying I should be practical. I urged them to find a way to guarantee my rights as a citizen.

Before long, Koh left, and I continued talking with Kin Moy. He began by praising me and saying how brave I was, but that sometimes the bravest act was to put one's emotions aside. I didn't understand what he was getting at. He also emphasized the benefits of the proposal: "Regarding the seven universities, I don't think they're that great either, but they're also not terrible."

"If they really want a good university for me," I said, "I think they'll find some excellent ones in Beijing or Shanghai. They shouldn't demand that I leave tomorrow for the hospital, because my family is not there. You all can go there with me, but when you leave, who will stay with me? Don't you think that's rather dangerous? If you ship me off to the hospital and then head home, that is sending a clear signal that you are handing me off to them. In that case, how would we know when—or if at all—my family would be allowed to come here, and under what conditions? Even if they are allowed to come here, we have no way of knowing what would happen when they got here.

"If something bad happens," I felt I had to point out, "there's no way to correct it. That's why I say that if they really want a resolution, they need to immediately cease the persecution of my family, bring my wife and children to Beijing, and then the central government can interview my wife about our treatment in Shandong over the past many years. After hearing what she has to say, if they respond appropriately, it will not be too late for me to go to the hospital. This, to me, is a reasonable way forward. Don't you agree?"

"Maybe," Mr. Moy said. "But you might not be aware that our time—"

"—is extremely tight," I finished for him.

He asked me how long it would take for my family to get to Beijing.

I said about eight hours by car. "Well, then, if it takes eight hours, I will go immediately," he said, and he soon left.

A little while later, Locke and Wang arrived. Everyone was a bit dejected, and it was getting late. I again expressed my fears that my safety and rights were not being guaranteed. "If you take me to the hospital," I said, "what guarantees will I have that you will be able to bring my family here, or that I will actually see them? And if you can't find me, what recourse will you have?"

"With this proposal," Ambassador Locke said, "you would be able to go to NYU's Shanghai campus after two years, or you could apply to another school."

"I understand the rationale," I said, "but in this scenario, what happens if they don't allow me to go at all? Clinton raised my case on more than one occasion, right? If I lose the upper hand, they'll do whatever they want. The only way to keep them to their word is to do everything under the light of the media—then they might worry about how their actions will be perceived. They don't care about anything that happens behind closed doors. In addition, I haven't seen any response to my demand that they immediately cease the persecution and guarantee my civil rights. I don't even have any basic freedom of speech. Demanding that I not have contact with the media for two weeks is completely unjustifiable. Contacting the media at whatever time I choose is my right."

I wondered if the Americans fully understood the power Chinese officials have over ordinary citizens. "If I can't speak out, then we've only changed the scenery," I told them. "At home they locked me up, took my cell phone, and prevented me from talking to anyone on the outside. From where you stand, it looks like there is a limit to their demand that I not speak to the media for two weeks in the hospital, but in reality, there is no way to say what they will do. It's just like when I was in jail: when I served out my term, I should have been free to live my life as I chose. But they threw me in their car, took me to my village, and locked me up at home."

I knew my negotiators were getting anxious that I wouldn't accept the proposal; they kept asking me what it would take for me to agree. I repeated my demands: "The Chinese government must immediately stop the persecution of my family, bring my family here, and both listen to what my family says about what has been going on in Shandong and acknowledge what happened there. Also, the authorities must promise to protect my rights when I leave the embassy. If they can make this known and protect my rights as a citizen, including my right to freedom of speech and my right to exit and enter the country, as well as my freedom of movement within the country, then I might consider their proposal. If they are not willing to concede anything, if there is nothing concrete, I can't agree to it."

When I had finished, the room was silent. Finally, Koh spoke: "A decision has to be made, regardless. Is there any other information you need to come to a decision?"

"Of course I need more information," I replied. "I have no information whatsoever except from what you tell me. I can't get in touch with my family or friends or get advice from friends who could help me, like Professor Cohen."

Koh left to try to get in touch with Jerry, and after a while they put me on the phone with him. I told him simply and directly what the situation was: that despite having no concrete promises regarding my rights or my safety, they—both the Chinese and the Americans—were trying to get me to leave the embassy. Professor Cohen replied, "Isn't safety the number one concern? You need to stay safe." Back in my room, the Americans repeated their statements about the benefits of the proposal and how if I chose to remain in the embassy my rights would be restricted and my family would continue to be abused.

I asked, "If they're not letting me go to NYU now, why would they change their minds a year from now? If they continue to interfere with my rights, who's to stop them? I know you are going to say that the U.S. government will continue to watch my case and will demand that they protect my rights. Why, then, can you not demand that my rights be protected now, at this time? If you think they won't respond now, why do you think they will respond later?"

Hours passed. Campbell came back to my room after he'd finished another meeting with Washington. "The proposal has come out of the last three days of intense talks," he said. "I want you to know that the White House, the State Department, and the secretary of state all support you. This is the first time you have really come into contact with the U.S., and you will find that this is a relationship that will last a lifetime. I know you withstood persecution and abuse, and I know your path has been extremely difficult and brave. You are a figure of tremendous latent power in China, and in the coming years, when the drama in China has shifted inexorably, you will be able to take your place. We have guarantees from the Chinese government, the U.S. government, and nonprofit organizations that you will have support going forward, and we will create a support system to help you in your life and in your future. We just finished talks with the Chinese government, and they will take care of the details of getting your family to Beijing. We also just went to the hospital, and they have prepared the best room for you. If you don't leave the embassy, the Chinese government will accuse you of treason, and then you won't be able to leave the embassy for many, many years or you will have to go to America on your own and leave your family behind. I ask for your trust. The American government and the Chinese government will take care of your case from the highest levels of government. This is the best way forward. We need you to leave tomorrow. You should know that hundreds of people back in the U.S. have been working on your case night and day. It's the best we can do, and I don't think we can do any more."

"I am so grateful," I said. "Originally, however, we should have been making demands that Chinese authorities protect my rights, but now the situation has turned so that they are making demands and will only act depending on what we do. It's quite bizarre!"

"They will do an investigation," Campbell said.

"I will leave only if I know they have already begun an investigation."

Campbell began to get agitated. "Mr. Chen, we need to be clear. After tomorrow, unless we have progress, they will accuse you of treason. That's why we have planned for you to reunite with your family tomorrow at the hospital, because they won't allow your family to come to the embassy. We support this proposal. Deputy Chief Wang will go with you to the hospital tomorrow. Secretary of State Clinton will be arriving, and she has assured us that she will raise your case with the highest levels of the Chinese government. Now that this has come to the light of day, they can't make a mess of this. If you leave here tomorrow, you will become a hero to the Chinese people. If you remain here, the Chinese government will accuse you of treason. You need to understand that in that situation, we will have no way of helping you. You would remain here as a foreigner, and we would not be able to help. You will still have issues with your government, and you will continue to struggle with them. There is no question of this.

"But now you have a big brother, the American government, on your side. And I can guarantee that you will not lose your big brother. You need to believe in us. Things are different now—you aren't in Shandong anymore. And you are no longer stuck in your tiny village surrounded by thugs who will beat you. There will be no thugs on the campus where you go to study. I can promise you that I will not leave China and I will not sleep until you are reunited with your family. This is today! You will be a hero to your people. The reason why the Chinese authorities want you to leave is that they are afraid of you. They are afraid of you because they know that you could become a very important figure in this country. You must be brave. You have to be brave."

"Can you please bring my family here first?" I asked.

Campbell took a deep breath. "I swear on my mother's name, on the name of my children, in the name of God, that Ambassador Locke and I will go to get your family. And tomorrow, you will leave here to go to the hospital. And you will also need to take one important step: to make a statement that the American government has been extremely helpful and that you completely trust us."

I thought about my excruciating escape and my flight to the one place in China that seemed safe: the American embassy. I hadn't expected that so many people on both sides would be working so hard to get me to leave, without guaranteeing my rights or my family's safety. No one seemed to be putting pressure on the Chinese Communist Party; instead, they were dumping shipping containers of weight onto my shoulders to get me to do their bidding. Suddenly I was overcome by sadness, and I wept.

Ambassador Locke comforted me. "You are going to meet your family," he said, "and I will go get them. You should let me know how much time you think your family will need to get ready and pack their things."

Didn't they know that we had nothing? Everything, down to the last pencil and smallest scrap of newspaper, had been confiscated or destroyed. We had only the clothes on our backs, which we had worn for years. By then, though, the thirty-six-hour deadline stressed by Campbell had arrived: Clinton would be landing in Beijing on May 2, and the U.S.-China summit was about to begin.

On the morning of May 1, Ambassador Locke and some others came to my room, told me they had made all the preparations for the move to the hospital, and asked if I was willing to go with them. No, I said, I am not. None of my rights are being guaranteed in the slightest. Ambassador Locke turned and left. A while later, Deputy Chief Wang stopped by and told me that Hillary Clinton would likely come by to see me around nine the next morning. "Think about what you want to say to her," he advised.

That afternoon, the Chinese authorities called American officials to see if I was in fact leaving the embassy. As I learned later, U.S. negotiators told them that I hadn't agreed to the conditions in the proposal. The Chinese side seemed anxious and asked for an explanation. "Mr. Chen doesn't trust you," replied the Americans. The Chinese authorities immediately announced they would bring my family to Beijing. I greeted this news cautiously and asked if embassy officials would be going to Shandong to pick up my family, as they had promised. No, they said, the Chinese side wouldn't allow it.

My heart sank as I considered the symbolic and practical implications of this change of plan. For one thing, it looked like the Americans had lost another fight, and by doing so they had relinquished control of the situation. Equally important, my family would be brought to Beijing surrounded by the very authorities who had persecuted us over so many years. This plan was fraught with dangers that the U.S. team apparently did not perceive.

Embassy officials assured me that they would be with me the entire time I was at the hospital, that they would stay in an adjacent room, but I now fully understood the precariousness of my position. The Americans either didn't understand what I had been through or were being easily deceived by their Chinese counterparts. I still held out hope that these officials had my best interests—my safety—at heart. But despite my repeated requests that we wait to see the party's true attitude before making a decision, Koh and Campbell would not change their minds and did not appear to heed my requests and listen to my concerns. Couched in various turns of phrase, their message was clear: "You have to take this deal."

Later that day, an embassy official asked me if I wanted to call Professor Cohen again, and of course I did. When he picked up the phone and heard it was me, he immediately blurted out, "I never said you had to reject their proposal!" Apparently, the American side had been pressuring him as well, wary of the counsel he had been giving me, and hoped he could talk me into leaving. Earlier I had asked to talk to various members of the U.S. House of Representatives—Nancy Pelosi, Frank Wolf, Jim McGovern, and Chris Smith—but apparently the embassy had not followed through.

My fate had now become a critical test case, watched by the world: could the Chinese government guarantee the rights of even a single Chinese citizen, and could the United States hold it accountable if it didn't? Basic inviolable freedoms, like the ability to be together with my family, were presented by the Chinese government as if they were magnanimous concessions. American hearts might be in the right place, but what was needed now was an iron will to persevere and negotiate hard.

My conversations with Campbell, Koh, and the others continued that evening, and we talked long into the night. As the time wore on, nerves became frayed. At one point, Campbell threw up his hands and said, "I'm so upset, I don't know how else to help you. We've been up for days and nights, and in Washington hundreds of people have been working on this. We can't keep talking about it!" Exhausted by the pressure and intensity, he, too, shed tears before storming out of the room.

On the morning of May 2, Kin Moy, a translator, and some others came to my room. They told me that staff from the Chinese central authorities had ordered provincial officers in Shandong to bring my wife and children up to Beijing. I would soon be meeting with Ambassador Locke, they said, and afterward I would be taken to the hospital. I protested that I had yet to agree to anything, but I was told I would be taken to the ambassador's office while staffers and officials began packing the few things in my room.

Over the past few days, I had requested numerous times to meet with China's top leaders, Hu Jintao and Wen Jiabao, but all anyone would say was that a high-level official would see me at the hospital. "Why can't they come to the embassy?" I asked. In lieu of such a meeting, I was told, I could write a letter to give to Hillary Clinton, who would personally hand it to Wen Jiabao and Hu Jintao during her visit. Though I knew from radio reports that Clinton had arrived in Beijing, our proposed meeting never materialized, and a letter seemed the only possibility on offer. The officials encouraged me repeatedly to write the letter, and so I did: sitting in Ambassador Locke's office, dictating to a translator, I detailed in three pages and for the thousandth time all that I'd been through. I cried as I wrote this letter, reliving seven years of suffering, the painful experiences surfacing once again.

At one point, Weijing called to let me know she had arrived at the hospital, adding that "things are just fine back home." This was the first time I'd spoken with her since leaving Dongshigu. I understood immediately that she was not able to speak freely, but I urged her to tell me what was going on. She said she was in a conference room, surrounded by the officials from Shandong—the very ones involved in our house arrest. Hearing this, I was infuriated: just as I had feared, the Chinese side was making every preparation to continue their control of my family.

While the translator was cleaning up the letter, other officials gathered around me again, urging me to leave the embassy, using all kinds of excuses and rationales. "Aren't you worried about your wife?" they asked me. "We know you want to protect her. You shouldn't stay in here hiding. Your family is already at the hospital." I was also told that Hillary Clinton would call me when I was in the car and headed to the hospital, another obvious nudge to get me out of the embassy. The American negotiators were unrelenting; only Ambassador Locke remained silent.

I asked to speak to Weijing a second time, and after ten minutes the call was put through. She urged me to leave the embassy because of my health, saying that the American officials were telling her that if I didn't leave within fifteen minutes the Chinese "would rip up the agreement." I could tell that she was still not able to speak freely. She had no way of knowing all the machinations at work, but I felt a deep obligation to protect her, to be with her in life or in death.

After an awkward pause, Harold Koh announced that we were running out of time—if I didn't leave within the next twenty minutes, the Chinese would accuse me of treason.

At this point, what could I do? I had reached the end of the road. Where else could I turn for justice? I had brought my case to China's highest authorities, to the American embassy, and to the world's attention, detailing seven years of blatantly criminal acts, detentions, tortures, and lies. But what troubled me most at the time was this: when negotiating with a government run by hooligans, the country that most consistently advocated for democracy, freedom, and universal human rights had simply given in. My heart ached. At home under house arrest, I had shed blood; at the embassy, I shed tears, the youthful idealism that had buoyed me through my most discouraging and painful times now giving way to colder, clearer realities. Nonetheless, I was and always will be grateful to the U.S. embassy in Beijing and its staff for protecting me and sheltering me. Without the embassy's help during that critical period, I have little doubt that I would have been sent back to Shandong to endure even greater torture and suffering than that which I had experienced before.

By noon, the wheels were in motion. I was given something to eat, but I was too depressed to take a bite. I heard people gathering in Locke's office; the embassy photographer moved around us snapping pictures. Someone must have had a video camera trained on us: Ambassador Locke spoke a few words to me, but from his voice I could tell that he was really addressing the millions of strangers who might be tuning in.

"Are you ready to leave the embassy of your own free will?" asked Ambassador Locke.

I didn't answer him directly, pausing a moment in suspended time as I contemplated where I stood. The immense pressure was excruciating, and it was clear that none would relent. I realized that I would have to be on my own, and yet there was no way for the ambassador or any of the Americans in the room to understand what I had been through or to fully appreciate the depths of my disappointment and despair.

Though I could not see them, I turned my face to each of the officials surrounding me, taking in each one in turn. Suppressing the emotion in my voice, I said, simply, "Let's go."

CHAPTER THIRTEEN

To a Land of Promise

Ambassador Locke held my left arm, while I leaned into the crutch under my right. Campbell lagged just behind us. I made a brave face as we moved toward the open air and the van that would take me to Chao-Yang Hospital. Standing next to the vehicle while photos were being snapped, I could feel heat emanating from underneath—the engine had been running for quite some time in anticipation of my exit.

Once we had all gotten inside the van, the team of American diplomats and officials were animated, talking excitedly to each other and to me. They returned my phone, though for some reason it now didn't work. Still parked at the embassy, they called Secretary of State Clinton to tell her I was in the van, then passed the phone to me. Clinton and I exchanged a few symbolic words, but there was no translator on the line. Having been told that she would be meeting with me, I stuttered out, "I want to see you now" in broken English, but I couldn't understand what she said in response.

As the van pulled out of the embassy compound, the officials offered to dial whatever numbers I could remember using their phones; one of them looked up the number for the *Washington Post* for me. I called my old lawyer Li Jinsong, who warned me against leaving the embassy; I couldn't get through to Yushan or Teng Biao. The drive to the hospital took only a few minutes, and the diplomats seemed happy to allow me the time to finish my calls; we all knew that I would be in the hands of the party as soon as the vehicle's door opened and I stepped outside, and no one could say for sure when I would have another chance to speak freely to the outside world.

Getting out of the van, I was guided into a wheelchair and then pushed through a swirling chaos of nurses, doctors, guards, and diplomats to an exam room on the ninth floor, where I was at last reunited with my wife and children. Despite the turmoil of the past twelve days, our reunion felt inhibited and uncertain—other people, most of them unknown to us, never seemed far away. Both children kept their distance; Kesi was upset by my condition, asking Weijing why I had to sit in a wheelchair, and Kerui, who hadn't seen us in over a year, held back, suspicious of this strange new environment and unsure of his place.

Weijing quickly filled me in on how she and the children had been brought to Beijing. The previous day, she had still been awake after midnight when two local officials appeared at our home and told her to pack up and make ready to leave the village immediately. Soon Weijing and Kesi were driven to Shuanghou, where they encountered two busloads of officials who were to accompany them to Beijing as reinforcements. Kerui, escorted by officials of his own, arrived a few minutes later, at which point Weijing and the children were put on one of the buses and driven to Qufu, the ancient home of Confucius. Still trailed by a group of police and officials, they boarded a train for Beijing.

Late that morning, Deputy Chief Wang and another embassy staffer met Weijing and the children at the Beijing train station, bearing flowers and toys. Weijing expected to go directly to the embassy, but she and the children were quickly surrounded by hospital staff, who drove them to Chao-Yang Hospital and then brought them up to the fourth-floor conference room, from where she had called me earlier. Everyone took a seat around a large oval conference table: my family and the embassy staff sat on one side, while hospital officials, officials from the Ministry of Foreign Affairs, and Shandong officials faced them from the other. Each time Weijing spoke to me by phone, the officials from the Ministry of Foreign Affairs made ready their own phones before allowing her to connect with me on Deputy Chief Wang's phone—clearly everyone was in agreement that these calls between us should be monitored.

Weijing told me that following our first conversation, embassy officials had taken another call, one that seemed to leave them extremely anxious. After they hung up, the officials told her that if I didn't leave the embassy within the next fifteen minutes, the Chinese government would "rip up the agreement," after which the American negotiators would be out of options and all their work over the past few days would be for naught. Hearing this, Weijing became extremely worried about me, which is why when we spoke for the second time she urged me to leave the embassy immediately.

Now, in the exam room, the hospital staff took my vitals and had me fill out some forms, while Deputy Chief Wang and Yang Junyi looked on. Technicians drew blood and prepared other tests; they X-rayed my right foot and discovered that I had broken three bones. After setting the bones and wrapping my foot in a cast, they moved us down to a guest suite on the first floor.

Twelve days had passed since my escape, and it had been almost one week since I'd entered the embassy. But the ordeal was far from over. Soon after my arrival, the authorities had sent a mass of riot police to the hospital, and the numerous supporters and journalists who had gathered were forced to move out of the hospital and across the street, where they were unable to reach me or report on what was happening. Wang and several others from the embassy had stayed with me during my initial consultation with the doctors, but as we settled into our suite on the first floor, I realized that everyone from the embassy had disappeared. Soon a text message came in from Wang on the cell phone Yushan had given me—mysteriously, the phone was now working—confirming that they had left. I was surprised and worried, having been told that for our safety they would stay with us the entire time I was at the hospital. I immediately tried to call Wang back, but no one answered; the other embassy numbers I called yielded the same result.

Guards now surrounded our room, and I had the familiar sense of a noose drawing tighter; we later found out that as many as four hundred police and security personnel were stationed in and around the hospital itself, some in uniform and many others in street clothes. Trying to stay calm, I told myself that Chao-Yang Hospital was not Dongshigu: here, at least, the world was watching us.

That evening, I called Hu Jia's wife, Zeng Jinyan, to tell her about my situation. She was extremely worried. "Do you know what it means to have left the embassy?" she asked anxiously. Certain that the call was being monitored, I simply said that I'd had no other choice. She replied that the only thing to do at this point was to contact as many journalists and media outlets as possible—the world needed to know the truth. She promised to get in touch with several reporters she knew, and I told her that if I couldn't protect my family we would have to leave the country. From our brief conversation, I inferred that the media had reported on the fact of my escape but that many details were getting mixed up in the retelling. "Did you say you wanted to kiss Hillary Clinton?" Zeng asked. "No, I said I wanted to see her," I replied.

Around six p.m. we asked for something to eat—by then, Kerui and Kesi were both crying from hunger and exhaustion. Predictably, we were not allowed out of the room, even to buy food. The authorities seemed intent on letting me know that I was back in the party's grasp.

While waiting for our meal, I again called a number of different embassy contact lines on my phone, but no one picked up. My mind was in turmoil. So many promises had been broken—whom could I trust? A blind man in an unfamiliar place, I was surrounded by strangers and extremely nervous. I kept hearing unusual noises, some of them reminding me of how they installed mobile phone jammers around us in Dongshigu. I assumed my phone was being monitored; whenever I got someone on the line, there was a strange little echo, and I often had trouble hearing the person on the other end, even when they could hear me just fine.

I finally managed to reach Teng Biao, who passed on greetings from other friends before turning deadly serious. "If you stay in China," he said, "you'll be in very grave danger." I said nothing in reply. He told me about the hard line taken publicly by China's Ministry of Foreign Affairs, which had just released a statement demanding a U.S. apology and an investigation into how I had gotten to the embassy. Teng Biao reminded me that many Chinese activists had been safe while in the spotlight, but when the world stopped paying attention they had been tortured or disappeared. "What should I do?" I asked. "You and your family should go back to the U.S. embassy immediately," he said, "and then you should go to America." I couldn't tell him on the compromised line that at this point there was no way I could return to the embassy.

At around nine that night our food was finally delivered, but by then the children had cried themselves to sleep. After my call with Teng Biao, we discovered that the phone no longer worked; now we felt completely trapped. More anxious than ever, and needing a more complete understanding of our precarious situation, I asked Weijing what had been happening back in the village. She then described the series of events that had unfolded after the authorities belatedly realized I had escaped.

The authorities took me away from my home and family on April 26, and I was held by the criminal police until the evening of April 28. On the third day of my captivity, the police insisted I record a video stating that they hadn't tortured me and indeed had treated me quite well. They told me that if I said what they wanted, they would let me go. Judging by their words and actions, I was pretty sure that by now Guangcheng was safe. But I was terribly worried about Mama and little Kesi, so in the end I made their video and signed a document "verifying" that I hadn't been the victim of torture while in their hands. Then they took me home.

As soon as I stepped through the gate, Kesi ran to me, hugging me and crying. I saw that the guards were now occupying all the rooms and the yard—whatever we did, they followed us closely. Kesi was not allowed to go to school, and that evening, when I went to turn out the light and shut the door, the guards began to bellow, shouting so wildly that my mother-in-law feared a terrible beating was coming and urged me to remain silent. All night long, while we tried to sleep, the guards stood only few feet away from us. The following morning, our captors photographed and measured every corner of the yard and then began installing security cameras. The guards swore at us, infuriating me, but my mother-in-law said to pay them no heed. Our dog barked at them, and a guard beat it with a pitchfork.

On the night of April 29, I received a visit from a group of city and provincial officials who were given a tour of our yard and the new equipment. The head of Yinan County Public Security explained that the seven new security cameras put up around the yard were high-tech and would allow the surveillance team off in Shuanghou or Linyi to see us clearly at night. After the officials left, the shift of guards who had watched our house for many years was switched out for a dozen new captors—six of them perched on the roof of the kitchen building, from where they could keep an eye on the yard, and another six stood on either side of the door to our house. Like the men before them, the new guards were dressed in plain clothes, but they seemed more seasoned than the usual thugs, and their accents made it apparent that they were neither local nor from Linyi.

The next morning, our captors began dismantling the security cameras. Over the next few days they installed and then dismantled the security cameras several times; they also continued their measuring and photographing. I had no idea what they were trying to do until I heard one of the guards say, "This will be great—with an electric net, even wings won't help them get away." Now I understood: they were planning to install a giant electrified net over the entire yard. Terrified by this new development, I found myself thinking, We might even die here . . .

Weijing finished her report by telling me that as soon as the Shandong officials picked her up for the trip to Beijing, they began pressuring her to tell me that everything was just fine, that the government was now treating my family well, and that I should leave the embassy. But her account of what had taken place over the past few days made it clear that things in Dongshigu were worse than ever, and that even while negotiating with the American diplomats, the Chinese authorities were planning to continue our brutal captivity. As things stood, I was certain that it was only a matter of time before we were all dragged back to our village and once again put under house arrest.

Reflecting on everything that had happened since my escape, I began to form an idea of what I should do. My family had suffered enough—how could I ask them to endure yet more? In my heart, I wanted to stay in China, but for the sake of their safety and my health, we would have to leave our country. We would have to go to America.

Once I had made my decision, I had to find a way to let it be known. Most of the time my phone either had no signal or malfunctioned with some sort of interference, which was worrying. I hadn't heard from anyone at the American embassy for a number of hours, and now I felt I had no way of reliably communicating with the outside. Then, early on May 3, a phone call suddenly came through from a foreign journalist, and I took the opportunity to pass on the news about my decision. After that first call, the phone rang almost constantly for several hours, except when the signal would cut out again for a time. I talked with netizens and journalists from CNN, the Associated Press, and other news outlets, telling them that I was abandoned, encircled, and in imminent danger. I told everyone who would listen that I was convinced that the party had no intention of fulfilling its promises and ensuring justice and that I had to leave for the United States with my family before it was too late.

One of the calls I received that morning came from Deputy Chief Wang, and I told him about my decision to go to the States. I also described the circumstances of the night before: how we had called the embassy but couldn't get through; how I had thought someone from the embassy would be staying next door to us; and the aggressive statement issued by the Chinese Ministry of Foreign Affairs that Teng Biao had told us about. Wang said he had never received any indication that we had called. And from that day on, we were no longer permitted to see embassy staff members unless Chinese officials were also present.

Later that morning, an interesting visitor arrived: Mr. Guo Shousong, who was accompanied by a secretary. Mr. Guo showed his ID to Weijing. "I'm the assistant head for citizen reception at the State Bureau for Letters and Visits," he said, referring to the petition office, that hopeless, peculiarly Chinese institution which I had encountered early in my own activism, way back in 1997. "Don't think of me as a nobody just because my position is not that prestigious," he added. "I've actually been sent by high-level central authorities."

Indeed, from the initial rounds of negotiations, the Chinese side had said that a high-level official would listen to my complaint, and now here he was. Absurd as it seemed, I began to tell him my story: how my family had suffered myriad persecutions, my nephew had been detained, my brothers beaten, my friends dragged away by the authorities. I demanded that the authorities return all of our stolen belongings and said that an investigation had to be conducted into the illegal treatment of my family, no matter what level of official was implicated or how many. Shaking his head in mild surprise, he made as if he'd never heard any of this before.

The secretary took notes on everything I said, and as Mr. Guo departed he told me to take care of myself. He left behind a large bouquet of flowers and a basket of fruit, including oranges, melons, and apples. I have a deep love for flowers and their magical scents, but I was not so easily mollified.

The following day, May 4, Mr. Guo and his secretary again came to my room. He said all the right things; he had clearly been preauthorized to do so. "The center has made their position clear. I will also make clear my position. No matter the level of official, anyone who has been involved in unlawful activities related to your treatment will be thoroughly investigated and publicly dealt with. All the surveillance cameras will be dismantled, and everyone guarding your house will be thrown out immediately." He also assured me that my family would no longer be harassed. "You can call your family back home to verify it," he said. I reiterated my demand that an investigation be undertaken with the participation of my lawyers and under the scrutiny of the media, and Mr. Guo readily agreed. As we finished our conversation, I asked Mr. Guo about a rumor I had heard that six buses of thugs had driven up to Beijing from Shandong and that their mission was to bring me back dead or alive. "Well, hopefully they won't get in!" he said, laughing stiffly.

As soon as Mr. Guo left, we began calling my family and neighbors back home. They confirmed my suspicions about the reality in Dongshigu. Elder Brother reported that he was living under house arrest and that except for the cameras in our yard the entire apparatus of surveillance and security remained in place. Other villagers told me that in the days following April 26, the cadres had been apoplectic, searching frantically up and down Dongshigu and Xishigu, still not believing that I could be in Beijing. Carrying wooden sticks, they thwacked everything that came within range, suspecting every cornfield, every bush, stone, and hole of sheltering me. Three separate teams of investigators looked into my disappearance, and all three concluded that a blind man could never have escaped to Xishigu without outside help. They hunted ruthlessly for my "accomplices," questioning a number of people for hours on end. Initially, Elder Brother and his wife were held in custody, as were Chen Kegui, Chen Hua and his father, Liu Yuancheng and his wife, and several other villagers.

Over the next few days, I had plenty of time to reflect on the visits from Mr. Guo. Was he trying to pull the wool over my eyes or was the local government deceiving the center? The answer hardly mattered. "When can I see my friends?" I had asked him.

"We'll let you see them soon, once things are a little less sensitive," Mr. Guo replied.

"When will the investigation start?" I asked.

"If laws have been broken," he said, "the center will investigate; however, it will take time."

Mr. Guo's visits were the Chinese government's sole response to my unceasing calls for justice.

In the early hours of May 4, an important opportunity came my way. I received a call from Washington, D.C., where the Congressional-Executive Commission on China was holding an emergency hearing on my situation. Suddenly I was able to make my case directly to Congress: in an unforgettable moment, I spoke to the assembled congressional representatives from my hospital bed in Beijing, thanks to a telephone connection with Bob Fu of ChinaAid, who was present in the hearing room. I told them plainly that I didn't feel safe in China and wanted to go to the United States. I also said that I still hoped to meet with Hillary Clinton, expressing my deepest thanks to the secretary of state for her decision to support me, despite the other pressures she was undoubtedly fielding.

The congressional hearing, which would play a decisive role in events to come, allowed me to communicate directly with the American people and to express my hope that their values would be represented in the way my case was handled. In every media interview, I made a point of thanking embassy officials and emphasizing all the good they had done, but I also didn't hesitate to offer a few more critical comments. After all, I had been pressured to leave the embassy, and the American people had a right to know that.

Now under enormous pressure from Congress and the American public, President Obama, Secretary of State Clinton, and the U.S. negotiators were forced to recalculate. I wasn't privy to the discussions, of course, but I believe that at this critical moment the voice of the American people made itself strongly felt at the bargaining table. Later in the day, a spokesperson for the Chinese Ministry of Foreign Affairs announced that I could "lawfully utilize the normal legal channels to process the paperwork for going abroad." That afternoon, I learned from embassy officials that the United States would prepare the entry paperwork as quickly as possible.

Without the concern of both the Chinese people and the American people, without the media attention and the congressional hearings, I don't know what would ultimately have happened—I might well have been detained, disappeared, or imprisoned and never heard from again. I had not been wrong about Chris Smith, Jim McGovern, Frank Wolf, and Nancy Pelosi: these members of Congress proved to be principled and fearless friends of the Chinese people. I didn't know—and I didn't care—if they were Democrats or Republicans: as long as they cared about freedom and human rights in China, that was enough for me.

For the moment, however, I remained in a kind of captivity. When could I leave for New York? When could I venture beyond my hospital room, let alone go outside? No one was allowed to visit me, and the media people were still trapped in the "interview area" outside, though I wasn't permitted to go there and give interviews. A man named Wang Zancheng served as our chief minder and caretaker, but was he an employee of the hospital, a functionary at the Ministry of Foreign Affairs, or something else? His English was remarkably fluent, and he was in many ways quite responsive to our basic needs, but we had no way of knowing to whom he answered.

And while I remained in limbo, what was happening to my family and friends? Teng Biao had come back to Beijing to see me, but as soon as he arrived Ministry of State Security personnel ordered him out of town. Yushan was detained multiple times, and ultimately he was forced to sign off on an account of his role in my escape. My friend and lawyer Jiang Tianyong, who had worked with me during the family planning campaign of 2005, was severely beaten and had his eardrum punctured.

May 4 happened to be Kerui's birthday, and that morning Deputy Chief Wang and Yang Junyi had come to the hospital to deliver gifts; they were not allowed to go to my room, so they met Weijing outside. Later, Yang told me that as he approached the hospital that day he had seen an assistant of Ai Weiwei's bearing a birthday cake for Kerui and being forcibly turned away, at which point the cake had been thrown to the ground. I also learned that once Yang was gone, several of the guards stationed around the hospital had restrained Ai Weiwei's assistant and carried her off to the police station, where they beat her and questioned her. Indeed, throughout my stay at the hospital I heard numerous accounts of well-wishers and petitioners who tried to see me but were blocked and then detained by the police for questioning. Many of them were subjected to physical violence.

From May 3 on, I spoke to embassy officials every day I remained in the hospital. Ambassador Locke called often—he was unfailingly considerate, always inquiring about my health and my family's well-being. I continued to feel that my phone was my only lifeline to the world outside, and shortly after our arrival at the hospital, I had asked Deputy Chief Wang to send me an extra cell phone in case I was unable to use the one I had. I was relieved and grateful when embassy staffers brought over several working phones on May 4 or 5, ensuring that I could always communicate with them.

Other foreigners also continued to express their concern and support. The British embassy called—their staffers' earlier help with our village well had not been forgotten. Representatives of several other Western countries, including France, Switzerland, Sweden, and Canada, called me to let me know that they were contacting the Chinese Ministry of Foreign Affairs. On May 8, Ambassador Locke arranged a phone call with Congresswoman Pelosi, who asked after my health and spoke encouragingly about the work I had done. I thanked her for her concern and her unfaltering support of human rights.

Mr. Guo continued to pay me regular visits, and one day he mentioned the government's proposal that I be given the choice of attending one of seven Chinese universities. I told him I was no longer considering these schools; instead, I had received a three-year invitation from New

York University and was planning to go to the States to study. After he left, I asked Weijing to bring me the letter of invitation Deputy Chief Wang had read aloud to me that day in the embassy garden. Weijing searched the belongings packed for me by the embassy staff but couldn't find it. We got in touch with the embassy to ask about the letter and were told that someone would bring it to the hospital.

Deputy Chief Wang came to the hospital a few days later to deliver NYU's invitation, but as before I was not allowed out of my room, and he was not allowed in to see me. Instead, Weijing was directed to one of the conference rooms in the hospital, where Wang handed her a form. As she read through it she discovered that the form indicated a one-year invitation, not three. She asked Wang about it; he replied the form was "just a formality, something to give to the Chinese government." Weijing had full faith in the embassy, so she brought the form back to the room and told me about it. I, too, trusted the embassy staff implicitly, so I didn't press them to bring NYU's original letter of invitation.

On May 14, Mr. Guo again came to see me, this time to discuss our passports. He returned the next morning with four Shandong Province police officials, and together they spent several hours preparing our passports, taking photographs of us, and filling out forms. During another meeting with Mr. Guo around this time, I reiterated my demands, especially with regard to my family's safety. I was particularly concerned about my nephew Chen Kegui; I feared that he would continue to be harassed and abused by the authorities.

That extended stay in Chao-Yang Hospital was extraordinarily difficult for my family, and the government authorities were almost entirely unsympathetic to my wife and children's needs. It was a major concession when they agreed to permit Kerui and Kesi to spend fifteen or thirty minutes in the hospital courtyard. Eventually Weijing was allowed to take both children into a small garden outside my room, always under the watch of hospital staff and a throng of unidentified people with cameras. Poor Kesi: she had been living under surveillance for so long that when she was told it was time to go back inside, she never questioned the directive, never asked why she and her brother couldn't stay outside longer.

* * *

Almost two weeks into my recuperation at the hospital, my health had stabilized; if it went on any longer, my stay clearly would have a political meaning, not a medical one. By this point, we had been given luggage for our few possessions, but without our passports I refused to get my hopes up.

In the end, I learned of our imminent departure from the media—no one else saw fit to tell us. On the morning of May 19, I was told that officials would soon be meeting at the hospital to discuss our situation, though I was not invited to participate in this conversation. Once I realized that these officials must be from the Ministry of Foreign Affairs, I knew it was just a matter of time before we would be released. Sometime before eleven a.m., Wang Zancheng, who had just returned from the meeting, told me it was time for us to pack our things and that we would be leaving for the airport around one p.m. I reminded him about the government's promise, reiterated by Mr. Guo, to investigate the crimes committed against me. He made no response.

I had wanted my mother to come with us, but she wouldn't hear of it, saying she couldn't leave so many sons and grandchildren behind. When I called her to tell her that we would soon be getting on the plane, she seemed so happy, as if maybe we could all live safely and peacefully now.

After lunch we began preparing for our departure, leaving some things at the hospital for friends to pick up and calling other friends to say good-bye. The Americans' original plan was for Ambassador Locke and Deputy Chief Wang to fly with me to New York, but the Chinese side objected for the usual reason: "Too high-profile." But as Deputy Chief Wang said, it really didn't matter who accompanied me, just so long as I got to the United States safely.

In the early afternoon, Wang Zancheng and a group of doctors and nurses escorted us out of the hospital and guided us into a little bus that was waiting outside. They drew the curtains to prevent people from seeing in and keep us from seeing out, as if they could still stop the world from learning the truth. After driving out of the hospital, the bus turned right and then traveled due north, following a road that would take us straight to the airport. Not a single car or stoplight impeded our progress—the authorities had closed down the road for us.

Police held traffic back at the intersections, long lines of cars standing in motionless homage as we sped along the empty boulevard past a city of twenty million souls. For a moment, with our seven-car convoy, you could almost imagine we were heroes, not captives.

I fielded calls on my phone all the way to the airport, all the way onto the plane. The callers were journalists, friends, supporters, and netizens from all over the world, wishing me happiness and a safe journey—"a single sail and a gentle wind," as we say. I wanted to stay on the line forever, taking every greeting and kind word in its turn.

We stopped at an airport outbuilding far from the regular terminal and were taken inside. There, Chinese Ministry of Foreign Affairs officials handed us our passports, only to confiscate them again after an American consul attached our visas. Our flight was delayed for hours, and while we waited we were pained to watch Kerui lying on the floor, weeping inconsolably at the idea of leaving home and all he knew behind. Nothing we did seemed to comfort him.

It was almost six p.m. before officials finally drove us out onto the tarmac in a shuttle bus, still keeping us apart from everyone else. Only after all the other passengers had boarded did the officials allow us to enter the plane. Two diplomats from the embassy, standing at the front of the cabin, handed back our passports with the visas inside, then took their seats across the aisle from us in business class; they would be accompanying us all the way to New York. Wang Zancheng, our mysterious minder, shook my hand and wished me a pleasant journey. The airplane crew came over, welcomed us on board, and gave plane badges to the children. Even the pilot stopped by to shake my hand and welcome us to America, though it was still thousands of miles away.

Several journalists had bought tickets so they could ride with us on the plane; a few were old friends who had traveled to Dongshigu during the darkest days. But by now I was too exhausted to give more than a few interviews. I tried resting, but my mind was still reeling. The sour and the sweet, the bitter and the spicy—at this tangled moment, I tasted all the flavors of life.

After the plane took off, the two diplomats periodically leaned over to offer advice and guidance about life in the United States. We spent thirteen hours in the air, and by the time we were approaching the east coast it was early evening. "You should look out and see where we are," I said to Kerui and Kesi. "Take a good look at America."

"We see a river," they said, "and we see trees and bridges." Like Weijing, they were accustomed to being my eyes, allowing me to see through their words.

And then at last we were landing and preparing to disembark at Newark airport. All the passengers around us, none of whom had seemed to notice or recognize me, now stood up and began to applaud. I was touched and grateful; the sincere warmth of the American people reminded me of the kindness exhibited by everyday people in China. As we got up to exit the plane, we were met at the cabin door by two staff members from the State Department. Also at the airport to greet us was my old friend Professor Cohen, who was waiting in a car; Jerry and I hugged each other and cried. "We've taken care of everything," he said, and I felt like a child in the embrace of a parent. Jerry had supported me and my work in so many ways over the years, and I was deeply moved to know that now I would be able to study by his side.

On the way into Manhattan, Jerry told me there would be a press conference as soon as we arrived at NYU. I had originally been told that this would take place at the airport and didn't know why there was a change; I worried that the many friends and supporters—some who had driven for hours to welcome us—wouldn't know where to go.

Carsick and battling a headache, I was overwhelmed by exhaustion as we entered the city, its invisible towers all around me. I learned that Representative Chris Smith of New Jersey had traveled to the airport to greet me and that he had later rushed to NYU to find me. I'm not sure why he wasn't told when we left the airport, and in the end my headache made me too miserable to visit with him for very long.

To all those who had gathered in NYU's Washington Square Village to welcome us, I said a few words, extending my deepest thanks to everyone who had helped and supported me over the years and made it possible for me to be there. "Justice and equality know no borders," I said, "and by joining hands together we can overcome all hardship." So many friends and supporters stood around us as I spoke; after I finished, their applause was warm and prolonged, and then there were flowers and toys for our children and kind words from old friends. I was sorry I couldn't speak to everyone who had come, that I couldn't grant an interview to each of the journalists. For now they would have to wait; the whole story would be told in time.

At long last we went upstairs to the place we would now call home, high above the streets of Manhattan. I began to make myself familiar with the room, memorizing its contours and learning its soundscape, as I always do. Our hosts had thought of everything, even oranges. Suddenly I remembered my mother—my mother, who would sometimes buy me oranges while I was under house arrest, no matter that they cost more than we could afford. Just now, I thought, she must be waking up in the little village of Dongshigu, on the other side of the world.

I had finally reached a free land. I was not yet able to feel pure joy, but in my divided heart and restless soul I did begin to feel something like release. Most of all, I felt an overwhelming fatigue, a weariness that penetrated to my very bones. For now I would rest, but tomorrow I would resume the fight.

A New Life

More than two years after I left my village, another summer is giving way to autumn. Weijing and I have made our home here in America, along with our children. Kerui is eleven years old; little Kesi is already nine. They now speak English faster than we can understand, having thoroughly embraced their new life with an unfettered joy. There was a time when Kerui would grow frightened at the sound of police sirens screaming down the Manhattan streets. "The white car takes Daddy away; the red car takes Mommy," he would say, recalling events he'd witnessed firsthand. Past traumas recede slowly, but time and freedom have their healing effects. Not always, but often, we now have the gift of normalcy.

We are still in constant communication with friends and family, so many of whom continue to suffer back home. The crackdown on human rights activists has only intensified since I left, and almost every prominent dissident or outspoken lawyer now faces persecution, house arrest, imprisonment, or violence; some have even been killed while in police custody. The notion that China is gradually liberalizing and improving its human rights record—as apologists and wishful thinkers would have it, in step with the party line—is simply untrue. The only question is how to get this unfortunate news past the censors in China so that it is accepted as truth by the leaders and citizens of Western nations.

In fact, it is vitally important that people of the West and other free nations of the world understand that nothing short of your democracies and your way of life are at stake at this critical juncture. Beyond the luxury hotels and showcase projects of Beijing and Shanghai sits a barbaric dictatorship masquerading as a government. Intoxicated by its own brawn, the Communist Party brazenly violates the constitution and the law daily, throwing up a smoke screen of economic triumph, bewitching the world, and gagging domestic opposition in the process. Like the dynasties of the past, in China today an elite enjoys rights and privileges available to no one else. The law thus becomes a mechanism crafted not to guarantee rights but to ensure the Communist Party's continued control over the people. From the central government down to the local districts, at every level, institutions and government bodies are beholden to party committees, which appear everywhere—in counties and towns, universities and grade schools—and wield ultimate power and yet carry no legal responsibilities whatsoever. No matter what the crime, the party and its representatives cannot be tried and cannot be held liable in lawsuits of any kind.

There is no doubt that in recent years the People's Republic of China has undergone inexorable transformation; what path the nation will take going forward remains open to speculation. Will the party hasten democratic change by embracing true reforms in governance, the rule of law, and ethics? Will democratic nations play a positive role in the transformation? And will they stand strong behind their commitments to human rights, or will short-term interests lay claim to public airwaves and closed-door negotiations alike? Whatever the answers, our country will fulfill its potential and take its place among the free and democratic nations of the world only through the dedicated participation of the sons and daughters of China, wherever they may be.

I firmly believe that as China goes, so goes much of the world, and that the fate of my country of origin will not be an isolated one. My every effort is bent toward a dream of justice and equality for the citizens of China and for all peoples; now let this one man's striving serve as a gesture of invitation for others to join with me. Each of us possesses a boundless strength within; together, may we move mountains.

Acknowledgments

Thanks to Danica Mills as well as the other collaborators who helped get my story into English, including my tireless editor, John Sterling.

I am indebted to those brave individuals who, in my times of crisis, willingly faced untold dangers to travel to Dongshigu to show their support, including Christian Bale, whose appearance outside our village drew immediate attention to our plight. I gratefully acknowledge the efforts of the myriad persons who, both from within China and all over the world and through various and often ingenious methods expressed their support and outrage from afar.

Thanks are due to those elected representatives from the United States Congress, European nations, and other countries across the globe who publicly voiced their support for me when I was in jail, and for my family during our extended persecution. I owe much to those media professionals whose persistent concern helped expose the truth, and to the efforts of the leaders and members of the many human rights organizations who stood up for my cause, including Bob Fu, whose timely intervention proved invaluable. My deepest thanks to Jerry Cohen for his mentorship and friendship over many years.

I will always be grateful to Hillary Clinton for her farsighted decision to take me in, and to the staff at the United States embassy in Beijing, whose care and compassion sustained me during my time there. Likewise, I am grateful to the countless people from across all walks of life who have supported me and my family since we arrived in the United States, in particular the American friend whom we know as Panda. Thanks as well to the U.S. Department of State for its ongoing support, and to New York University, which hosted me so generously when I came to the United States.

Words cannot express my gratitude for those friends, neighbors, and relatives who fearlessly and selflessly stepped forward on my flight to freedom to bring me to safety with no prior warning or preparation. To the many villagers and extended family who have buoyed me over the years, your kindness and uprightness will remain with me always.

To Li Jinsong, Li Fangping, and my many many lawyer friends in China: you are fearless, you are brave, you are heroes.

And lastly, boundless thanks are due my family—my mother and father, my brothers and their families, my wife, and my children: your love is an unbreakable force.

To all these friends, near and far: without you, I would have no today.

Index

extracts reading groups
competitions books new
discounts extracts
competitions extracts discounts
books
new
events books
extracts new reading groups
interviews
events extracts books
discounts events
new books events
events new
discounts extracts discounts
www.panmacmillan.com
extracts events reading groups
competitions books extracts new